IMAGINATION FOR CRIME PREVENTION:

Essays in Honour of Ken Pease

Graham Farrell
Kate J. Bowers
Shane D. Johnson

and

Michael Townsley

editors

Crime Prevention Studies
Volume 21

Criminal Justice Press
Monsey, NY, USA

Willan Publishing
Cullompton, Devon, UK

ISSN (series): 1065-7029.
ISBN-13 (cloth): 978-1-881798-70-5.
ISBN-10 (cloth): 1-881798-70-4.
ISBN-13 (paper): 978-1-881798-71-2.
ISBN-10 (paper): 1-881798-71-2.

Printed on acid-free and recycled paper.

CRIME PREVENTION STUDIES

Ronald V. Clarke, Series Editor

Crime Prevention Studies is an international book series dedicated to research on situational crime prevention and other initiatives to reduce opportunities for crime. Most volumes center on particular topics chosen by expert guest editors. The editors of each volume, in consultation with the series editor, commission the papers to be published and select peer reviewers.

*   *   *

Volume 1, edited by Ronald V. Clarke, 1993.

Volume 2, edited by Ronald V. Clarke, 1994.

Volume 3, edited by Ronald V. Clarke, 1994 (out of print).

Volume 4, *Crime and Place*, edited by John E. Eck and David Weisburd, 1995.

Volume 5, *The Politics and Practice of Situational Crime Prevention*, edited by Ross Homel, 1996.

Volume 6, *Preventing Mass Transit Crime*, edited by Ronald V. Clarke, 1996.

Volume 7, *Policing for Prevention: Reducing Crime, Public Intoxication and Injury*, edited by Ross Homel, 1997.

Volume 8, *Crime Mapping and Crime Prevention*, edited by David Weisburd and J. Thomas McEwen, 1997.

Volume 9, *Civil Remedies and Crime Prevention*, edited by Lorraine Green Mazerolle and Jan Roehl, 1998.

Volume 10, *Surveillance of Public Space: CCTV, Street Lighting and Crime Prevention*, edited by Kate Painter and Nick Tilley, 1999.

Volume 11, *Illegal Drug Markets: From Research to Prevention Policy*, edited by Mangai Natarajan and Mike Hough, 2000.

(continued)

Contents

(continued)

Contents

Foreword — Just Say Pease

Ken Pease is the British boffin behind Crime Science. He, more than anyone else, inspired the idea of importing serious scientific methods into crime reduction. He has sparkled with original ideas, fizzed with energy, and thrown himself enthusiastically not merely into groundbreaking research but into the task of explaining his revolutionary message to anyone who would listen. And despite what at first seemed an unorthodox approach people *have* listened, including government ministers and police chiefs. If you have a crime problem, just say Pease.

Remarkably for a man with so much knowledge to impart, he is an exceptionally good listener and absurdly humble. But most importantly, working in a field in which policymakers are at the mercy of political and sociological whimsy, he has helped to create the foundations of a truly methodological approach to discovering what works and what doesn't. This book charts some of his remarkable achievements. With one significant exception his expertise spans the whole field of crime prevention, from finding patterns in offending (such as geographic hot-spots, vulnerable products and services, or his seminal work on repeat victimisation which identified a hitherto unnoticed group of people who are especially at risk from crime), to finding solutions, including changing policing methods and detection processes, improving product design, and reshaping corporate and public policy.

The exception to his expertise is illuminating. Ken is first and foremost a professor of psychology, a discipline that focuses on people and their social interactions. Perhaps because of this he is aware how difficult it is to change human individuals: we are what we are. So he turned his back on the great tradition of criminology and its fascination with the social and psychological make-up of individual offenders. Instead, he has worked on changing the circumstances in which citizens find themselves, arguing that people's predisposition to offend is only one factor in crime, and generally it happens to be the least amenable to manipulation. Ken's interest has been to remove the temptations and opportunities that lead or allow people to offend. Essentially that means making crime harder to commit and harder to get away with. Yet his elegant solutions do not lead to more locks and bolts; indeed, as with good engineering, the answers often seem surprisingly simple and graceful.

When he started down this path he was in the company of little more than half a dozen like-minded senior academics around the world. Some were interested in sharpening police methods ("problem oriented policing"), some in reshaping everyday experiences so as to strip out opportunities for crime ("situational crime prevention"), and others in improving the experimental rigour of social sciences (now epitomised by the international Campbell Collaboration). I coined the term Crime Science to encompass all these approaches in a new multidisciplinary school, but I shall always consider Ken to be the epitome of it all, the father of Crime Science. It was through his encouragement and ability to enthuse me and others that the world's first college of Crime Science was established: the Jill Dando Institute at University College London.

Ken is a brilliant innovator in his field and a kindly and diffident colleague who prefers that credit goes to others; but no scientist can be measured by his or her professional achievements alone. He is a warm-hearted husband and devoted father (whose daughter, Katie, has been inspired to follow in his professional footsteps), and equally devoted lover of dogs. Any unwanted mutt near his home in north-west England, however difficult, disfigured or downright dangerous, could find sanctuary in the Pease household until the family ran out of space to take in more. The Crime Scientist in Ken knows he can never reform his guests; but he can arrange life so that even his most unstable and belligerent hounds behave themselves – at least most of the time.

I hope that one day Crime Science will be as much of an established discipline as Economics, Town Planning, Industrial Design, Statistics or Engineering, or any other of the many subjects on which it relies; and that students and practitioners will take down this book and marvel that so much bears the hallmark of Ken Pease.

Nick Ross

Editors' Introduction — Ken Pease (1943-): A Prospective Obituary

by

Graham Farrell
Midlands Centre for Criminology and Criminal Justice,
Loughborough University

Kate Bowers

Shane Johnson

and

Michael Townsley
Jill Dando Institute of Crime Science,
University College London

"Being ever of a maudlin disposition (I dug graves in the vacations) I read every obituary in all the journal issues I ever opened." (Pease, 1998a, p. 163)

Those of you who knew Ken Pease will not be surprised at his failure to conform in time for this obituary. It will have to serve as a draft, and we welcome his further input for a revised version. However, this leaves us in the disappointing and methodologically challenging position of writing a prospective obituary. It is therefore serendipitous that, to our knowledge, such a prospective-retrospective has not been previously applied as methodology in a criminological context, and we claim it as an original contribution. Were he with us today, Ken would be proud. Then he would speedily edit the material, adding value and insight throughout while thoughtfully correcting us grammar.

Since this is not a posthumous volume at time of going to press, it is clear that we come here not to bury Pease but to praise him. For the former of these two acts would, in present circumstances, lead to somewhat incredulous choking on his part. However, we know this would be accompanied by praise for our foresight and efficiency in completing the task in advance of the traditional deadline. This *festschrift* belatedly marks Ken's official, if rather early, retirement in 2003, and pays tribute to his various criminological contributions to date. This is despite the fact that we predict these contributions will, no matter how hard we protest, continue for many years to come.

Pease Popularity Problem

It was always clear that Ken Pease's ridiculous popularity would present a problem for editors seeking to compile a single volume. It has been our frequent wish that Ken was not so collegial, so prolific, so generous of co-authorship, had not mentored so many students or assisted so many colleagues in various tasks, with such consistency and distinction for so long a period. That he unfortunately did so presented us with the unenviable task of being able to invite only a fraction of those who would have wished to contribute. That Ken were less giving of his time and skills, less generous with his ideas, sparkling imagination, extensive knowledge and outrageous capacity for methodological innovation, would clearly have been desirable. However, it was not within our capacity to produce the Encyclopaedia Peasia in 26 volumes. While we realise Ken may not forgive this lack of capacity on our part, we ask the forgiveness and understanding of colleagues we were unable to ask to contribute. We thank and applaud those who did for making this what we hope is also a substantive contribution to knowledge and crime prevention practice.

Popularity, however, was only one of Ken's many problems. A lack of respect for the academic establishment and its practices was evident through his career. This was nowhere more obscure than in his singular preference to appear as last author on his publications, despite so often being both intellectual driving force and principal writer. We refute Nick

Ross's description of Pease as "absurdly humble" in the Foreword to this volume, and prefer to categorise him as wilfully anarchic, verging on unprofessional. That Pease had a somewhat crude lack of materialistic greed, frequently spurning his consultancy fees and preferring to pass it to a needy research assistant or churn it back into his research, was overcome upon retirement only by the need to purchase food and clothes. Were it not for the scope and impact of his academic work, and the respect it engendered in such a range of colleagues and institutions, such fundamental flaws would surely have precipitated his more rapid demise. In his academic work, far too many were the times when Pease elected to constructively build upon the work of others, offering sound advice and encouragement, when a damning indictment would have been less arduous and more publishable. It is a wonder that he survived so long without the hardnosed attitude characteristic of so many academics, and we look forward to the day when this flagrant abuse of academic tradition is practised no longer.

Criminal Careers and Career Criminologist

Born 5th August 1943, the precocious intellect of Kenneth George Pease was in evidence from the outset. At the age of 11 he scored the highest exam result (for the legendary British "eleven plus") in the county of Cheshire. When offered sponsorship to attend the venerable Westminster School in London, he rejected it in favour of a more local establishment. After being tempted to read for an undergraduate degree in Psychology at University College London, the young Pease returned to northwest Britain, where he then remained despite a range of efforts to entice him away. Utilising a prospective model of residential locations (based on Johnson et al., 2004), we predict with near certainty that he will remain in this location. This is not least due to the proximity of the soccer grounds of Manchester City, Stockport County and Stalybridge Celtic: It was long clear that Ken's pursuit of the underdog applied to sport as much as to canines that occupied his time and residence.

To his credit, Pease was always an advocate of clarity and truth in the visual display of quantitative information. He had a penchant for the work of Edward R. Tufte (e.g., Tufte, 1992). We think they would be proud of the way we have shaped Figure 1, making it somewhat squarer than a traditional chart in order to exaggerate the aggressiveness of the publication trajectory. Note how the same chart with a more typical x-axis would not produce quite the same erection. By the time of publication

Figure 1: Pease Cumulative Publications 1968-2004

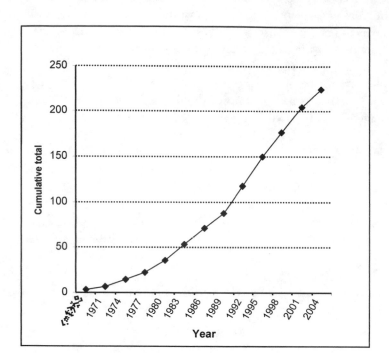

of this volume, Pease will almost certainly have published more than 250 works of various types. We were only able to obtain data on 224 publications by 2004 as he "has lost track" of some of them in recent years. This simple counting of publications masks significant variation in terms of articles, books and monographs (Table 1). This analysis understates the widespread impact of Pease's work, the reading of which some commentators have argued was more contagious than a cold on a damp winter morning, if slightly less likely to require antihistamines.

In their tribute to Leslie Wilkins (to which Pease contributed), Gottfredson and Clarke (1990) analysed publication patterns and identified two types of Wilkins. The first was the British civil servant, and the second the American academic, with the latter slightly more prolific. Our examination of the trajectory of the Pease publication rate suggests, rather, three stages of an ongoing criminal career. After onset, even as an initiate, Pease's involvement in crime was frequent. Prolific and serious subsequent

Table 1: Pease Publications by Type over Time (3-Year Periods)

Publication Type	≤1968	-1971	-1974	-1977	-1980	-1983	-1986	-1989	-1992	-1995	-1998	-2001	-2004
Book	0	0	1	0	1	0	4	0	1	0	0	3	10
Article	3	1	6	5	7	7	3	9	16	15	10	8	9
Book chapter	0	0	0	0	4	1	7	1	7	7	11	11	0
Monograph	0	0	0	3	2	1	0	2	2	5	3	5	0
Other	0	3	0	0	0	8	4	5	4	5	3	1	0
Total	*3*	*4*	*7*	*8*	*14*	*17*	*18*	*17*	*30*	*32*	*27*	*28*	*19*
Cumulative	*3*	*7*	*14*	*22*	*36*	*53*	*71*	*88*	*118*	*150*	*177*	*205*	*224*

involvement with periods of both generalism and specialism have led to a seeming reluctance to desist. The period we characterise as onset and initiation lasted until around 1977. During this period, Pease fenced his criminal wares at Manchester University, then as Senior and Principal Research Officer at the Home Office (1972-1976). The value of his average annual offence rate, lambda, was approximately 2.11 (19 publications over nine years). In stage 2, Pease was a persistent, prolific and serious offender through the 1980s as Head of the School of Sociology and Social Policy at Ulster Polytechnic (1981-1983), and upon return to his old stomping ground at Manchester University as Senior Lecturer (1983-1986), then Reader (1986-1995). From 1978 to 1989 inclusive, Pease's offending lambda was 5.5 (66 publications in 12 years). The latest epoch of Pease's career commenced at the start of the 1990s (136 publications over 15 years), which saw an escalation of offending with an annual lambda of 9.1. Numerous career advancements – appointment to a Professorial Chair at the University of Manchester in 1995, acting Head of the Home Office Policing and Reducing Crime Unit (1999-2000) and setting up the successful Applied Criminology Group (1995-2003) at the University of Huddersfield – failed to stop Pease from collaborating with a range of co-offenders. As visiting professor at University College London and at Loughborough University, he appears both relentless and unrepentant. Over the years he ruthlessly pressed initiates into service, and apprentices into more serious work. The Pease criminal career resulted in a protracted series of grave offences against previous ways of thought, method, policy and practice. It is noteworthy not only for its duration but also for its particular trajectory. While desistance is commonly at a younger age for most offenders, it is clear that Pease continues to be offensive well beyond his sixtieth birthday.

A career of such profligacy and seriousness is rare. It landed Ken in hot water on countless occasions. He was frequently retained by the police and held at Her Majesty's pleasure. Both he and his work were routinely processed the length and breadth of the criminal justice system. Pease-related crime writings hold an unusually high re-sale value on the black market of policy and practice. They appear unusually accessible, durable and – a particularly odd characteristic – useful. Perhaps it was his interaction with Interpol or the UN, or perhaps the rise of mutual extradition treaties, but Pease was frequently deported to countries around the world, only to escape and return to hunt in his native Stockport. And despite numerous appearances before the Parole Board since 1987, like many such organisations, they were reluctantly obliged to release Pease on his own recognisance. The result was that few contemporary criminals were on first name terms with so many senior police, criminal justice and crime policy-making figures as the fugitive Ken Pease. Though he never broke bail or other agreements, his "Wanted" mug-shot and by-line appeared in diverse communication media around the world. Even that tabloid rag *The Economist* demanded he write about his imprisonment experiences for their annual global review (Pease, 1989). Amongst the harsher of many sentences meted out, Pease was condemned to be a Fellow of the Royal Society of the Arts from 1995, and shackled by the Order of the British Empire (OBE) in 1997 for services to crime prevention. Note the arresting and familiar orientation of Photo 1 when Pease successfully infiltrated the grounds of Buckingham Palace. Since the abolition of capital punishment, the OBE is one of the severest sentences that can be bestowed upon a U.K. citizen. Only placing him in the stocks at the Tower of London would be more fitting, and we know of only a handful of academic criminologists warranting this or similar measures: Sir Anthony Bottoms, David Farrington OBE, Roger Hood CBE, Pat Mayhew OBE, the late Sir Leon Radzinowicz, Nick Tilley OBE, and Paul Wiles (Order of the Bath). A rogue's gallery if ever there was one.

Some unpublished career highlights should not go unrecognised. In 1980, as expert consultant to the Sixth United Nations Crime Congress, Pease sat on the podium in Caracas, Venezuela, in front of the diplomatic missions of the world. Suddenly, eyes from around the globe alighted upon him. With a brief delay for the Chinese translation to which he was inadvertently listening through his earpiece at the time, he heard his name mentioned and realised he had been asked a question. The world's finest diplomats awaited his pronouncement as he shifted uncomfortably in his seat and, in an effort to avoid international dispute, strove to answer the unheard question with the profundity and insight upon which his reputation was built. Never a prouder moment for the pioneering analyst of the early UN crime surveys.

Among Ken's more irritating habits was his ability to persistently inspire others. Few among us can say they have not, after even only a few minutes with Ken, been left with a new research idea, a fresh momentum and spirit, or even a whole new research agenda. We have lost count of the number of people who should, but rarely do, blame Pease for their peculiar career path. And he was as generous with his ideas as his time. And, while we talk of intellect, that is not to detract from his professionalism.

Photo 1: Pease Steals OBE Award from Buckingham Palace and Celebrates with Family in 1997 (left to right: Nick, Judy, Ken, Katie)

INVESTITURE AT BUCKINGHAM PALACE

His ability to draw criminological insight from *The Simpsons* TV show is legendary.

In truth though, we write of an academic sports star. A meet was better attended and more successful if Ken was in the starting line-up. He had the talent that turns heads. Peers and onlookers watched with awe. Few have his mental agility to turn on the spot and play the unanticipated through-pass that cuts open the defence. Fewer still have the creativity combined with that lightning burst of pace. Unique was his ability to bring such qualities to the field with consistency, disarming ease, and grace. The crowd roared.

So What? Was Pease Effective?

Peer citation is a commonly used indirect measure of intellectual impact. For the period 1991-1995 Pease topped the citation rankings for the *British Journal of Criminology* after the British Crime Survey main reports personified by Pat Mayhew and Mike Hough.[1] This was a move up the charts from eighth-place for 1986-1990 (Cohn and Farrington, 1998). We confidently anticipate a high ranking if analysis were conducted for more recent years. Reflecting this trajectory, plus decreased international insularity due to the Internet, we would anticipate a significant promotion in relation to non-British journals over the last decade. This would be despite the Pease habit of pursuing useful applied work, a refusal to resort to grandiose theory, plus an eschewal of large academic conferences and the limelight generally. Moreover, we note the absence of publication frequency and citation analysis for the field of crime prevention, where we anticipate Pease would be on the podium.

What could be called the "pioneer's paradox" is that truly influential work becomes normalised to the extent that, to future generations, it appears commonplace. The best work appears so obvious that the work achieves public ownership. In the late 1970s and 1980s, Pease was probably the leading scholar of community service orders (including Pease, 1975, 1978, 1985a; Pease et al., 1977; McWilliams and Pease, 1980). His work on judicial sentencing (Thorpe and Pease, 1976; Hine, McWilliams and Pease, 1978; Fitzmaurice and Pease, 1981, 1986; Wasik and Pease, 1986), crime seriousness (Wagner and Pease, 1978; Pease, 1988), probation (Pease, 1985b, 1999; Laycock and Pease, 1985; McWilliams and Pease, 1990; Humphrey and Pease, 1992; Humphrey, Carter and Pease, 1992, 1993), and prison populations (Pease, 1980; Harvey and Pease, 1987), falls into this category. For a couple of decades Pease was arguably one of the few real universalists, foraging across broad swathes of the criminological steppes, his crime prevention interest always evident but taking time to emerge as a specialism. Note that only a smattering of Pease publications and topics are mentioned above, and others include various areas of policing, parole reconviction predictors, evaluation methodology, incapacitation, the uses of criminal statistics, reconviction predictors, domestic violence, obscene phone calls, community safety legislation, rape, child abuse, threats, and the utility of DNA evidence. His dozens of studies of repeat victimisation mean the subject now appears laughingly obvious. Since Ken directed the pioneering Kirkholt burglary project (Forrester et al., 1988; Pease, 1991), his work on repeats influenced local, national and international crime prevention and policing policies (see Gloria Laycock's [2001] "repeat victimisation story"). One result was that the work of victim services and victim support agencies was re-conceived. The "Biting Back" project was the first to develop responses to crime that were graded according to risk (Chenery, Holt and Pease, 1997). It is now difficult, or perhaps just foolish, to study crime without accounting for repeats. His empirically-driven policy analyses (e.g., Pease, 1998b) spurred the investigation of spatially-near repeats, tactical repeats undertaken by the same modus operandi, and virtual repeats of similar places, products and other targets. His studies of how offenders repeat crimes, and the resultant detection possibilities, bridged the gap with criminal career research. To prevent crime by addressing some dimension of repetition ought to be termed a "Pease response" to capture the general notion.

Yet if there was a concern about Pease-led crime prevention projects it has always been that their implementation success may have been due to his particular vision and captaincy. Such ingredients are hard to replicate. Over a quarter of a century ago, Pease recognised that who implements wins:

> [T]he cause of unease about the state of crime prevention is not with the lack of solutions, but with the lack of incentive to apply solutions. The most sophisticated technology available is useless in the absence of an adequate system to deliver it to the right place at the right time to prevent crime. (Pease, 1979, p. 233)

Other indirect indicators of impact are apparent. Longevity, though it takes various forms, can indicate influence. One specific example is Kuhn and Willi-Jayet's (2005) test of a sentencing hypothesis proposed a quarter of a century earlier by Pease and Sampson (1977). Another would be that there can be few if any authors who published more than Pease using the data from the British Crime Survey and the United Nations Survey of Crime Trends and Criminal Justice Systems, and certainly none who wrote more imaginatively, for a quarter of a century to date.

It is difficult to capture the influence of the observation that prison population per capita, the measure used by most studies, may be highly misleading as a comparative measure of punitiveness (Pease, 1994, see also Nuttall and Pease, 1994). Our notion of crime displacement was transformed by Pease's re-conceptualisation of the issue including: (1) Displacement is a good thing because it shows, first and foremost, that crime can be prevented; (2) displacement should be proactively used to deflect crime from some situations and to shape crime patterns in others; and (3) offenders can be "displaced" to licit activities (Barr and Pease, 1990). "Self-selecting offenders" was his favourite term for those people whose minor legal infringements flagged their more serious offences – so aptly encapsulated in a study of illegal parking in disabled bays. Both drivers and vehicles were far more likely than the control group to have outstanding warrants or additional violations (Chenery, Hernshaw and Pease, 1999). These are just illustrative examples from a long list.

Pease wrote with flair and concision. When combined with his tendency to a most un-academic clarity of expression, a talent for insightful metaphor, and a preference for scientific method, it is a wonder his work is read at all. One of the more personal anecdotes we located is this opening of a book chapter:

> As a student, I had the great pleasure of being taught by the statistician A. R. Jonckheere, originator of the eponymous trend test. I held him in awe at the time because I was told he could play Scrabble well in seven languages. His insistence on prediction was remorseless. He described a visit he had made to the laboratory of the eminent ethologist Nikolas Tinbergen. Jonckheere said the two men stood in front of a tank of sticklebacks, and he challenged Tinbergen to predict the behaviour of one fish in five-second units. Jonckheere said that Tinbergen came out reliably better than chance according to the sign test which he conducted in his head.
>
> Criminology has not consistently engaged with the future . . .
> (Pease, 1997, p. 233)

This seemingly innocuous tale introduced a study which outlined an agenda for anticipating criminal opportunities. It trail-blazed the prediction of crime futures. Ken's work with the U.K.'s Foresight programme inspired the crime and technology research programme of the Engineering and

Physical Sciences Research Council (EPSRC).[2] Along the way Pease introduced concepts and themes that underpin much of this growing area (see also Pease, 1998c, 1998d; Association of British Insurers, 2000; Foresight, 2000a; Davis and Pease, 2000; Pease, 2005). The study of the future is one of the threads that drove him to nurture a concept of crime science as the prevention of crime via all appropriate disciplines. Crime prevention as crime science should include engineering, biotechnology and other hard sciences, all of which have a major role to play in addressing crime. Ken may not forgive us for the fact that the bulk of present contributors derive primarily from the social sciences. However, for the fact he did not co-author or edit his own tribute volume, and for the detrimental effect this lack of input had upon many of the contributions, he only has himself to blame.

The Contributors

Rarely have we seen such an able set of academics so motivated to see the back of someone. The obvious dedication with which the chapters were compiled is merely one tribute to the unspoken desire to see the discipline rid of Ken Pease. That he continues to linger, making repeated and fruitful contributions, is somewhat disappointing to the bulk of the competitors herein. To speed the process, the only guidelines we gave contributing authors for this volume was that this was a Pease festschrift to be published in the *Crime Prevention Studies* series. Half a dozen of the contributing authors completed their doctoral theses under Ken's supervision (Armitage, Everson, Farrell, Moss, Shaw, Tseloni). Most of the remaining have worked with, co-authored or frequently consulted and collaborated with Ken in some capacity. While some of the chapters are personalised (though this was not a requirement), the chapters went through the peer-review process in keeping with the series' guidelines.

Nick Ross, whom we thank for so eloquent a Foreword, is the ground-breaking journalist and founding presenter of the monthly BBC television programme *Crimewatch*, now in its third decade. In 1993, Ross and Pease met when they sat on the select National Crime Prevention Board of the U.K.'s Home Office. Their collaboration contributed to the development of the Jill Dando Institute of Crime Science based at University College London. Gloria Laycock, director of that institute, and Nick Tilley, both long-term Pease collaborators, outline crime science in their contribution. Paul Ekblom's progressive thinking about rational choice theory provides insights into offenders which will inform crime science. Per-Olof Wik-ström examines pitfalls in inter-agency work on crime prevention as well as criminality prevention, and proposes that the gulf between research into crime causation and into identifying preventive mechanisms for crime is not necessarily broad.

A key facet of Ken Pease's work was that, no matter how sophisticated the underlying methodology, the product would be grounded in practical application. Ken's work has been as influential in local areas as in national policy and internationally-recognised developments in methodology. Among the sound-bites that could be lifted from his work is the notion that that *crime should be prevented by all locally appropriate means.* Three of the present chapters have a local or regional focus with broader implications. Kate Moss-Brookes and Jenny Ardley develop an index to measure the risk of burglary in Nottingham. Steve Everson and Pete Woodhouse examine the impact of Section 17 of the 1998 Crime and Disorder Act, with particular reference to police Architectural Liaison Officers. And Rachel Armitage examines the impact of Secure by Design upon crime in housing.

A willingness to produce work contrary to academic fashion, where appropriate, is a frequent feature of Ken Pease's work. The chapter by David Farrington, Trevor Bennett and Brandon Welsh evaluates an "un-successful" CCTV scheme. Crime was not prevented in this particular application of the technology, and it is clear that rigorous evaluation of "unsuccessful" projects can be tremendously informative.

The prediction of crime, crime's unequal distribution, and innovative crime analysis techniques are areas that feature prominently in Ken Pease's work. Prediction is a necessary if not sufficient step towards prevention. Shane Johnson and Kate Bowers contribute their work on prospective hotspots, which they developed with Ken Pease. John Eck, Ron Clarke and Rob Guerette add "Risky Facilities" to the lexicon of terms that encapsulate crime's tendency to pursue repetitive patterns. Machi Tseloni provides our most sophisticated quantitative tribute, using multivariate analysis to examine area variations. Mandy Shaw and Sylvia Chenery exam-ine the aftermath of victimisation, while Michael Townsley and Graham Farrell further the study of repeat victimisation in relation to prison in-mates. Ken Pease drove research and practice on crime's tendency to repeat, which led Wesley Skogan to comment:

> Probably the most important criminological insight of the decade has been the discovery in a very systematic fashion of repeat multiple victimization. This has tremendous implications both for criminological theory and . . . practice in the field. (Skogan, 1996, p. 3)

Concluding Comments

With the seemingly pessimistic insight for which Ken Pease is known amongst colleagues, Richard Dawkins once noted:

> I am lucky to be in a position to write [a book], although I may not be when you read these words. Indeed, I rather hope that I shall be dead when you do. Don't misunderstand me. I love life and hope to go on for a long time yet, but any author wants his work to reach the largest possible readership. Since the total future population is likely to outnumber my contemporaries by a large margin, I cannot but aspire to be dead when you see these words. (Dawkins, 1998, pp. 3-4)

We therefore conclude with the optimistic note that we anticipate Pease making a significant posthumous contribution to the study of crime and its prevention. It would perhaps be too cheerful to hope that you are reading it when he (or more preferably, all editors and contributors) has long passed. While it is regrettable that the inception of a posthumous Pease contribution continues to be delayed by his unrelenting vitality, this is something we will endure. While this rough effort at an obituary is unsatisfactory, it will, at least, allow us to consult the subject on further details, analysis and measurement techniques, respectively.

Postscript

Ken Pease (1943-) is rarely missed by his wife Judy (née Judith Anne Parker), son Nick (Nicholas John), daughter Katie (Catherine Sally), and a small but loud pack of dogs. This volume is titled "Imagination for Crime Prevention" because imagination is the talent Ken believed most necessary, if often sadly lacking, in crime prevention research. It is but one of the qualities he brought to bear and without which his passing will be so much sweeter.

Address correspondence to: Graham Farrell, Midlands Centre for Criminology and Criminal Justice, Loughborough University LE11 3TU, UK; e-mail: g.Farrell@lboro.ac.uk

NOTES

1. As well as being the most-cited *BJC* authors, Pat and Mike are two of the many colleagues who, in writing this section, we realize would have willingly contributed to this volume.
2. For documentation of the connection see the presentation by Alasdair Rose of EPSRC (Rose, 2004), which acknowledges the Foresight Crime Prevention Panel review (Foresight, 2000b) as the starting point for the EPSRC initiative.

REFERENCES

Association of British Insurers. (2000). *Future crime trends in the United Kingdom.* ABI General Insurance Research Report No. 7 (written by K. Pease, M. Rogerson, & D. Ellingworth).

Barr, R., & Pease, K. (1990). Crime placement, displacement and deflection. In M. Tonry and N. Morris (Eds.), *Crime and justice: An annual review of research*, vol. 12. Chicago: University of Chicago Press.

Chenery, S., Holt, J., & Pease, K. (1997). *Biting Back II: Preventing repeat victimisation in Huddersfield.* Crime Detection and Prevention Paper 82. London: Home Office.

Chenery, S., Hernshaw, C., & Pease, K. (1999). *Illegal parking in disabled bays: A means of offender targeting.* Policing and Reducing Crime Briefing Note 1/99. London: Home Office.

Cohn, E. G., & Farrington, D. P. (1998). Changes in the most cited scholars in major international journals 1986-90 and 1991-95. *British Journal of Criminology*, 38(1), 156-170.

Davis, R., & Pease, K. (2000). Crime, technology and the future. *Security Journal*, 59-64.

Dawkins, R. (1998). *Unweaving the rainbow.* London: Penguin Books.

Fitzmaurice, C. and Pease, K. (1981). On measuring distaste in years. In J. Gunn & D. P. Farrington (Eds.), *Abnormal offenders, delinquency and the criminal justice system.* Chichester, UK: Wiley.

Fitzmaurice, C. T., & Pease, K. (1986). *The psychology of judicial sentencing.* Manchester: University of Manchester Press.

Foresight. (2000a). *Just around the corner.* Foresight Crime Prevention Panel consultation document. London: Department of Trade and Industry.

Foresight. (2000b). *Turning the corner: Crime Prevention Panel Consultation Recommendations Report. Final report and recommendations – Using science and technology to prevent crime.* London: Department of Trade and Industry (www.foresight.gov.uk).

Forrester, D., Chatterton, M., & Pease, K. (1988). *The Kirkholt Burglary Prevention Project, Rochdale*. Crime Prevention Unit series paper no. 13. London: Home Office.

Gottfredson, D., & Clarke, R. V. (1990). The criminologist from the small backroom. In D. M. Gottfredson & R. V. Clarke (Eds.), *Policy and theory in criminal justice: Contributions in honour of Leslie Wilkins*. Aldershot, UK: Avebury Press.

Harvey, L., & Pease, K. (1987). The lifetime prevalence of custodial sentences. *British Journal of Criminology, 27*(3), 311-315.

Hine, J., McWilliams, W. W., & Pease, K. (1978). Recommendations, social information and sentencing. *Howard Journal of Criminal Justice, 17*, 91-100.

Humphrey, C., & Pease, K. (1992). Effectiveness measurement in probation: A view from the troops. *Howard Journal of Criminal Justice, 31*, 31-52.

Humphrey, C., Carter, P., & Pease, K. (1992). A reconviction predictor for probation officers. *British Journal of Criminology, 22*, 33-45.

Humphrey, C., Carter, P., & Pease, K. (1993). *Changing notions of accountability in the Probation Service*. London: Institute of Chartered Accountants.

Johnson, S. D., Bowers, K. J., & Pease, K. (2004). Prospective hot-spotting: The future of crime mapping? *British Journal of Criminology, 44*(5), 641-658.

Kuhn, A., & Willi-Jayet, A. (2005). 'Doing Time and Marking Time' twenty-five years later: A Swiss confirmation of a British hypothesis. *Howard Journal of Criminal Justice, 44*(2), 167-171.

Laycock, G. (2001). Hypothesis-based research: The repeat victimisation story. *Criminal Justice: The International Journal of Policy and Practice, 1*(1), 59-82.

Laycock, G., & Pease, K. (1985). Crime prevention within the Probation Service. *Probation Journal, 32*(1), 43-47.

McWilliams, W. W., & Pease, K. (1980). *Community service by order*. Edinburgh: Scottish Academic Press.

McWilliams, W. W., & Pease, K. (1990). Probation practice and an end to punishment. *Howard Journal of Criminal Justice, 29*, 14-24.

Nuttall, C. P., & Pease, K. (1994). Changes in the use of imprisonment in England and Wales 1950-1991. *Criminal Law Review*, 316-323.

Pease, K. (1975). *Community service orders*. Home Office Research Study 29. London: Her Majesty's Stationery Office.

Pease, K. (1978). Community service and the tariff. *Criminal Law Review*, 269-275.

Pease, K. (1979). Some futures in crime prevention. *Home Office Research Bulletin*, pp. 31-35. London: Her Majesty's Stationery Office.

Pease, K. (1980). *Prison populations: Using statistics to estimate the effects of policy changes*. London: Open University Press.

Pease, K. (1985a). Community safety orders. In M. Tonry and N. Morris (Eds.), *Crime and justice: An annual review of research*, vol. 6. Chicago: University of Chicago Press.

Pease, K. (1985b). A five year plan for probation research. In *Probation, direction, innovation and change in the 1980s*. London: National Association of Probation Officers.

Pease, K. (1988). *Judgements of crime seriousness: Findings from the 1984 British Crime Survey*. Research and Planning Unit paper 44. London.

Pease, K. (1989). Going to prison in 1990? In *The world in 1990*. London: Economist Publications.

Pease, K. (1991). The Kirkholt Project: Preventing burglary on a British public housing estate. *Security Journal*, 2(2), 73-77.

Pease, K. (1994). Cross-national imprisonment rates: Limitations of method and possible conclusions. *British Journal of Criminology*, 34, 116-130.

Pease, K. (1997). Predicting the Future: The roles of routine activity and rational choice theory. In G. Newman, R. V. Clarke and S. Shoham (Eds.), *Rational choice and situational crime prevention: Theoretical foundations*. Aldershot, UK: Dartmouth Press.

Pease, K. (1998a). Obituaries, opportunities and obsessions. In S. Holdaway and P. Rock (Eds.), *Thinking about criminology*. New York: Routledge.

Pease, K. (1998b). *Repeat victimisation: Taking stock*. Home Office Research and Planning Unit Paper 90. London: Home Office.

Pease, K. (1998c). Crime, labour, and the wisdom of Solomon. *Policy Studies, 19* (3/4), 255-265.

Pease, K. (1998d). "Changing the context of crime prevention." In P. Goldblatt & C. Lewis (Eds.), *Reducing offending: An assessment of research evidence on ways of dealing with offender behaviour*. Home Office Research Study 187. London: Home Office.

Pease, K. (1999). The probation career of Al-Truism. *Howard Journal of Criminal Justice*, 38, 2-16.

Pease, K., Billingham, S., & Earnshaw, I. (1977). *Community service assessed*. Home Office Research Study 29. London: HMSO.

Pease, K., & Sampson, M. (1977). Doing time and marking time. *Howard Journal*, 16, 59-64.

Rose, A. (2004, May). *Think crime*! Presented to a conference on "How Can Science Support the Home Office in Reducing and Detecting Crime, Improving Security, Controlling Immigration and Managing the Prison Service?," The Royal Society, London (available via: http://www.foundation.org.uk/discuss.htm).

Skogan, W. G. (1996). The decade's most important criminological insight. In *Measuring what matters, Part I: Measures of crime, fear and disorder*. National Institute of Justice Research in Action series. Washington, DC: U.S. National Institute of Justice.

Thorpe, J., & Pease, K. (1976). The relationship between recommendations made to the court and sentences passed. *British Journal of Criminology*, 16, 393-394.

Trickett, A., Osborn, D. R., Seymour, J., & Pease, K. (1992). What is different about high crime areas? *British Journal of Criminology*, 32, 81-89.

Tufte, E. R. (1992). *The visual display of quantitative information*. Cheshire, CT: Graphics Press.

Wagner, H., & Pease, K. (1978). On adding up scores of offence seriousness. *British Journal of Criminology*, 18, 175-178.

Wasik, M., & Pease, K. (1986). *Sentencing reform: Guidance or guidelines?* Manchester: University of Manchester Press.

From Crime Prevention to Crime Science

by

Nick Tilley

and

Gloria Laycock
Jill Dando Institute of Crime Science,
University College London

Abstract: *This paper offers a first history of crime science, a term originally coined by Nick Ross to reflect his concerns at what he saw as the failure of the criminal justice system to respond effectively to crime and the potential of a more scientific approach to its control. We begin by describing more fully what is distinctive about the methods and aspirations of crime science. We then move on to discuss streams of existing research that have provided the main foundations of and rationale for the new discipline. Having looked to its past, we then turn to the developing agenda for crime science. Here we lay out the promising areas that are likely, we think, to prove fruitful in coming years.*

We write this paper from the Jill Dando Institute of Crime Science (JDI). The JDI comprises the first and currently the major research organisation whose mission is explicitly to do crime science. At the JDI crime science is construed as an applied discipline, bringing the methods and findings of the sciences to the practical business of ethical crime prevention, crime reduction and crime detection. It is attempting to do for crime what medical science aims to do for the treatment of disease, the prevention of illness and the promotion of health. In its avowed commitment to the methods of science and to improvements in crime prevention and detection, crime science distances itself from much of what is produced as conventional criminology.

Ken Pease is one of the main intellectual and institutional progenitors of the JDI. We would in this sense not be where we are working today without Ken Pease's inspiration, imagination and hard work. And we are profoundly grateful! The idea for the Institute grew from conversations between Ken and Nick Ross, a U.K. broadcaster and journalist who had been a co-presenter, with Jill Dando, of the U.K. television programme *Crimewatch*. It was Jill's murder in 1999 which provided the focus for the institute which bears her name.

For the purposes of crime science, science is taken to involve:

1. Identifying regular patterns in data;
2. Formulating theories and testable hypotheses relating to the mechanisms through which patterns are generated;
3. Trying empirically to test hypotheses;
4. Rejecting or revising explanatory theories that are untestable, and theories that fail rigorous tests;
5. Achieving cumulation in understanding, building on past research to create more powerful explanations, with diminishing error; and,
6. Aspiring to objectivity and the avoidance of bias in tests of theory and the development of practice

The applied concerns of crime science mean that it is far from value-free. Crime science values detection of criminals and the prevention of crime harms, just as medicine values the curing of illness and the prevention of sickness and its consequences. Criminologists and medical sociologists, as onlookers observing the practical business of dealing with crime and illness, may ask pointed questions about the meaning of crime, security, health and illness and may try to locate assumptions about these in prevailing cultural contexts. These issues, though important, are of lesser direct interest to those engaged in the sciences themselves, who are attempting to improve medicine and crime control.

The term "crime science" is, of course, only a recent coinage. It captures, though, an emerging approach to crime that has become increasingly distanced from most conventional criminology and from traditional assumptions about ways to control crime. Ken Pease has been, and continues to be hugely influential in its development.

The History of Crime Science

Leslie Wilkins provided the first stimulus to crime science. Ken was one of his greatest fans, and Leslie Wilkins was delighted to see the formation of the Jill Dando Institute of Crime Science shortly before his death in 2001 (Laycock, 2005). Prior to coming to social research and thence to the Home Office, Wilkins had been in the Royal Air Force, looking at accidents. He distinguished between issues of culpability for crashes and the conditions that seemed to facilitate accidents. He looked carefully at accident data, seeking common patterns. He looked to what conditions led to greatest injury in the event of accidents. He analysed near accidents to see what might have been different to provide for their avoidance. He brought science to the investigation and prevention of accidents (Wilkins, 1997). It is just this radical, critical, analytic, cool, blame-avoiding examination of the conditions that enable crimes to occur that marks off crime science from everyday discussions of crime.

During the 1970s, on both sides of the Atlantic, scientific research was casting doubts about the effectiveness of traditional responses to crime. The common sense assumption had been that crime control was the responsibility of those within the criminal justice system – the police, the courts, prison and the probation service. It was up to these agencies to identify, convict, punish and rehabilitate or deter offenders. In this sense it was assumed that crimes were committed by bad people, or people who had something bad within them that needed to be expunged. Insofar as there was an interest in the conditions that might encourage crime, it was assumed that these had to do with poverty and deprivation – something wrong with society whose correction would bring about substantial falls in crime committed by the needy and excluded. Confidence in this set of beliefs was challenged in part by research findings and some key summaries of suites of research findings.

The notion that offenders could be reformed through treatment (Martinson, 1974; Brody, 1976) or that a simple increases in police numbers would reduce crime (Clarke and Hough, 1984; Kelling et al., 1974) was questioned on the basis of empirical research findings. Assumptions that linked levels of absolute social deprivation to crime were losing credibility. Crime rates were rising steadily in spite of improvements in welfare. The falling confidence in the power of criminal justice agencies, treatment providers and improvement in welfare benefits even to stem crime rises let alone to reduce levels of crime, opened the door to fresh thinking about means to prevent crime, as well as ways of understanding crime patterns.

A "situational turn" took place in British approaches to crime prevention from the mid-1970s, as a result of Home Office research (Mayhew et al., 1976; Mayhew et al., 1979; Clarke and Mayhew, 1980; Clarke, 1980; Heal and Laycock, 1986). This suggested that in the face of specific crime problems, changes in the immediate situation for crime – increasing risks, reducing rewards or increasing efforts for the prospective offender – would lessen the likelihood that crimes would be committed. It also cast doubt on the assumption that crime could only be prevented by lessening offenders' basic dispositions to commit crimes.

On the other side of the Atlantic, Newman (1972) argued that "defensible space" was critical to the prevention of crime in and around buildings; Jeffery (1971) suggested that the physical environment could be configured in ways that would design out crime; the Brantinghams (1981, 1984) developed models and methods of spatial crime analysis that explained crime patterns and pointed to potential means to control them; Cohen and Felson (1979) produced a compelling account of crime trends in the United States through their "routine activities theory" that explained patterns across time and space by the supply distribution and movement of "capable guardians," "suitable targets," and "likely offenders"; and Goldstein (1979) presented a vision of "problem-oriented policing" that advocated an analytic, scientific approach to police work, questioning traditional police methods (Goldstein, 1990; Eck and Spelman, 1987; Braga, 2002).

These approaches were less concerned with individual pathology and individual disposition, social pathology and social reform, and criminal justice and the criminal justice system. In relation to traditional preoccupations with crime, the concerns outlined here with place, space, procedure, and everyday life practices, alongside the silences about offender disposition, responsibility, punishment and treatment, created a substantial distance in understanding and interest from traditional criminology.

The switch from the old criminology to the new methods of understanding crime and trying to control it could loosely be called a paradigm shift. It is certainly the case that the questions, methods, theories, debates, and rationales for the work were very distinctive and different. Questions about guilt, responsibility, disposition, punishment and treatment – the staple diet of traditional criminology – are not asked. The focus is no longer primarily on criminality and its emergence. The primary questions concern patterns of criminal events, ways in which they are generated as unintended consequences of changes in space, routines and products, and means by which crime harms can be lessened in the short as well as longer term. More specifically:

- The primary purpose is to inform prevention or reduction of crime rather than to understand offenders or the criminal justice system.

- The primary focus is on crime events rather than criminals or delinquents.

- The primary theories revolve around opportunity and rational choice rather than disposition and disadvantage.

- The primary methods include action research, case studies, and victimisation surveys.

- The research draws as much on the disciplines of geography, planning, mathematics, design, engineering, medicine and economics as it does on sociology, psychology, psychiatry and law.

- The potential users include the likes of planners, managers, designers and architects rather than being confined to those within the criminal justice system and welfare services.

- Good work is that which explains event patterns in ways that will inform effective preventive or harm-reducing interventions rather than that which better explains factors associated with criminality or careers through the criminal justice system.

What marks out a new paradigm in Kuhnian terms is a new set of questions, theories, methods, research priorities and criteria of success (Kuhn, 1962). The emerging approaches to crime provided radical departures from the old in all these respects. Its discontinuities with preceding ways of understanding and dealing with crime are striking. Kuhn refers to the "incommensurability" of successive paradigms – the ways in which paradigms talk past each other, populating the world of interest with different phenomena, asking different questions of the relevant world, employing different theories, using different methods and having different criteria of success. In all these senses the new paradigm differs from its predecessors. The new paradigm has also brought with it those infrastructural arrangements Kuhn noted. There are conferences, notably the annual

Environmental Criminology and Crime Analysis (ECCA) meeting. There are two publication series, Crime Prevention Studies, in the 21st volume of which this paper appears, and a new Crime Science Series. There are training courses, for instance those run by the Jill Dando Institute of Crime Science. There are exemplary pieces of work that are generally taken to have been formative, for example Mayhew et al. on crime and opportunity (1976), Clarke and Mayhew on suicide (1988), Mayhew et al. on motorcycle helmets (1989), Barr and Pease on displacement (1990), and Pease on repeat victimisation (1998).

In spite of all this, why do we say that the change could only *loosely* be termed a paradigm shift? The reason is that for Kuhn in the natural sciences a babble of competing approaches preceded the emergence of the mature discipline. Once one dominant paradigm comes to prevail it defines the community of researchers, including what they can take for granted and their research questions, until anomalies in findings accumulate to the point at which a crisis of confidence precipitates a revolution. There is then a period of intellectual turmoil prior to the emergence of a new dominant paradigm to cement the disciplinary community. In contrast to this, in criminology the babble has been incessant. The new methods of understanding crime in this sense comprised no more than another voice, competing for attention. Rather than a paradigm shift carrying with it a body of scholars who had previously coalesced around some earlier specific orthodoxy, the new methods of crime science initially comprised no more than an interesting new set of ideas to add to the existing range. Moreover, the practices undertaken in the name of crime prevention have been informed as much by the kinds of assumption embodied in traditional criminological discourses as they have been in the new "paradigm." That is, they have involved probation, social work, community work, treatment, welfare reform, educational programmes, social inclusion initiatives, preschool provisions, after school clubs, play projects, sports activities and so on designed in some way to reduce criminal disposition, protect from risk factors associated with criminal involvement, or to correct social malfunctions deemed to lie behind criminality. The new paradigm has triumphed neither as research orthodoxy nor as policy or practice foundation.

What marks out a productive paradigm is what Imre Lakatos, writing from a somewhat different position from Kuhn, called its "scientific research programme" (Lakatos, 1978). Progressive scientific research programmes turn out new questions, insights, discoveries and ideas, against a set of core ideas. Limitation in the core ideas may ultimately mean that new findings cease to be produced when a new research programme may emerge. Let us turn now to what has happened within the new approach to crime. Do we see progress, cumulation, new understandings, and new discoveries? It is, perhaps, easiest to illustrate what has taken place with a few key examples:

1. The theoretical framework for situational crime prevention

The theoretical framework for situational crime prevention has been steadily elaborated and extended since the mid-1970s. What began as an observation that crimes could be prevented by blocking opportunities rather than attending to underlying dispositions has been followed by a series of cumulative developments.

- Classic studies showing the role of opportunity in creating unwanted behaviour by enabling it (Clarke and Mayhew [1988] on gas-supply and suicide; Mayhew et al. [1989] on helmet wearing legislation and theft of motor cycles, Felson and Clarke [1998] on opportunity as a cause of crime);

- The incorporation of rational choice as an underlying mechanism explaining the role of opportunity in crime and the removal of opportunity in prevention (Cornish and Clarke, 1986);

- A developing framework elaborating types and techniques of situational crime prevention (Clarke, 1992; Clarke and Homel, 1995; Cornish and Clarke, 2003);

- Large numbers of case studies illustrating the potential explanatory power of opportunity and the effectiveness of situational measures to block them; and,

- The incorporation of attention to diffusion of benefits as a recurrent side effect of situational measures and exploration of mechanisms behind diffusion effects.

2. Repeat victimisation patterns

Repeat victimisation describes a pattern of crime events: the tendency for crimes to be concentrated on a smaller than expected number of victims in a given period and the tendency for repeat events to occur relatively quickly. Graham Farrell (1995) traces the history of research into repeat victimisation and shows it to have surfaced first in 1973 specifically in relation to gunshot wounds, and to have been looked at first more generally in 1977 (Sparks et al., 1977). There has, though, since 1988 been a more or less continuous programme of research associated with the preventive possibilities furnished by the phenomenon of repeat victimisation much of it carried out or supported by Ken Pease (Laycock, 2001):

- A domestic burglary reduction project in Rochdale which noticed that those victimised were at heightened risk of revictimisation (Forrester et al., 1988, 1990), and that this could usefully inform the targeting of preventive interventions;

- Studies finding repeat victimisation in relation to a wide range of offence types as well as across offence types (Farrell and Pease, 1993, 2001);

- Projects attempting to reduce repeat victimisation as a means of addressing various crime problems (for example, Chenery et al. [1997] for burglary and car crime across a police division, Tilley and Hopkins [1998] for crimes against businesses in two specific local areas, Hanmer et al. [1999] for domestic violence in one local policing area);

- Discovery that high crime areas are partially created through a concentration of repeat victims (Trickett et al., 1992; Bennett and Durie, 1995; Johnson et al., 1997; Townsley et al., 2000);

- Discovery that repeat victimisation is associated with return crimes by prolific offenders (Everson and Pease, 2001); and,

- Realisation that crime concentrates not only in space but also in time – there are "spates" of burglaries and "near" repeats (Johnson and Bowers, 2004; Townsley et al., 2003).

3. *The focus on products*

Studies initially noted that some products attracted crime and mooted the possibility that redesign could lessen crime (Southall and Ekblom, 1985). Since then there has been growing understanding

- of the attributes of those products (Clarke, 1999),

- the careers of criminogenic products (Pease, 1997), and,

- the means of leveraging attention to design issues (Houghton, 1992; Pawson, 2002).

4. *Methods of analysis*

There has been a growing number of interrelated methods and techniques of analysis specific to the new paradigm. These include:

- Using a range of standard approaches and methods, including action research, crime surveys, and non-obtrusive methods;

- Analysis of crime sets (Poyner, 1986);

- Repeat victimisation measurement (Trickett et al., 1992; Farrell, 2002; Morgan, 2001);

- Use of geographical information systems to capture spatio-temporal patterns (e.g., Radcliffe, 2004); and,

- Use of techniques from epidemiology to study near-repeats (Liu et al., 2005).

There is a community of scholars cumulatively building a body of knowledge against a shared background set of questions, theories, and methods. Because this has occurred against the continuing background babble of conventional criminology, in which the new paradigm has little interest, the question of separate development arises. Rather than competing with or trying to convert those engaged in debates about a radically different business, it might be more sensible to construe the new paradigm as a different discipline, one that has more to do with science than what passes for the standard fare in criminology. The new paradigm in this account would amount to the foundational paradigm of an emerging new discipline – crime science.

The Crime Science Agenda

There are a number of directions in which the crime science agenda might develop. Thoughts are set out below under four headings:

- Broadening the range of social science involvement

- Broadening the involvement of hard sciences, including issues of technology transfer and multidisciplinary effort

- Broadening the range of responses to crime, disorder and terrorism

- Adapting to evolving crime conditions.

Broadening the Range of Existing Social Science Involvement

There is more work to be done on the prevention of crime, much of which is an extension of the environmental criminology agenda. Crime mapping, closely associated with environmental criminology, is in its infancy and there is a whole list of potential studies associated with its further development. Much of this development involves taking techniques common in geography, a well established existing discipline, and applying them to the crime field. At the same time the studies need to be interpreted in the light of existing knowledge about crime. In other words, it is not simply a matter of established geographers applying their geographical expertise to crime rather than, say, to marketing toothpaste. The geographers need to better understand crime and its genesis, which would put them in a stronger position to apply their geographical expertise to crime prevention.

The same is true of a number of other aspects of the developing crime science agenda. A great deal of the work of the social psychologist is relevant to criminal behaviour, particularly that of young people. What might seem common knowledge in social psychology comes as a flashing revelation when applied to the crime field. It was established in the 1970s, for example, that when groups of people make decisions, as opposed to individuals, there is often a "shift" in the risky direction (see for example Feldman (1977) for a brief discussion of this in relation to crime). This risky shift is of obvious relevance when considering the processes of decision making by young people as they hang around on street corners wondering what to do next. The work of Clarke and others on offender decision making, and the extent to which that decision process is influenced by judgements of risk, is ample illustration of the importance of factoring in the risky shift process, and of finding ways in which to counter it.

A discipline with considerable claim to the crime science field is criminology, and the development of techniques for crime detection, which are clearly needed, could reasonably be seen as the preserve of criminologists. Such developments would make sense, however, if they were to be carried out in collaboration with forensic scientists. And it is collaborations of this kind that crime scientists, with their sympathy for rather than sometimes antithesis toward science, might be better placed to deliver.

The above examples speak to the notion that crime science is multidisciplinary. The intersection of other disciplines with crime control does not necessarily mean that we need a new discipline, it may be that collaborations and cross-disciplinary working practices are all that are needed. It is, however, notoriously difficult to deliver cross-disciplinary working. That may not be sufficient to justify the development of a whole new discipline to overcome the problem! Whether it does or not may depend on the cost of not doing so. We would argue that the current focus of crime control is *so* misplaced as to at least raise the need for realignment on this scale.

Broadening the Involvement of Hard Sciences

Greater association with the techniques and approaches of the hard sciences might stimulate new thinking in relation to crime control. One area of potential influence is in the more detailed specification of the problem. It is perhaps a moot point but some of the greatest advances in science have come about because the right question was asked. You have to wonder why apples fall in order to home in on the notion of gravity. There are some examples in the crime field of similarly significant questions. As much is learned from asking why people stop offending as from asking why they start (see for example, Sampson and Laub, 1993), but in doing so, the assumptions associated with both questions can be articulated and investigated. In some branches of science it is the search for regularities in data that leads on to asking significant questions about the world about us. Trying to explain regularities is what much science is about. A similar emphasis on looking for and explaining regularities in data within the crime field would almost certainly take us to an empirically based approach driven by hypothesis testing. This, then, is one area of potential development for crime science – a much greater emphasis on specifying problems, based on observations about regularities in data that lend themselves to empirical test.

Another lesson from the hard sciences is the importance of transferring technology from the university test bench to the market place or from one area of application to another. It can be big business, and many universities, commercial organisations and governments have supported specific departments to facilitate the process (see, for example, http://www.itiworld.org/WATTO/; accessed 22/3/05). The existence of a separate discipline of crime science can facilitate this technology transfer process specifically in the crime reduction field. It could, for example, raise the profile of non-criminal justice responses to crime and encourage the scientific community to think about the application of their technologies to crime. This is a process that could happen without the encouragement of a crime scientist, as happens in many other fields of potential application. But we would argue that crime-related applications do not spring immediately to mind because of the stranglehold the criminal justice system seems to have as the primary crime control response.

In England and Wales, the Engineering and Physical Sciences Research Council (EPSRC) launched a major funding programme to encourage scientists and engineers to think about the application of science to crime prevention and detection. They began in 2002 with a "Think Crime" Conference, at which Ken Pease gave a keynote speech. This initiative, which in 2005 is in its fourth round, has proved very successful in attracting bids and providing research funds. University College London was successful in attracting support for a Crime Science Network, which is intended to encourage dialogue between police (and law enforcement agencies more generally) and the scientific community. The network is operated through the Jill Dando Institute at UCL and the authors are closely involved in its development. We see it as providing an almost unique opportunity to bring practitioners from the full crime control field together with scientists, including social, physical and computer scientists. We are particularly keen to ask practitioners to talk about the problems they face in reducing crime – both preventing and detecting it – and giving the scientists the opportunity to consider whether we are simply (not that this is so simple!) facing a problem of technology transfer or whether there are more fundamental gaps in scientific knowledge.

One reason we felt this network was needed was to expose the extent to which science might contribute to the reduction of volume crime – theft, burglary, car crime – and not just to the detection of terrorism or other serious threats, which had tended to be the focus of many of the applications for funding support to the EPSRC on its crime prevention and detection programmes.

The EPSRC programme is, in our view, a highly significant and welcome innovation and its roots can be traced back to the influence of Ken Pease. Ken was one of the few academics to sit on the Department of Trade and Industry's Foresight Programme. This is a programme which supports "forward looks" at a whole range of public policy issues and emerging opportunities. Crime prevention was one such programme. One of the key recommendations put forward in their report (Department of Trade and Industry, 2000) was the need for a more co-ordinated financial framework to support research in crime prevention and detection.

The involvement of the hard sciences in crime control, we would argue, brings advantages. But it is not a one-way street. Since the Al Qaeda attacks of September 2001 terrorism and its threat have generated a huge investment of resources. Much of that investment has been in hard science applications. The webpage of the U.S. Department of Homeland Security (http://www.whitehouse.gov/homeland/; accessed 27 March 2005), to take what's probably an extreme example, makes the following claims:

- President Bush signed into law Project BioShield, *an unprecedented, $5.6 billion effort to develop vaccines and other medical responses to biological, chemical, nuclear, and radiological weapons.*

- The Bush Administration is *investing more than $7 billion across all aspects of biodefense.* In the last three years, the Administration has created the BioWatch program to monitor major cities for a biological release, procured sufficient smallpox vaccine for all citizens, and significantly increased stocks of antibiotics against anthrax.

- State and local health systems have been provided more than *$4.4 billion to bolster their ability to respond to public health crises.*

- The Bush Administration undertook several initiatives to *detect radiological materials being smuggled into our Nation,* issuing thousands of portable radiation detectors to border control personnel and installing radiation detection portals at ports of entry.

- *Security and research to protect the Nation's food supply from terrorists has increased,* adding millions of dollars in funding and hundreds of food inspectors.

Sums on this scale for research of this kind are unprecedented, but are not matched with similar funds on the social science side. Crime science offers a balance between the almost militaristic approach to prevention – which in some respects relies upon generating fear, and can summon huge sums in its support – and the "softer" but possibly more effective and longer-term approaches offered by the social sciences. (For a brief but interesting discussion of these issues see Bellavita, 2004.)

Broadening the Range of Responses to Crime, Disorder and Terrorism

If you believe that the primary means of crime control revolves around identifying offenders and bringing them to justice, then your response to increasing crime rates, or a rising fear of crime, will be to argue for more of the same; more police (or police associates) on the streets, more efficient courts, more prisons. The more liberal view might look to alternatives to custody and perhaps advocate community sentences or restorative justice – but the solution to crime would remain with the criminal justice system, in some form or another. One of the advantages of crime science is a widening of the response options.

Crime science brings as great an emphasis on prevention as on the response to crime. This is based on the observations that opportunities cause crime and that the immediate situation is a powerful determinant of what we do – including committing crimes. This clearly offers a much wider range of options for crime control. Furthermore, these options can be located within a number of mutually reinforcing theoretical approaches to crime prevention such as situational crime prevention (Clarke, 1983) and routine activity theory (Felson, 2002).

For example, fly tipping – the dumping of rubbish of various kinds – is illegal. This can range from mattresses and other unwanted domestic trash left on street corners or waste ground to contaminated materials being dumped on an industrial scale. Illegal dumping is increasing. The Environment Agency in the U.K., which has responsibility for dealing with these matters, reports that in 2003/04 it won 174 successful prosecutions against fly-tippers (http://www.environment-agency.gov.uk; accessed 8/4/05). This is against a background of 5,000 offences reported to the Environment Agency, but with some local authorities dealing with as many as 15,000 cases each. The Environment Agency estimates that the cost of fly tipping to them and to local authorities and landowners is between £100 and £150 million each year. The traditional approach of detection and prosecution is not effective in dealing with offending of this kind.

Webb and Marshall (2004) have carried out a careful analysis of the characteristics of fly tipping on behalf of the Environment Agency. They made a number of recommendations that they felt would significantly improve matters and reduce offending, most of which did not involve the criminal justice system. For example, they described the opportunity structures which enabled fly tipping to happen and suggested ways in which that structure might be changed. This included identifying locations at risk and protecting them, measures to improve the capture and disruption of offender activities, and making the duty of care system – the legal requirement that producers of waste ensure that it is disposed of safely and is only transferred to someone who is authorized to receive it – work effectively.

A further example comes from prisons, where it is commonly assumed that when offenders are committed to prison their offending behaviour stops – they are incapacitated. This assumption is wrong. Offending continues, with robbery, drug dealing, bullying, theft (including theft from cells, which might be called burglary outside the prison system) and assaults of various kinds continuing to happen. Wortley and Summers (2005) describe a range of initiatives taken in a young offender institution in the U.K., which had problems of bullying, shouting out of the windows and assaults on staff in the form of scalding them with hot water that was provided in the evenings to make tea in cells. They describe a range of solutions, most of which involved creative thinking rather than increased enforcement. The staff scalding, for example, was dealt with by giving the prisoners sealed thermos flasks for their water, which had the added advantage of keeping it hot for longer, and a number of the other problems were reduced with the introduction of TV sets in the cells.

Finally, although clearly not criminal, cheating in exams has been a longstanding issue within the education sector. The classic experiment by Hartshorne and May (1923) demonstrated that left unsupervised children fell into three categories – those who never cheated, those that always cheated, and the vast majority in the middle who cheated if they thought they could get away with it. Cheating has been controlled by the placement of exam desks at a suitable distance from each other and the presence of invigilators. New technologies have, however, introduced a new set of challenges to the prevention of cheating. Plagiarism, which is facilitated by the Internet, has made it much easier for students to copy the work of others directly into essays. This is now being countered by the introduction of sophisticated software to compare the text of essays submitted by students with extensive data bases of essays and other material on the Internet. The existence of these detection techniques is widely publicised throughout colleges and universities as a deterrent.

Adapting to Evolving Crime Conditions

Crime scientists take the view that crime evolves (Ekblom, 1997; Pease, 1997). As a consequence they expect to have to keep up with the changing crime scene and to anticipate new crimes and take effective preventive measures at the design stage. The crime scenario is littered with examples of cases where crime waves might have been eliminated or reduced if prevention had been "planned in" to the design of goods, services, management systems and even legislation at an earlier stage.

A good example is offered by the Internet, which has grown exponentially in use over the last decade. With it has come a huge growth in a range of crimes, facilitated or created by the proliferation of the Internet (see Newman and Clarke, 2003; see also, http://www.cybercrime.gov/). The list includes:

- Trading copyrighted songs
- With the advent of broadband, illegal downloading of movies
- Software piracy (theft of intellectual property)
- Electronic funds transfer fraud
- Hacking
- Identity theft
- Child pornography.

So we need to be alert to the potential for criminal exploitation of the developments throughout society. Optimistically we can not only keep the new crime threats under some control, but do so in ways that are both ethically and aesthetically acceptable. Notwithstanding our best efforts however, as Ken Pease (2005) says: "Crime will remain the hum in the machine of emotional, social and economic life." The trick is to keep the hum down to the lowest possible level.

A Final Note

This chapter, indeed this book, is intended as a tribute to Ken Pease. It is difficult in our view to do him justice. He has contributed to if not led many of the developments that have culminated in the establishment of crime science. His intellect is huge; it reminds us of the line from Oliver Goldsmith's poem "The Deserted Village" – "And still they gazed and still their wonder grew, that one small head could carry all he knew." Ask him almost anything and he will know about it and add value! He started life as a psychologist but could pass as an eminent statistician, criminologist and now crime scientist. It is perhaps as a scientist in the most fundamental sense that he is most comfortable. Really great scientists not only know the skills of their trade – they can collect the data, do the sums, and ask the questions – but they also have an undying curiosity, a need to know and understand the world about them. That is Ken Pease. He has been the midwife for crime science, and when we think of its future we find his thoughts inescapably informing our own.

But Ken is more than a straightforward scientist! He is a hugely generous man in not only sharing ideas but giving them away in all directions to students and colleagues alike. It is not always easy to detect the extent of his influence, given his insistence on coming last in almost every co-authored paper he has written. I (GL) am proud to say that when Ken and I wrote a short paper for the Australian Institute of Criminology about repeat victimisation, on which he is the world's leading authority, I managed to get him down as first author by threatening to take my name off the paper altogether (Pease and Laycock, 2002) if I did not get my way.

We cannot close this chapter without noting that in the midst of all his research activities, his student support and his teaching he finds time for his dogs – all of them – and even the occasional moment for his long suffering wife!

Address correspondence to: NickJTilley@aol.com

REFERENCES

Barr, R., & Pease, K. (1990). Crime placement, displacement and deflection. In M. Tonry and N. Morris (Eds.), *Crime and justice: A review of research*, vol 12. Chicago: University of Chicago Press.

Bellavita, C. (2004) *Preliminary notes on reducing the threat of terrorism by using research* (http://www.usc.edu/dept/create/team.php; accessed 27 March 2005).

Bennett, T., & Durie, L. (1995) Identifying, explaining and targeting "hot spots." *European Journal of Criminal Policy and Research*, 3, 113-123.

Braga, A. (2002). *Problem-oriented policing and crime prevention*. Monsey, NY: Criminal Justice Press.

Brantingham, P. J., & Brantingham, P. L. (1981). Notes on the geometry of crime. In P. J. Brantingham & P. L. Brantingham (Eds.), *Environmental criminology*. Beverly Hills, CA: Sage.

Brantingham, P. J., & Brantingham, P. L. (1984). *Patterns in crime*. New York: Macmillan.

Brody, S. (1976). *The effectiveness of sentencing*. Home Office Research Study No. 35. London: Her Majesty's Stationery Office.

Chenery, S., Holt, J., & Pease, K. (1997). *Biting Back II: Reducing repeat victimisation in Huddersfield*. Crime Detection and Prevention Paper 82. London. Home Office.

Clarke, R. V. (1980). Situational crime prevention: Theory and practice. *British Journal of Criminology*, 20, 136-147.

Clarke, R. V. (1983). Situational crime prevention: Its theoretical basis and practical scope. In M. Tonry & N. Morris (Eds.), *Crime and justice: A review of research*, vol. 4. Chicago. University of Chicago Press.

Clarke, R. V. (1992). Introduction. In R. V. Clarke (Ed.), *Situational crime prevention: Successful case studies*. Albany, NY: Harrow and Heston.

Clarke, R. V. (1999). *Hot products: Understanding, anticipating and reducing demand for stolen goods*. Police Research Series Paper No. 112. London: Home Office.

Clarke, R. V., & Homel, R. (1995). A revised classification of crime prevention techniques. In S. Lab (Ed.), *Crime prevention at the crossroads*. Cincinnati, OH: Anderson.

Clarke, R. V., & Hough, M. (1984). *Crime and police effectiveness*. Home Office Research Study 79. London: Her Majesty's Stationery Office.

Clarke, R. V., & Mayhew, P. (1980). *Designing out crime*. London: Her Majesty's Stationery Office.

Clarke, R. V., & Mayhew, P. (1988). The British gas suicide story and its criminological implications. In M. Tonry & N. Morris (Eds.), *Crime and justice: A review of research*, vol 10. Chicago: University of Chicago Press.

Cohen, L. E., & Felson, M. (1979). Social change and crime rate trends: A routine activity approach. *American Sociological Review, 44*, 588-608.

Cornish, D. B., & R. V. Clarke (Eds.), (1986). *The reasoning criminal: Rational choice perspectives on offending*. New York: Springer-Verlag.

Cornish, D., & Clarke, R. V. (2003). Opportunities, precipitators and criminal decisions: A reply to Wortley's critique of situational crime prevention. In M. Smith and D. Cornish (Eds.), *Theory for practice in situational crime prevention*. Crime Prevention Studies, vol. 16. Monsey, NY: Criminal Justice Press.

Department of Trade and Industry. (2000). *Turning the corner*. Report of Foresight Programme's Crime Prevention Panel. London: Department of Trade and Industry. Downloadable from: www.foresight.gov.uk/previous_rounds/foresight_1999_2002/crime_prevention/reports/index.html

Eck, J., & Spelman, W. (1987). *Problem-solving: Problem-oriented policing in Newport News*. Washington, DC: Police Executive Research Forum.

Ekblom, P. (1997). Gearing up against crime: A dynamic framework to help designers keep up with the adaptive criminal in a changing world. *International Journal of Risk, Security and Crime Prevention, 2*, 249-265.

Everson, S., & Pease, K. (2001). Crime against the same person and place: Detection, opportunity and offender targeting. In G. Farrell and K. Pease (Eds.), *Repeat victimisation*. Crime Prevention Studies, vol. 12. Monsey, NY: Criminal Justice Press.

Farrell, G. (1995). Preventing repeat victimisation. In M. Tonry & D. Farrington (Eds.), *Building a safer society*. Crime and Justice: A Review of Research, vol. 19. Chicago: University of Chicago Press.

Farrell, G., Sousa, W., & Lamm Weisel, D. (2002). The time-window effect in the measurement of repeat victimisation. In N. Tilley (Ed.), *Analysis for crime prevention*. Crime Prevention Studies, vol. 13. Monsey, NY: Criminal Justice Press.

Farrell, G., & Pease, K. (1993). *Once bitten, twice bitten: Repeat victimisation and its implications for crime prevention*. Crime Prevention Unit Paper 46. Home Office: London.

Farrell, G., & Pease, K. (Eds.), (2001). *Repeat victimization*. Crime Prevention Studies, vol. 12. Monsey, NY: Criminal Justice Press.

Feldman, M. P. (1977) *Criminal behaviour: A psychological analysis*. Chichester, UK: John Wiley and Sons.

Felson, M., & Clarke, R. V. (1998). *Opportunity makes the thief: Practical theory for crime prevention*. Police Research Series, Paper 98. London: Home Office.

Felson, M. (2002) *Crime and everyday life* (3rd ed.). Thousand Oaks, CA: Sage.

Forrester, D., Chatterton, M., & Pease, K. with the assistance of Robin Brown (1988). *The Kirkholt Burglary Prevention Project, Rochdale*. Crime Prevention Unit Paper 13. London: Home Office.

Forrester, D., Frenz, S., O'Connell, M., & Pease, K. (1990). *The Kirkholt Burglary Prevention Project, Phase II*. Crime Prevention Unit Paper 23. London: Home Office.

Goldstein, H. (1979). Improving policing: A problem-oriented approach. *Crime & Delinquency, 25*, 236-258.

Goldstein, H. (1990). *Problem-oriented policing*. New York: McGraw-Hill.

Hanmer, J., Griffiths, S. & Jerwood, D. (1999). *Arresting evidence: Domestic violence and repeat victimisation*. Policing Research Series Paper 104. London: Home Office.

Hartshorne, H., & May, M. A. (1923). *Studies in deceit*. New York: Macmillan.

Houghton, G. (1992). *Car theft in England and Wales: The Home Office Car Theft Index*. Crime Prevention Unit Paper 33. London: Home Office.

Heal, K., & Laycock, G. (1986). *Situational crime prevention: From theory to practice*. London: Her Majesty's Stationery Office.

Jeffery, C. (1971). *Crime prevention through environmental design*. Beverly Hills, CA: Sage.

Johnson, S., & Bowers, K. (2004). The stability of space-time clusters of burglary. *British Journal of Criminology, 44*, 55-65.

Johnson, S., Bowers, K., & Hirschfield, A. (1997). New insights into the spatial and temporal distribution of repeat victimisation. *British Journal of Criminology, 37*(2), 224-244.

Kelling, G., Pate, T., Dieckman, D., & Brown, C. (1974), *The Kansas City Preventive Patrol Experiment*. Washington, DC: Police Foundation.

Kuhn, T. (1962). *The structure of scientific revolutions*. Chicago: University of Chicago Press.

Lakatos, I. (1978) *The methodology of scientific research programmes*. Cambridge, UK: Cambridge University Press.

Laycock, G. (2001). Hypothesis based research: The repeat victimization story. *Criminal Justice: The International Journal of Policy and Practice, 1*(1), 59-82.

Laycock, G. (2005). Defining crime science. In M. J. Smith & N. Tilley (Eds.), *Crime science: New approaches to preventing and detecting crime*. Crime Science Series. Devon, UK: Willan.

Liu, L., Xuguang, W., Eck, J., & Liang, J. (2005). Simulating crime events and crime patterns in a RA/CA model. In F. Wang (Ed.), *Geographic information systems and crime analysis*. Reading, PA: Idea Publishing.

Martinson, R. (1974). What works? Questions and answers about prison reform, *Public Interest, 35*, 22-54.

Mayhew, P., Clarke, R. V., Burrows, J. N., Hough, J. M., & Winchester, S. W. C. *Crime as opportunity*. London: Her Majesty's Stationery Office.

Mayhew, P., Clarke, R. V., & Elliott, D. (1989). Motorcycle theft, helmet legislation and displacement. *Howard Journal of Criminal Justice 28*, 1-8.

Mayhew, P., Clarke, R. V., Sturman, A., & Hough, M. (1976). *Crime as opportunity*. Home Office Research Study 34. London: HMSO.

Morgan, F. (2001). Repeat burglary in a Perth suburb: Indicator of short-term or long-term risk. In G. Farrell & K. Pease (Eds.), *Repeat victimization*. Crime Prevention Studies, vol. 12. Monsey NY: Criminal Justice Press.

Newman, O. (1972). *Defensible space: Crime prevention through urban design*. New York: Macmillan.

Newman, G., & Clarke, R. (2003). *Superhighway robbery*. Cullompton, Devon, UK: Willan.

Pawson R. (2002). Evidence and policy and naming and shaming. *Policy Studies, 23*, 211-230.

Pease, K. (1997). Predicting the future: The roles of routine activity and rational choice theory. In G. Newman, R. Clarke, and S. Shoham (Eds.), *Rational choice and situational crime prevention*. Aldershot, UK: Dartmouth.

Pease, K. (1998). *Repeat victimisation: Taking stock*. Crime Detection and Prevention Series Paper 90. London: Home Office.

Pease, K. (1997) Predicting the future: The roles of routine activity and rational choice theory. In G. Newman, R. V. Clarke and S. Shoham (Eds.), *Rational choice and situational crime prevention*. Aldershot, UK: Dartmouth.

Pease, K. (2005) Science in the service of crime reduction. In N. Tilley (Ed.), *Handbook of crime prevention and community safety*. Cullompton, Devon, UK: Willan.

Pease, K., & Laycock, G. (1999). *Revictimisation: Reducing the heat on hot victims*. Trends and Issues in Crime and Criminal Justice series, paper # 128. Canberra: Australian Institute of Criminology.

Poyner, B. (1986) A model for action. In K. Heal & G. Laycock (Eds.), *Situational crime prevention: From theory into practice*. London: Her Majesty's Stationery Office.

Radcliffe, J. (2004) The Hotspot Matrix: A framework for spatio-temporal targeting of crime reduction. *Police Practice and Research 5*, 5-23.

Sampson, R. J., & Laub, J. H. (1993). *Crime in the making: Pathways and turning points through life*. Cambridge, MA: Harvard University Press.

Southall, D., & Ekblom, P. (1985). *Designing for car security: Towards a crime free car*. Crime Prevention Unit Paper 4. London: Home Office.

Sparks, R., Genn, H., & Dodd, D. (1977). *Surveying victims*. London: Wiley.

Tilley, N., & Hopkins, M. (1998). *Business as usual: An evaluation of the Small Business and Crime Initiative*. Police Research Series Paper 95. London: Home Office.

Townsley, M., Homel, R., & Chaseling, J. (2000). Repeat burglary victimisation: Spatial and temporal patterns. *Australian and New Zealand Journal of Criminology, 33*(1), 37-63.

Townsley, M, Homel, R., & Chaseling, J. (2003). Infectious burglaries: A test of the Near Repeat Hypothesis. *British Journal of Criminology, 43*, 615-633.

Trickett, A., Ellingworth, D., Osborn, D., & Pease, K. (1992). What is different about high crime areas? *British Journal of Criminology, 32*, 81-90.

Webb, B., & Marshall, B. (2004). *A problem-oriented approach to fly-tipping*. Jill Dando Institute Report (http://www.jdi.ucl.ac.uk/publications/adhoc_publications/fly_tipping_report.php).

Wilkins, L. (1997). Wartime operational research in Britain and situational crime prevention. In G. Newman, R. Clarke & S. Shoham (Eds.), *Rational choice and situational crime prevention*. Aldershot, UK: Dartmouth.

Wortley, R., & Summers, L. (2005). Reducing prison disorder through situational prevention. In M. Smith & N. Tilley (Eds.), *Crime science*. Cullompton, Devon: Willan.

Making Offenders *Richer*

by

Paul Ekblom[1]
Design Against Crime Research Centre,
University of the Arts London

Abstract: *Ken Pease is one of those rare individuals who spans the entire field of criminology. A key aspect of this breadth is his ability to switch focus between situational and offender-oriented causes and interventions. This chapter aims to develop this theme by charting the evolving concept of the offender in crime science – from the two-dimensional figure of rational offending models to complex adversary. The aim is more to stimulate discussion than to produce a definitive framework, but undoubtedly crime science needs such a framework if we are to cope with, and exploit, the range and diversity of causes and interventions at an equally varied set of levels and perspectives suggested by this brief review of the enriched offender concept. These include the rational "view from the offender"; the wider phenomenological equivalent; the causal-mechanism "view of the offender"; and the ecological perspectives of Routine Activities Theory, the Conjunction of Criminal Opportunity, opportunity structures and niches. Ashby's (1957) Law of Requisite Variety says that for a model to be useful and usable in capturing and manipulating some aspect of the world, it must itself be sufficiently complex internally to handle and reflect enough of the variety in the reality it is intended to represent. Cautiously enriching the model of the offender is a task that should repay investment.*

Enriching the offender is something that honest folk and/or crime scientists strive to avoid. But enriching the *model* or concept of the offender is something that, although it has been happening piecemeal and by stealth, we should consider embracing more deliberately. The model of the offender at the heart of crime science stems from situational prevention. It was intentionally impoverished by its originators, to make the then-radical case that much of crime could be understood, and prevented, if we forgot traditional offender-related issues – such as wickedness, psychopathology, personality and their development through social conditions – and focused instead on causes and interventions in the immediate crime situation. Thus the offender (like the evil twin of those cardboard cut-out police officers formerly fashionable in anti-shoplifting projects) shrank to a minimalist two-dimensional figure characterised only by Rational Choice based on perceived risk, effort and reward (Cornish and Clarke, 1986, 2003), and a Routine Activities Theory (RAT; Cohen and Felson, 1979) concept of "likeliness."[2]

The minimalist offender made sense when situational prevention was first trying to stake out a conceptual, and practical, territory for itself in a sceptical criminological environment. But does it still make sense to minimise the offender, or is this stance now holding us back? Like the Hitchcock film *The Trouble with Harry*, the body will not go away. I think that cautiously fleshing out the offender can contribute to situational prevention itself; allow crime science to explore certain kinds of offender-oriented intervention consistent with its core interest in understanding, and manipulating, proximal causes; cover a wider range of crimes, including more complex and sophisticated ones; address higher-level strategies for crime reduction, give some wider perspectives on displacement and strengthen the conceptual and methodological links between its concerns with both prevention and investigation of crime. It also enables re-examination of fundamental concepts like "the situation" itself.[3]

In all this, we are only following the logic of the problem-oriented approach to prevention (Goldstein, 1990; Bullock and Tilley, 2003; Clarke and Eck, 2003), which subordinates choice of method to nature of crime problem and context. We should also aim to be as conceptually- and practically-rounded as Ken Pease himself. Although frequently heard to complain about practitioners' and policymakers' uncritical and automatic recourse to "social" interventions centred on offenders and their life circumstances at the expense of situational methods, he shows himself well-capable of changing orientation when evidence and strategy suggest it could be worthwhile. Examples abound but are epitomised by the Kirkholt project, which evolved from pure situational interventions against burglary to uncovering and addressing local social factors motivating offenders to steal (Forrester et al., 1988, 1990); the repeat victimisation strategy that in appropriate circumstances allowed a focus on catching the persistently-returning offender (Chenery et al., 1997); and more recently the revelation of how serious criminals can be efficiently detected through such indicative misbehaviour as parking in bays for disabled drivers (Chenery et al., 1999).

Starting from the *Rational* and *Routine* offender we can enrich the model by adding features. Many are familiar, but only as sidelines or backdrops. The aim is not to review these features in depth but – by reversing "figure and ground," to identify new angles for those involved in situational prevention and wider crime science to consider; and to broaden the connections between these fields and wider criminology and psychology.

The features overlap, because they represent different facets of the same complex entity, and (for once) I make no attempt to organise these ideas into a consistent schema. Some have, though, appeared in the Conjunction of Criminal Opportunity (CCO) framework (Ekblom, 2000, 2001), which explicitly brings together situational and offender perspectives, and links are made with the categories of offender-based causation it uses.

The Reactive Offender

The offender is not only a (more or less) rationally-calculating decision-maker, but also a social and emotional being, capable of being prompted, permitted or provoked into action by stimuli in the immediate situation (Wortley, 2001). This perspective is now partly incorporated within the 25 techniques of situational prevention – e.g., Clarke and Eck, 2003). But there is more to explore than "precipitation" of criminal behaviour (as Wortley [1996] notes) – for example how the capacity for *empathy* might be exploited to understand and manipulate feelings towards potential victims in the crime situation, and inhibit attacks on people and their property. This could be pursued through identification of *situational* features that raise or lower empathy, including aspects of victims' appearance or behaviour (Wortley's [1996] techniques of "increasing victim worth"). Interventions could also seek to influence *offenders'* predispositions or resources for avoiding offending that can make them more empathetic or less, including social skills that might be teachable. Application of such skills would have to "fight it out" with the "neutralisation" skills (Sykes and Matza [1957]) of the *Rationalising* offender.

The emotional side of decision-making itself is important from a wider perspective. Wright and Decker (1994) indicated the importance of "psyching-up" for offenders at the point of choosing whether or not to burgle a house. In such conditions, the deterrent or discouraging message from situational prevention interventions would have to be particularly intense. As one lead, Cusson (1993) pointed to the role of *fear* in specific situations, as an influence on offending distinct from the perceived risk of being caught and punished at some later stage. This has rarely been exploited in crime prevention.[4] More positive emotions can also drive offenders. When Martin Gill (personal communication, 2005) asked robbers how they felt when actually committing a robbery the commonest responses were excitement, nerves and a rush of adrenalin.

Neurological research (e.g., Bechara, 2004) further suggests that our capacity for rational decision-making relies more on emotional reactions than we think. Most theories of choice assume decisions derive from purely cognitive and calculated assessment of the future outcomes of various options through intuitive cost-benefit analysis. But studies of decision-making in certain brain-damaged patients unable to process emotional information normally, suggest that people make judgments not only by evaluating the consequences and their probability of occurring, but also at a gut-feeling or *emotional* level. Such damage has been found to seriously compromise the quality of decisions (criminal or otherwise) in daily life.

How far crime science should re-establish criminological links with psycho- or neuropathology is an interesting question that should be revisited now that neurological and cognitive science offer a far sharper, richer and more objectively-measurable picture of processes in normal and abnormal brains than was available when this interest was "ditched" at the inception of situational prevention in the 1970s. People with detectable and significant brain-damage are rare enough for interventions to be centred on neurological or psychological treatment. But to the extent that neurologically-impaired decision-making, whether genetic or environmental in origin, is widespread in the population it may be worth considering situational "boosters" to honest choice such as clearer flagging up of responsibilities for payment at supermarket checkouts, in the spirit of "inclusive design."[5] This would presumably also be relevant for children whose moral development had not yet matured. Here, recent findings pose a particular practical and moral challenge – Dahl and Spear (2004), for example, describe changes in adolescents' brains associated with a sequence of disorganisation and increased risk-taking and reward-seeking, followed eventually by higher reorganisation of the capacity for social perception and reasoning.

The Remorseful Offender

Offenders of course can react emotionally to perceptions of *themselves* and their actions. Wortley's other important contribution (1996) has been to draw attention to the significance for offender decision-making, of criminals' capacity to feel guilt and shame, and to guide their choices to avoid these negative emotions. This is partly captured, under "removing excuses," in the 25 techniques of situational prevention (Clarke and Eck, 2003), but there is more scope for developing this area. Wortley distinguishes between the *self*-condemnation of guilt and the *other*-condemnation of shame. Wikström (2004) also develops the self-monitoring moral side of the offender in his model of causation of criminal acts.

Offenders do not operate in a social vacuum. Crime *preventer* roles as defined in the CCO framework include *handlers* (borrowed from Felson, 1995; Clarke and Eck, 2003), people who make crime *less* likely by exerting some restraining influence over offenders, whether in the crime situation or beforehand. For handlers to succeed in their influence, though, offenders need "handles" (cf., Felson, 1986) – something in their head that renders them susceptible. The capacity to *feel* shame, and the requisite *relationship* with people (whether strangers or significant others) who can awaken that shame, are both important. Likewise for shame or guilt to work requires a capacity for criminals to restrain their behaviour through an "executive function" (Wikström, 2004) or self-control (Gottfredson and Hirschi, 1990).

In the light of these issues we can envisage a multi-pronged assault on certain crimes, centred on the theme of shame. *Situational* interventions could:

- Mobilise people as *preventers/handlers* in advance of any incident by alerting, motivating and empowering them to act as "shamers";

- Make shame *salient* before or during the offence (e.g., through posters); and,

- Ensure that appropriate shamers will be *present* or otherwise learn about the misbehaviour, and be visible to the offender.

Offender-oriented interventions could include those that:

- Focus offenders' minds on the shame of earlier crimes and bring home the social consequences – with scope for connection with the processes of reintegrative shaming (Braithwaite, 1989) and restorative justice (see, e.g., www.restorativejustice.org – retrieved May 2, 2005);

- Develop their capacity for self-control, i.e., to enable them to act positively on their feelings of shame at contemplated crime; and,

- Establish social relations/bonds with appropriate handlers whose anticipated condemnation (and approval) would be important to the offender.

Some elements of this integrated package of possible interventions are untested proposals and rest on uncertain knowledge of how much guilt and shame offenders may actually feel as they go about their business. The interventions also go far beyond situational prevention, but they still come under the *proximal* causes of criminal events that crime science targets. However, we might also consider supplementing them with:

- Some careful *cultural engineering* to potentiate the feelings of shame and acts of condemnation, as with recent changes in norms on the unacceptability of drink-driving. This admittedly involves remote or distal changes, but the point is *only to contemplate them when we have a clear picture of how they end up as active causes present in or near crime situations*.

The Ready Offender

The notions of the Reactive and the Remorseful offender reflect criminals' susceptibility to emotion-inducing stimuli in the immediate crime situation, or to their own, internal moral response to particular contemplated acts, anticipated or experienced whilst in that situation. By contrast, the concept of *Readiness* (in CCO terms) refers to those temporary motivational or emotional states that are often awakened *before* the offender arrives in the crime situation – such as a need for money, an angry mood or sexual arousal – and which then "program" how the offender might tend to behave once there; or which may even cause the offender to seek out or create particular situations to achieve some instrumental or expressive goal. The distinction between Reactive and Ready is not, though, clear-cut because one can envisage a gradation of alternative dynamics. Consider an offender who either:

- becomes angry *before* entering a nightclub "looking for trouble," and once there, attacks some hapless person who spills his drink; or,

- is made angry *whilst at* the club with the same result; or,

- is immediately provoked into aggression *"out of the blue"* by the collision (perhaps reflecting a "thin-skinned" predisposition to provocation); or,

- who does nothing at the time but plans vengeance on the victim *later*.

These may seem subtle distinctions, but the preventive interventions to cope with them may be different, and designers of such methods would need to envisage the *range* of phenomena and causal mechanisms they should aim to tackle when, in this instance, seeking to reduce violence in pubs and clubs. Single strategies covering single contingencies are unlikely to suffice.

Focusing just on states *prior* to the crime situation, what makes a person motivationally ready to offend? The answer may involve a number of explanatory levels, each predominating as the source of variance in different circumstances.

- Various forms of physiological or neurological *need* such as hunger, craving for a drug or boredom may create a motivational state (as well as affecting perception of risk, etc.). These may derive, in turn, from prior circumstances characterised by absence of food, affordable drugs or decent play facilities (and even further back may relate to *dispositional* factors acquired through *developmental* processes such as early learning or addiction, or *genetic* factors acquired through biological evolution). The *Resourceless* offender may lack legitimate means of meeting those needs (as described in CCO). Some needs may be partly social in origin – perceived relative deprivation could engender envy; unfair treatment could awaken a burning desire for justice which might have violent expression; an overdue debt to a drug dealer may drive theft via fear.

- Other *current life circumstances* such as longer-term stresses from poor housing or shorter-term ones from that morning's crowded commuter train may likewise cause emotional arousal or a "short fuse." This should perhaps be taken into account when designing transport infra-structure or even the procedures for inspecting tickets – to avoid both the original pressure and the last-straw precipitation of some kind of "rail rage" incident.

- At the level of interpersonal or intergroup relationships, prior *conflicts* can produce powerful motivations which are persistent and targeted –

and thus might help predict the degree and direction of displacement. They should thus be considered when designing situational interventions to reduce provocations (Clarke and Eck, 2003) from disputes and other triggers (e.g., the design of queueing systems in areas of social tension). The same processes that may generate conflicts between groups may also generate powerful allegiances and pressures to conform within them – including criminal or terrorist groups. Wilson (2002) writes at length on humans' adaptedness to group living.

- Two powerful and persistent sets of conflict motives give us the *Revengeful* offender and the *Righteous* offender (driven by religion, ideology, the need for satisfying justice or culturally-formed notions of honour). In the wrong circumstances and to the wrong degree, these can generate violence and damage (Roach et al., 2005). The need for justice and revenge, for example, although culturally-mediated, may ultimately be explicable in terms of an *evolutionary* history of preserving a population tendency towards altruism by developing an inherited capacity to detect and punish cheats (e.g., Cosmides and Tooby, 1992; Wilson [2002] links revenge and religion in a wider evolutionary view). Intervening in such remote causes is arguably beyond the scope of crime science, but understanding them helps crime preventers appreciate their strength and pervasiveness, and understand what lies behind the uphill struggle to sell rational crime prevention to public and politicians who focus on justice and punishment.

- Such understanding can also guide the identification of immediate environmental stimuli which might trigger or attenuate them, suggesting situational interventions.

- Farrington's (1991) review of psychological explanations of criminal behaviour distinguishes between *excitatory* and *inhibitory* processes. Other models explicitly or implicitly make the same distinction (e.g., Gottfredson and Hirschi's [1990] self-control and Wikström's [2004] executive function are both inhibitory); and they come under the CCO's *resources to avoid offending*. These mental resources may act in the immediate crime situation (as with being stopped by shame at the thought of striking the person standing before them) or earlier, e.g., by stopping the offender from seeking a fight. *Disinhibitors* interfere with self-control. Those such as alcohol, of course, have direct physiological effects on the nervous system, and while exact causal mechanisms are debatable the association among alcohol, risk-taking and aggression is beyond dispute. Certain kinds of loud music, lighting and crowd conditions, and even colour and smell, may have related effects (and often go together). *Restricting* disinhibitors is classed (e.g., by Clarke and Eck, 2003) as a situational technique. However, I would see it as an offender-oriented *mechanism* which involves directly intervening in physiological causes residing in the offender; it is implemented through a situational *method* that is some way "upstream" of the *crime* situation.

Wortley's (e.g., 2001) precipitation model is a two-stage affair, with *precipitation* covering the short-term arousal of motivation/emotion, and *opportunity* acting as regulator by defining available choices. Cornish and Clarke (2003) attempt to assimilate and accommodate Wortley's ideas to their Rational Choice model. Their own two stages are, by contrast, both cognitive, perceptual and decision-making affairs – the first being the strategic, perhaps standing, decision to offend (what *they* term "readiness"), and the second the immediate choice to commit a specific criminal act. Revealing some pretty fundamental preferences of level and perspective, they extol the virtues of treating the offender as an active agent rather than one who is merely the "victim" of causal influences which tug on the motivational puppet strings. There is surely room in crime science for both views, properly articulated together.[6]

The "Root-cause" Offender?

The offender's predisposition for criminality is a complex concept, best defined as a *potential* to behave criminally which an individual brings to every situation, but which may be *called forth* only in some. The term "root cause" is, however, often used in a way that is uncritical and dismissive of other, implicitly "shallower," causes. It is also unclear where situation ends and predisposition begins. Ekblom (1994) and more fully Wikström (2004) have both indicated how *ways of perceiving*, including the tendency to see criminal opportunities in various situations, are actually part of predisposition.

If crime science seeks to sharpen up on situations and to explore proximal offender-oriented intervention it needs a way of articulating these issues and those discussed under Readiness. Making rather a flying leap, the concept of *epigenesis* in developmental biology may help provide a key underpinning idea. Epigenesis covers the "bootstrapping" process whereby an organism's genotype is gradually converted to the phenotype by a process of building on a succession of cumulative and ever-more subtle interactions with the environment.

The Rational Offender Revisited

Typical discussion of the rational offender centres on immediate decisions to commit specific crimes, although more strategic choices are also mentioned (e.g., Cornish and Clarke, 2003), usually in the context of persuading offenders to renounce their criminal careers because they don't pay relative to risk and effort.

Perception and decision are not the only significant aspects of rationality. We must consider the offender's goals. Logistically complex crimes such as "professional" bank robberies are best understood in terms of Cornish's (1994) concept of scripts and scenes, but these are drawn together even better if viewed as a flowchart of goals for offenders to achieve (Case the joint, and if successful, Steal getaway car and Obtain weapons, and if successful, Proceed to bank . . .). Organised crime is particularly susceptible to this kind of analysis (Ekblom, 2003; Levi and Maguire, 2004), which virtually by definition informs goal disruption strategies.

Finally, we should note that even the calculus of rationality may vary as a function of emotional arousal, which in turn is a product of situational-dispositional interactions including intoxication, conflicts and so forth (see Exum [2002] on causation and phenomenology of violence).[7] And subculture may conspire with chaotic life circumstances to enhance an impulsive lifestyle (Wright and Decker, 1994).

The Resourceful Offender

Ekblom and Tilley's (2000) extension of the concept of crime facilitators (e.g., Clarke and Eck, 2003) covers not just weapons and tools but cognitive, social, biological and emotional qualities such as skills, knowledge, contacts and collaborators, strength, courage, and capacity to neutralise emotional "distractions" such as guilt and empathy. Gill (2005) also develops this field. Resources shape and define the opportunities available to the offender, which are therefore not "pure" situational entities (an open window three floors up is only an opportunity to offenders with agility, courage and/or a ladder; and the capacity to "tune in" to the possibilities) but ecological ones irreducibly linking offender and environment. Restricting offenders' resources is a preventive strategy yet to be fully applied beyond attempts to control weapons, or limiting children's access to spray-cans. One field with scope for wider application of this kind of intervention is organised crime (why else do criminals organise, if not to pool the quantity and variety of resources?). Another is counter-terrorism (Roach et al., 2005), where considerations of materiel and expertise for chemical, biological, radioactive and nuclear attack, easy-to-fly aircraft and etc., come readily to mind.

The Responsive Offender – Displacement and Adaptation

Combining Ready, Rational and Resourceful yields the *Responsive* offender, well-positioned for making countermoves to prevention: *displacement* in the short term, and perhaps an *adaptive player in the arms race* with preventers in the longer term (Ekblom 1997, 1999, 2005a). Early debates on situational versus offender-oriented prevention referred to so-called "hydraulic" models of human motivation – where, if the motive to offend is thwarted at one time and place, it will simply resurface elsewhere. These were roundly dismissed (e.g., Clarke and Cornish, 1983); but we must acknowledge the subtler challenge that situational prevention faces in the medium to longer term from adaptable and goal-directed offenders. We also face offending *cultures* where learning can transfer from experts and innovators to followers, and criminal *organisations* whose adaptive capacities can be far greater than individuals'.

CONCLUSION

Enriching the model of the offender is a trend, as said, already started within situational prevention. Writing this chapter rather surprised me how far enrichment has come. It brings with it the prospect of situational intervention methods more finely-tuned to problem and context, and wider in scope; and "design against crime" interventions that are specified with a sophisticated model of the abuser/misuser in mind. For the bolder researcher, it allows cautious exploration of tangible changes we could attempt to make in specific qualities of the offender and in their immediate life circumstances.

Not all the causes of crime discussed here may be easily, reliably, rapidly or ethically manipulated via proximal factors in the situation or offender, and so fall outside the self-imposed scope of Crime Science. Causes identified through evolutionary psychology may be a particular case in point. However, understanding such a broader field of causation may be important for understanding what triggers criminal acts, and for purposes of targeting, contextual adjustment, and anticipating and countering displacement. And in any case, what is manipulable may change with new science and technology (a current U.K. Foresight project [Office of Science and Technology, 2004] is examining the future of brain science, including drug sensitivity and addiction and how it might be tackled bio-chemically [see also, Ahmed et al., 2003]).

Further perspectives and levels need to be brought into Crime Science to support understanding and contextual nuancing as much as to widen the scope for interventions. The Rational Offender view of Cornish and Clarke (e.g., 2003) gives a "view *from* the offender" – albeit a narrow, decision-making one focused on the agenda of risk, effort, reward and (with a little self-perception, also emphasised by Wortley, 1996) shame and guilt. *Phenomenologies* such as Katz (1988) give a richer subjective view that should not be forgotten. Wortley's (e.g., 2001) "crime precipitation" perspective is a view *of* the offender, allowing a detached, *causal-mechanism* interpretation. Routine Activities Theory (e.g., Cohen and Felson, 1979) focuses purely on *ecological* causes, explaining the occurrence of criminal *events* in terms of the coming together in time and space of its three principal ingredients, as are the *opportunity* and *opportunity structure* of Clarke (e.g., 1997) and the *niches* of Paul and Jeff Brantingham (1991; longer-term regularities of opportunity for appropriately-resourced/adapted offenders). Wikström (2005) also focuses on causal mechanisms, but his "cross-level Situational Action Theory" links both to individual offenders and their development, ecological setting, perceived situation and criminal *acts*.

The Conjunction of Criminal Opportunity (e.g., Ekblom, 2000, 2001) is both ecological (it stemmed from Routine Activities Theory) and built on causal mechanisms, integrating both offender and situational causes and focusing on *events* (which are not exclusively centred on the offender but symmetrically involve the other actors and physical ingredients caught up in them). It, too, has a phenomenological, decision-making element taken from the Rational Offender, and links to developmental processes. It has also begun to offer (e.g., in Ekblom, 2005b, Table 1) a set of alternative views – causes dissected analytically ("anatomy"), causal mecha-nisms viewed dynamically ("physiology"), and a hierarchy of complex emer-gent causal entities covering market, niche, network, etc. Both dynamics and emergence link to Cornish's (1994) procedural analysis of "scenes and scripts" (Ekblom, 2003).

But the task is not yet complete. More of Wortley's and Wikström's ideas could be taken in – perhaps in a new, combined framework. There are additional levels to consider, briefly raised in this paper: evolutionary and neurological, for example. The capacity to articulate all these different perspectives, identify which one we are thinking in at any given moment, and deliberately flip between them is something we should explicitly develop: evolutionary to ecological to developmental to decision-making to goal-directed to causal-mechanism-based. The composite model suggested may sound complex, but if its purpose is integration then it could replace a whole repository of simple sub-models, each with their own terminology to learn, their own implicit level and perspective, and each poorly fitting with the others. Here it is worth recalling Ashby's (1957) Law of Requisite Variety – which essentially says that for a model to be useful and usable in capturing and manipulating some aspect of the world, it must itself be sufficiently complex internally to handle and reflect enough of the variety in the reality it is intended to represent. It is the difference between, say, long, clumsy and imprecise sentences in a simple language versus concise ones in a more sophisticated tongue with which takes more time to acquire but repays the investment in the end.

This chapter has turned over the soil rather than grown a new, integrating framework. But undoubtedly Crime Science needs one if we are to cope with, and exploit, the range and diversity of causes and interventions at an equally varied set of levels and perspectives suggested by this brief review of the enriched offender. Whatever the case, my main aim has been to stimulate discussion, to which hopefully Ken Pease will long continue to make his uniquely enriching contributions.

Address correspondence to: p.ekblom@csm.arts.ac.uk

Acknowledgements: I am grateful for comments and/or material to Ron Clarke, Andrew Curry, Martin Gill, Keith Hayward, Jason Roach (who supplied quips too) and anonymous referees.

NOTES

1. Professor and Co-Director, Design Against Crime Research Centre, Central Saint Martins College of Art and Design, University of the Arts London.

2. For a critique of the impoverished offender of rational choice theory and situational prevention, see Hayward (2004).
3. Due to the popularity of the Ken Pease Tribute Book Club, there is insufficient space to pursue the last three themes here. A longer version ("Making offenders even richer") is available from the author.
4. Apparently only comic-books have applied it – those of a certain age may recall the adoption of the silhouette of the Bat by the Caped Crusader, because it "strikes terror into the criminal mind."
5. See e.g., www.inclusivedesign.org.uk (retrieved Dec 19, 2005).
6. Wilson (2002) makes the useful distinction between "ultimate" explanations for some physical or mental feature of a living being in terms of evolutionary adaptation and "proximate" ones in terms of how the adaptive feature is created and operated within the individual organism. Interestingly, he accuses rational choice theorists as a whole (not just the criminological subset) of mistakenly attempting to place their theory in the latter, "productive" frame: they use rational choice to explain detailed mechanisms of thought and behaviour, when it should really be located in the former, "predictive" frame – describing a generic cost-benefit calculus that is incorporated through a range of possible mechanisms in the control of behaviour, because however it is mediated, it confers adaptive advantage on the agent that uses it.
7. One is tempted to paraphrase the movie *Apocalypse Now*: "The subtlety, the subtlety!" How far these subtleties are open to manipulation is a moot point, but failure to understand them may derail interventions.

REFERENCES

Ahmed, B., Driver, J., Friston, K., Matus, A., Morris, R., & Rolls, E. (2003). *Advanced neuroscience technologies.* Foresight Cognitive Systems Project – Research Review. Retrieved May 2, 2005 from: http://www.foresight.gov.uk/Previous_Projects/Cognitive_Systems/Reports_and_Publications/Research_Reviews/Research_Reviews__Life_Sciences/2_Advanced_Neuroscience_Technologies.html

Ashby, W. R. (1957). *An introduction to cybernetics.* London: Chapman & Hall Retrieved May 2, 2005 from: http://pcp.vub.ac.be/books/IntroCyb.pdf

Bechara, A. (2004). The role of emotion in decision-making: evidence from neurological patients with orbitofrontal damage. *Brain and Cognition, 55,* 30-40.

Braithwaite, J. (1989). *Crime, shame and reintegration.* Cambridge: Cambridge University Press.

Brantingham, P. L., & Brantingham, J. (1991). *Niches and predators: Theoretical departures in the ecology of crime.* Paper presented at the Western Society of Criminology meeting, Berkeley, California.

Bullock, K., & Tilley, N. (Eds.), (2003). *Crime reduction and problem-oriented policing.* Jill Dando Institute Crime Science Series. Cullompton, UK: Willan Publishing.

Chenery, S., Henshaw, C., & Pease, K. (1999). *Illegal parking in disabled bays: a means of offender targeting.* Policing and Reducing Crime Briefing Note 1/99. London: Home Office.

Chenery, S., Holt, J., & Pease, K. (1997). *Biting back II: Reducing repeat victimisation in Huddersfield.* Crime Detection and Prevention Series Paper 82. London: Home Office.

Clarke, R. V., & Cornish, D. B. (1983). *Crime control in Britain: A review of policy research.* Albany, NY: State University of New York Press.

Clarke, R. V. (1997). Introduction. In R. V. Clarke (Ed.), *Situational crime prevention: Successful case studies* (2nd ed.). Monsey, NY: Criminal Justice Press.

Clarke, R. V., & Eck, J. (2003). *Become a problem solving crime analyst in 55 small steps.* London: Jill Dando Institute, University College London. Retrieved May 2, 2005 from: www.jdi.ucl.ac.uk/publications/manual/crime_manual_content.php

Cohen, L., & Felson, M. (1979). Social change and crime rate changes: A routine activities approach. *American Sociological Review, 44,* 588-608.

Cornish, D. (1994). *The procedural analysis of offending and its relevance for situational prevention.* Crime Prevention Studies, vol. 3 (pp. 151-196). Monsey, NY: Criminal Justice Press.

Cornish, D., & Clarke, R. (Eds.), (1986). *The reasoning criminal: Rational choice perspectives on offending.* New York: Springer-Verlag.

Cornish, D., & Clarke, R. (2003). *Opportunities, precipitators and criminal decisions: A reply to Wortley's critique of situational crime prevention.* Crime Prevention Studies, vol. 16 (pp. 41-96). Monsey, NY: Criminal Justice Press.

Cosmides, L., & Tooby, J. (1992). Cognitive adaptations for social exchange. In J. Barkow, L. Cosmides, & J. Tooby (Eds.), *The adapted mind: Evolutionary psychology and the generation of culture.* New York: Oxford University Press.

Cusson, M. (1993). *Situational deterrence: Fear during the criminal event.* Crime Prevention Studies, vol. 1 (pp. 55-68). Monsey, NY: Criminal Justice Press.

Dahl, R., & Spear, L. (Eds.). (2004). Adolescent brain development: Vulnerabilities and opportunities. *Annals of the New York Academy of Sciences,* 1021.

Ekblom, P. (1994). *Proximal circumstances: A mechanism-based classification of crime prevention.* Crime Prevention Studies, vol. 2 (pp. 185-232). Monsey, NY: Criminal Justice Press.

Ekblom, P. (1997). Gearing up against crime: A dynamic framework to help designers keep up with the adaptive criminal in a changing world. *International Journal of Risk, Security and Crime Prevention, 2,* 249-265.

Ekblom, P. (1999). Can we make crime prevention adaptive by learning from other evolutionary struggles? *Studies on Crime and Crime Prevention, 8,* 27-51.

Ekblom, P. (2000). The Conjunction of Criminal Opportunity – A tool for clear, "joined-up" thinking about community safety and crime reduction. In S. Ballintyne, K. Pease and V. McLaren (Eds.), *Secure foundations: Key issues in crime prevention, crime reduction and community safety.* London: Institute for Public Policy Research.

Ekblom, P. (2001). *The Conjunction of Criminal Opportunity: A framework for crime reduction toolkits*. Retrieved May 2, 2005 from Crime Reduction website: www.crimereduction.gov.uk/learningzone/cco.htm

Ekblom, P. (2003). Organised crime and the Conjunction of Criminal Opportunity framework. In A. Edwards & P. Gill (Eds.), *Transnational organised crime: Perspectives on global security*. London: Routledge.

Ekblom, P. (2005a). Designing products against crime. In N. Tilley (Ed.), *Handbook of crime prevention and community safety*. Cullompton, UK: Willan Publishing.

Ekblom, P. (2005b). How to police the future: Scanning for scientific and technological innovations which generate potential threats and opportunities in crime, policing and crime reduction. In M. Smith and N. Tilley (Eds.), *Crime science: New approaches to preventing and detecting crime*. Cullompton, UK: Willan Publishing.

Ekblom, P., & Tilley, N. (2000). Going equipped: criminology, situational crime prevention and the resourceful offender. *British Journal of Criminology, 40*, 376-398.

Exum, M. (2002). The application and robustness of the rational choice perspective in the study of intoxicated and angry intentions to aggress. *Criminology, 40*, 933-966.

Farrington, D. (1991). Psychological contributions to the explanation of offending. *Issues in Criminological and Legal Psychology, 1*, 7-19.

Felson, M. (1986). Linking criminal choices, routine activities, informal control, and criminal outcomes. In D. Cornish and R. Clarke (Eds.), *The reasoning criminal: Rational choice perspectives on offending*. New York: Springer-Verlag.

Felson, M. (1995). Those who discourage crime. In J. Eck and D. Weisburd (Eds.), *Crime and Place*. Crime Prevention Studies, vol. 4 (pp. 53-66). Monsey, NY: Criminal Justice Press.

Forrester, D., Chatterton, M., & Pease, K. (1988). *The Kirkholt Burglary Prevention Project, Rochdale*. Crime Prevention Unit Paper 13. London: Home Office.

Forrester, D., Frenz, S., O'Connell, M., & Pease, K. (1990). *The Kirkholt Burglary Prevention Project, phase 2*. Crime Prevention Unit Paper 23. London: Home Office.

Gill, M. (2005). Reducing the capacity to offend: restricting resources for offending. In N. Tilley (Ed.), *Handbook of crime prevention and community safety*. Cullompton, UK: Willan Publishing.

Goldstein, H. (1990). *Problem-oriented policing*. New York: McGraw-Hill.

Gottfredson, D. and Hirschi, T. (1990). *A general theory of crime*. Stanford, CA: Stanford University Press.

Hayward, K. (2004). *City limits: Crime, consumer culture and the urban experience*. London: Glasshouse Press.

Katz, J. (1988). *Seductions of crime*. New York: Basic Books.

Levi, M., & Handley, J. (1998). *The prevention of plastic and cheque fraud revisited*. Home Office Research Study 182. London: Home Office.

Levi, M., & Maguire, M. (2004). Reducing and preventing organised crime: An evidence-based critique. *Crime, Law and Social Change, 41*, 397-469.

Office of Science and Technology. (2004). *Brain science, addiction and drugs*. Retrieved on May 2, 2005 from website on Foresight Project: http://www.foresight-.gov.uk/Brain_Science_Addiction_and_Drugs/index.html

Roach, J., Ekblom, P., & Flynn, R. (2005). The conjunction of terrorist opportunity: A framework for diagnosing and preventing acts of terrorism. *Security Journal, 18*(3), 7-25.

Sutton, M., Schneider, J., & Hetherington, S. (2001). *Tackling theft with the market reduction approach*. Crime Reduction Research Series Paper 8. London: Home Office.

Sykes, G., & Matza, D. (1957). Techniques of neutralization. *American Sociological Review, 22*, 664-670.

Wikström, P O. (2004). Crime as alternative: Towards a cross-level situational action theory of crime causation. In J. McCord (Ed.), *Beyond empiricism: Institutions and intentions in the study of crime*. New Brunswick, NJ: Transaction.

Wikström, P-O. (2005). The social origins of pathways in crime. Towards a developmental ecological action theory of crime involvement and its changes. In D. Farrington (Ed.), *Integrated developmental and life course theories of offending*. Advances in Criminological Theory, vol. 14. New Brunswick, NJ: Transaction.

Wilson, D. S. (2002). *Darwin's cathedral: Evolution, religion and the nature of society*. Chicago: University of Chicago Press.

Wortley, R. (1996). *Guilt, shame, and situational crime prevention*. Crime Prevention Studies, vol. 5 (pp. 115-132). Monsey, NY: Criminal Justice Press.

Wortley, R. (2001). A classification of techniques for controlling situational precipitators of crime. *Security Journal, 14*, 63-82.

Wright, R., & Decker, S. (1994). *Burglars on the job*. Boston: Northeastern University Press.

Doing Without Knowing: Common Pitfalls in Crime Prevention

by

Per-Olof H. Wikström
University of Cambridge

Abstract: *This paper discusses the need for, and the value of, a more knowledge-based approach to crime prevention. I will argue the case not by presenting scientific evidence about how we can better prevent crime, but rather by pointing out the many problems caused by the lack of a knowledge-based approach in crime prevention. I will highlight the many pitfalls that, in my opinion, characterise much current crime prevention policy and practise, and discuss how these problems can be rectified by adopting a more knowledge-based approach to crime prevention. I can think of no better topic to address in a* festschrift *celebrating the life and work of Ken Pease,[1] who during his distinguished career relentlessly has championed a scientific approach to the study and prevention of crime.*

"Most interventions to prevent crime are based on untested ideas rather than upon systematic basic or applied research demonstrating that the interventions produce the intended effects and that they are cost-effective. They are rarely conceived and implemented by scientists or specialists in human and organizational engineering. Rather, they are conceived and initiated by administrators and practitioners of private organizations and government agencies who base them on their assumptions about what causes crime, what interventions will affect those causes, and how to organize and implement the intervention." (Reiss, 1992, pp. 6-7)

Crime is a serious social problem. Serious social problems should be taken seriously. To take a social problem seriously means allocating major resources into research and development in order to increase the understanding of its causes and the best ways to tackle the problem. Without fundamental knowledge about *why* the problem occurs and, based upon that, *how* it can be tackled, most of our efforts to minimise crime and disorder will continue to fail and the money we spend will be largely wasted.

Although politicians and practitioners (the police, housing authorities, social welfare authorities, etc.) may take the problem of *crime* seriously, they generally do not take the problem of *crime prevention* seriously. Crime is commonly identified as a serious problem that we have to *do* something about. New measures are proposed and implemented all the time, often rushed and poorly co-ordinated with other measures and many times with a weak knowledge-base and no prior demonstrable effects. However, crime is rarely identified as a serious problem that we have to *know* more about in order to be able to know what to do. There is less demand for and limited resources allocated to serious research and development, and there are no systematic and large-scale research programs with the aim to forward our knowledge about crime causation. In other words, *doing*, rather than *knowing*, appears to be the mantra guiding the crime prevention activities of most politicians and practitioners. The thought that *doing without knowing* may sometimes make the situation even worse seems to rarely enter the equation.

The particular kind of research that does seem to have most support among politicians and policy-makers are studies that aim to tell us how much crime we have, how victimisation varies among different social groups and crime events vary among different geographical areas (or places), and, particularly, whether the level of crime increases or decreases. Although this is important knowledge, it does not tell us much about *why* people commit crime and *what* causes the crime rate to change. At best it is only a starting point for raising questions about causes and prevention. This research only helps us define the problem, but not to explain what causes it or what to do about it.[2]

I submit that to achieve real improvements in the area of crime prevention, politicians and policy-makers need to *prioritise* the allocation of resources to *research programs* that advance knowledge of the causes of crime and, based on the outcomes of this research, to target resources to the *development* of effective methods of crime prevention (including organisational and technological aspects of implementation) in areas where interventions have the prospect of making a real difference. That is, to recognise that research and development is *the core technology of crime prevention* (Reiss, 1992).

In this paper my first aim is to identify and discuss some current key problems in creating effective crime prevention. The main point of departure for this discussion will be my own (and others') observations of the strategies, organisation and activities of local crime prevention partnerships, primarily based on experiences from Sweden and the U.K. My second aim is to briefly discuss the changes needed to move towards a more knowledge-based approach to crime prevention and why this can help us better address and deal with the problem of crime and its prevention.[3]

However, before addressing the two main topics of this paper I shall start with defining knowledge and evidence and their relationship, since these two concepts (and their relationship) will play a crucial role in my discussions.

IN LACK OF EVIDENCE: THE IMPORTANCE OF THE KNOWLEDGE-BASE

To advance crime prevention we need to utilise the best knowledge and the best evidence available. *Best practise* in crime prevention may be defined as when policy and practise deals with the problem based on the best available knowledge about the causes of crime and the best available evidence about the effectiveness of particular interventions (as they apply to particular types of individuals in particular types of social and moral contexts). I shall argue that the stronger the knowledge-base is, the more likely we are to direct our efforts to *important areas* in crime prevention, and the better the evidence-base is, the more likely we are to *do the right thing* in addressing the key causes of crime identified by the knowledge-base.

The *knowledge-base* may be defined as the *best knowledge* we have, at any given time, about the causes of crime, based on the best available analytical work (theory) and its supporting empirical study. Scientific knowledge is by its nature *general* in character. At best it assists us in better understanding the social, developmental and situational *mechanisms* (processes) that influence individuals' crime involvement. The main importance of the knowledge-base for crime prevention is that it helps *direct attention* to the social, situational and developmental processes where intervention can make the greatest impact in preventing or reducing crime. The extent to which theory and research can identify the basic social, developmental and situational mechanisms that influence individuals' crime involvement is the degree to which it can guide crime prevention activities to focus on interventions with the greatest potential to make a difference. However, a common problem with current crime prevention efforts is that policy-makers and practitioners often lack a guiding (scientific) knowledge-base when devising their strategy and making action plans to prevent crime. As a consequence many interventions are directed to areas (or implemented in a way) in which they have no or little chance of having any greater impact on the causes crime.

The *evidence-base* may be defined as the *best evidence* we have, at any given time, about the effectiveness of particular prevention measures based on scientific evaluation (preferably experiments). The main role of the evidence-base is to guide the selection of *particular measures* for implementation to address the causes of crime identified by the knowledge-base. Some major problems with the current evidence-base are that it is patchy,[4] frequently show conflicting outcomes for a particular measure, and that the findings of many evaluations are founded on weak designs and/or poorly implemented measures (e.g., Sherman et al., 2002).[5] Therefore, the overall value of the current evidence-base as a guide for crime prevention practise is often limited. Moreover, even where evidence exists about a particular measure, policy-makers and practitioners do not always use it. Often programmes that have no demonstrable effects are introduced and kept running even though the evidence shows (or indicates) that they are ineffective.[6]

In my opinion, current crime prevention efforts are often hampered by a too strong focus on the (rather patchy and weak) evidence-base at the neglect of the knowledge-base. The fact that the current evidence-base lacks comprehensiveness and many evaluations are of poor quality suggests that *only* basing crime prevention strategy and policies on available "evidence" may not always be the best course of action to create the most effective crime prevention possible. In fact, in the current state-of-affairs it may actually be wiser to take the knowledge-base (rather than the evidence-base) as *the point of departure* for devising a strategy and particular policies to prevent crime. I submit that such an approach makes it more likely that we will focus our attention on the social, developmental and situational processes in which intervention has the greatest potential for success, with the additional benefit that in building the evidence-base (through trial and error) we will focus on systematically developing measures and evaluating interventions that are likely to target the main causes of crime (Figure 1). In other words, to advance current strategy and policies the *first* question for crime prevention should be, "*How does it work?*" and only the *second* question should be, "*What works?*"[7]

Theory building and theory testing (building knowledge) are often detached from crime prevention development and practise, that is, disconnected from the devising, implementing and testing of particular interventions (building evidence). To advance crime prevention we need: (i) a better interplay between the generation of knowledge about the causes of crime (key mechanisms and processes) and the building of evidence as regards the effectiveness of particular interventions (to target these mechanisms and processes); and, (ii) a stronger guidance of crime prevention practise by the knowledge-base. I shall now consider some of the main current obstacles to such an agenda.

LOCAL CRIME PREVENTION PARTNERSHIPS: A GOOD IDEA THAT WENT WRONG, AND WHY

In countries like Sweden and the U.K. (and many others) there is a current focus on delivering crime prevention through the work of local partnerships (e.g., Local Crime Prevention Councils in Sweden and Community Safety Partnerships in the U.K.). I will share some of my own (and others')

Figure 1: The Ideal Relationship between the Knowledge-base, the Evidence-base and Action

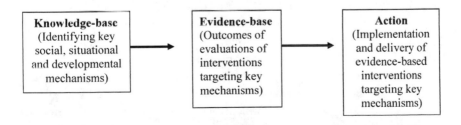

| Knowledge-base (Identifying key social, situational and developmental mechanisms) | Evidence-base (Outcomes of evaluations of interventions targeting key mechanisms) | Action (Implementation and delivery of evidence-based interventions targeting key mechanisms) |

observations of some common problems with the strategies, organisation and activities of local crime prevention partnerships as a way of illustrating the many obstacles that face the creation of effective crime prevention.

The idea of local crime prevention partnerships is fundamentally a good one because effective delivery of crime prevention requires the active involvement and contribution of a large range of local actors (parents, teachers, neighbours, police officers, social workers, doctors, shop-keepers, city planners, etc.). At the end of the day it is largely a question of what local actors do (or don't do) which determines whether or not crime prevention is effective. The effectiveness of crime prevention is ultimately dependent on how efficient the front-line is in successfully intervening in the processes that cause individuals to get involved in acts of crime.

Just bringing together local actors in a partnership does not automatically help them know what social, situational and developmental processes to target and, based upon that, what interventions to select and implement. This requires access to in-depth knowledge about the causes of crime and the effectiveness (or promise) of particular interventions. As a rule, most partnerships lack such knowledge, and therefore the starting point for their crime prevention policy and practise is often flawed. Let me give a few real life examples of what consequences this may have.

The most extreme example I have come across in my professional life is when the members of a partnership could not agree on the causes of crime and therefore it was suggested that they should take a vote on which are the main causes. The idea that one could democratically establish causation is quite fascinating, but probably would not make a fruitful foundation for policy.

A less extreme and more common situation is the one in which actors from various agencies have different *opinions* and cannot agree on what are the key causes of crime, and therefore they decide in a democratic fashion (to avoid conflict and to be able to move forward) to address all (or at least many) of the suggested causes. In fact, in my experience, actors in the crime prevention field (like most people) have quite strong and often differing opinions about the main causes of the problem, even if the word "cause" is less commonly used. A problem arises when ideas put forward about the key causes are not grounded in knowledge, or are contradictory (e.g., the idea that interventions should be minimised because they do more harm than good versus the idea that it is important with strong reactions to deter), or highly implausible. The most extreme example of an implausible cause I have come across in a partnership context is a police officer who suggested plastic surgery as a crime prevention tool, because he was of the opinion that many persistent criminals engaged in crime because of their ugly looks[8] (this was not a joke).

However, probably the most common situation is when the problem of causation is not explicitly addressed by the partnership, and as a result "policy" becomes a question of addressing identified problems and governmental priorities by *unsystematically picking and choosing interventions from all kinds of various sources* (like tool-kits, conference presentations, newspaper articles, looking at what other partnerships have done, etc.). For example, "We have a problem with vandalism; does anyone know of any good ideas how to reduce vandalism?" or, "The government has asked us to prioritise vehicle crimes; does anyone know of a good measure to prevent vehicle crimes?"

Local action plans are often drawn up without any guiding knowledge framework.[9] Typically, they are an exercise in trying to match particular problems/priorities with any suggested intervention that can be identified. Rarely is the question asked *how* this particular intervention would prevent crime (or a particular type of crime). A useful exercise I have conducted with some partnerships is to go through the list of interventions that constitute their action plan and ask the question for each intervention, *"How would this particular intervention prevent crime?"* The outcome of this exercise has so far always been that one can agree that the overwhelming majority of the measures in the action plan are unlikely to have any great impact on crime (or the particular type of crime they are supposed to target). The crucial question is: *Why do we have so many local action plans that list poorly co-ordinated measures, most of which are unlikely to significantly contribute to crime prevention?*

THE LACK OF A SHARED KNOWLEDGE-BASE

I submit that the lack of a shared organising framework of knowledge of the causes of crime is the most fundamental obstacle to the advancement of effective policy and practise in the field of crime prevention.

The lack of a knowledge-based strategy tends to promote a reactive approach where "priorities and problems of the day" are targeted, and "flavours of the day" and "tool-kits" are the basis from which programmes and measures are selected to deal with the problems and priorities. This tends to result in a large number of short-term projects that often lack a sound grounding in knowledge and evidence, and to result in patchy and poorly co-ordinated action. (For examples and discussions of these kinds of problems in the U.K., Sweden, Finland and Australia, see, e.g., Home Office, 1991; Liddle and Gelsthorpe, 1994a, 1994b; Walters, 1996; Wikström and Torstensson, 1999; Phillips et al., 2002; Byrne and Pease, 2003; Bullock and Tilley, 2003, pp. 112-124; and Savolainen, 2005.) In turn, this tends to detract from the role of more fundamental factors and therefore promote a focus on factors of less importance, often resulting in little or no long-term impact on the crime situation.

There are many reasons why knowledge- and evidence-based approaches to local crime prevention are less common. One key reason is the *lack of sufficient knowledge* about the causes of crime and the effectiveness of various crime reduction initiatives among those who formulate local strategies and action plans. This tends to promote an unsystematic and patchy approach and often detracts attention away from addressing more fundamental causes. Another key reason is the *bureaucratic organisation* of the different agencies involved in partnerships (which often tends to make well co-ordinated strategies and effective implementation difficult) and the *structure of funding* (which often tends to sponsor short-term projects). This tends to promote a "let thousand flowers bloom" approach and result in spreading resources thin. A third important reason is *external demands* from the media and pressure groups (and sometimes governmental funding bodies) to show that one is taking immediate action to deal with particular problems. This tends to promote a reactive approach combined with "a sense of urgency" and a focus on action rather than content.

Let's consider in some detail (but in no particular order) the common "deadly sins" that tend to occur as a result of the lack of a guiding knowledge framework and which often precludes the creation of the most possible effective crime prevention.

Urgency: It Has to Happen Today, or If Not, at Least Tomorrow

Long-term, well-thought-out strategies and carefully devised action plans require time and knowledge. Among politicians and practitioners there is often an understandable feeling of urgency to deal with serious problems such as crime and disorder. The demand for immediate action from the media and particular pressure groups may also be strong and, at times, highly emotionally charged (to take a somewhat extreme example, "people may die if we do not act"). However, to create lasting and significant results one has to withstand these feelings of urgency and the demand for quick action. Otherwise there is an apparent risk of implementing (and wasting money on) interventions that make little or no contribution, or even make the situation worse (that is, people would die anyway, or even more people would die). To identify a problem is not the same as knowing what to do about it (regardless how serious it is judged to be).

A Focus on Action Rather Than Its Content

Combined with "a sense of urgency," the opinion held by many partnership actors that *it is always better to do something than to do nothing*[10] may intensify the problem of doing the right thing.[11] There is no guarantee that *any* action will produce the desired outcome. On the contrary, it is important to realise that when "doing without knowing" there is, "a risk that resources will be spent on measures which may prove to be ineffective and costly, and which may, at worst, lead to a deterioration of the situation." There is also an apparent risk that, "untried but promising measures will be introduced in an over-hasty manner without having been sufficiently thought through – the result being that these measures are subsequently erroneously rejected" (Reiss, 1992). In other words, "doing without knowing" may not be the best thing to do. Sometimes it may be advantageous (in the shorter term) not to act upon emerging problems until their causes are better understood.

The strong action focus of many policy-makers and practitioners may make it difficult for them to see the benefits of grounding crime prevention practise in analytical and empirically-based knowledge about the causes of crime. One typical comment I have come across is that the contribution of academics to crime prevention is, "Intelligent but useless." A good illustration of this point is the following example; after I had finished a session with a group of practitioners on crime causation and prevention, a police officer approached me and said, "This is all fine, but we need names."

Let a Thousand Flowers Bloom – Too Patchy Actions

Without clear directions on what are the most important areas of prevention to target, programs risk developing a "let a thousand flowers bloom approach," with the hope that *if one does many different things at least some of them may give a positive result*. Lack of a directing knowledge-based frame of reference, in combination with "a sense of urgency" and a strong action orientation are factors that promote this kind of approach. This generally results in patchy and poorly co-ordinated action that lacks a sound grounding in knowledge and evidence. Sometimes it appears that the longer the list of interventions included in an action plan, the better it is judged. A partnership member once told me proudly, "We have addressed all problems and priorities in our action plan." The question whether the interventions were relevant (knowledge-based) adequate (the dosage and duration) and effective (evidence-based) in addressing the problems and priorities appeared to be of less interest. In other words, having a plan rather than its potential effectiveness was the main concern.

Spreading Resources Thin - Too Many Projects

Small pots of money spent on many minor short-term projects are less likely to make a significant difference. It may just be a waste of money. Spreading resources thin is often a consequence of lacking a directing knowledge-based frame of reference, in combination with a bureaucratic organisation and a structure of external funding that sponsors short-term projects. "Democratic demands" from various agencies and external organisations that they should have a share of the pot is another problem that may contribute to spreading resources thin.

In general, I would argue that a focus on "projects" should be avoided. Instead the aim should be on actions leading to permanent change in the way institutions or individuals operate and act. The role of projects should only be to test out and perfect interventions before implementing them on a larger scale. However, local partnerships are often caught up in running numerous of short-term projects that never become "mainstreamed," to use popular jargon.

The potential impact of a particular type of crime prevention initiative generally depends on: (i) the quality of the knowledge and evidence upon which it is based, (ii) the quality of implementation, (iii) the dosage (e.g., number of parenting sessions or frequency of police patrols), and (iv) the duration over time of the initiative. Many crime prevention initiatives appear to suffer from poor or weak implementation and/or small dosages and short duration. In such instances few or no discernible effects are to be expected even if the type of programme, in principle, is effective. Poor implementation generally renders outcome evaluations useless and does not contribute to building a solid evidence-base.

In addition, particular programmes may work better in some settings than in others, that is, their effectiveness may be context-dependent. It is therefore important to consider (build evidence concerning) in which contexts a particular programme may be effective. Currently, such evidence is scarce.

Too Reactive: Responding to "Problems of the Day"

There is always a risk that localised community safety and crime prevention work may become too reactive. There are many reasons why this may happen. One reason is that there may be a local demand for immediate action relating to particular "problems of the day" voiced by groups of residents, the media, local politicians, etc. Another reason is central guidelines or demands to prioritise certain types of crimes that may, or may not, be tied to available funding opportunities. This may promote a focus on quick-fix short-term actions and detract attention from the "bigger picture" of more fundamental problems that need to be addressed. I have been in many situations in which representatives from governmental or local agencies want to learn more about what to do about a specific problem, e.g., "What can we do about youth robberies?" In my experience they mostly want a specific and simple measure that can be implemented right away with immediate effect (like on-the-spot fines[12]) and, if such a measure does not exist, as a rule they quickly lose interest (particularly if it is suggested is that we need more knowledge before acting: "Academics always wants more money for research").

An obvious risk of a strongly reactive approach is that it may lead to a predominant focus on short-term law enforcement and situationally-oriented solutions, whereas structural problems such as concentrated disadvantage in residential areas and more long-term socially oriented programmes of action may be neglected. Most local action plans are dominated by short-term law enforcement and situational measures. In fact, in my experience, for many local partnerships crime prevention has almost become synonymous with law enforcement and situational measures.

Not Targeting Fundamental Causes

Although law enforcement initiatives and situationally-oriented techniques of crime prevention are important elements of a comprehensive local crime prevention strategy, I would argue that they have their limits. They are (in most cases) unlikely to have any long-term major impact on more fundamental factors that generate crime. This, I would argue, is a particularly important consideration in communities that include many residential areas with high levels of disadvantage. While in affluent areas the main attention of a local community crime prevention strategy and action plans may be appropriately focused on situationally-oriented measures, in less affluent communities this is not likely to be enough to make a major impact on the crime situation. Instead there is a need to address *structural factors* (concentrated disadvantage), and develop *extensive social preventative programmes* targeting the role of key players like the family and the schools in the socialisation of children and youth and their development of lifestyles, backed-up by *targeted law enforcement and situational techniques of prevention.*

I submit that influencing the day-to-day operation of families and schools and the wider organisation of social life and control in the local community are the keys to making a lasting difference as regards the problem of crime and disorder.

CREATING A MORE KNOWLEDGE-BASED APPROACH TO CRIME PREVENTION

To create a more knowledge based approach to crime prevention, local partnerships (and national actors for that matter) need to redefine their role in crime prevention. I shall conclude this paper by briefly describing what I believe are the key necessary changes in how partnerships approach their role in crime prevention and what developments are required to give them the support they need to successfully make such transformations.

The Main Role of Partnerships Should be Implementation and Delivery

Most individual members of local partnerships do not have any specific in-depth knowledge about the causes of crime and techniques of crime prevention.[13] Therefore they may not be the best-placed body to lay the foundations of a knowledge-based crime prevention strategy and action plans. In fact, I believe it is quite unfair to ask a group of professionals ("the partnership") to take on a task for which they (in most cases) are neither adequately educated nor trained.

I would argue that the *key role of the partnership should be to deal with issues of organisation, funding and co-ordination of crime prevention activities and their implementation.* Producing the knowledge- and evidence-bases upon which the local organisation and implementation of a crime prevention strategy and action plans are (or should be) based is not a task for which a partnership of practitioners are well suited. This is rather something that partnerships should be assisted with (preferably) by a national forum (a centre of excellence) of experts in crime causation and evaluation research.[14] Unfortunately, such a national forum does not, to my knowledge, exist in any country and, I would argue, is desperately needed to help advance crime prevention.

Partnerships Should Avoid Involving Local Residents in Devising Strategy and Action Plans

A difficult and sensitive question is whether, or to what extent, the local residents should be actively consulted and engaged in devising a local crime prevention strategy and action plans. A sometimes-voiced opinion is that the *local residents know best what their problems are and what should be done about them.* The extent to which this is likely to be entirely true is questionable. Although local residents may be a good source of information about visible local crime problems (and should be used as such), *it is less obvious why residents would have any specific knowledge about what would be the best course of action to deal with problems of crime and disorder.* The involvement of local residents in community safety and crime prevention work should therefore focus on making sure that their problems are identified and effectively addressed and dealt with, rather than involving them in the process of finding solutions to the problems (despite the fact that many times engaging and influencing the actions of local residents, as parents, teachers, etc., may be a crucial part of successful prevention).

Reiss (1995, p. 113), in reference to the problems of creating effective crime prevention, observes, "one finds it difficult to imagine that advances in modern medical practise would have been achieved were every local practitioner to have been a problem solver with his or her patients."

Local Strategy and Action Plans Should Not Be Problem-oriented

I submit that devising a local strategy and action plan based on identified problems (by the partnership, the public, the media, pressure groups, etc.) and governmental priorities (which currently mostly seem to be set as reactions to identified problems) tends to create a strategy and action plan that is patchy and mainly focuses on addressing *symptoms* rather than the underlying causes.[15] I argue that a much better starting point for devising local strategy and action plans to effectively prevent crime is to ask what are the fundamental causes (i.e., what are the key social, developmental and situational processes) that needs to be targeted to prevent or reduce individuals crime involvement. In other words, I believe that a "*cause-oriented approach*" (at least in the longer term) will turn out a much more effective way of organising and creating effective crime prevention strategy and action plans than a "problem-oriented approach."[16] While identifying a problem does not tell us much about how it can be prevented, identifying its causes do.

The Causes Are the Same, But the Problems Are Not

Local partnerships face very different realities. The problem profiles vary considerably. It is natural that this should be reflected in the partnerships' strategy and action plans. However, the fact that problems are different does not mean that the underlying causes of particular problems are different. I submit that the causes are the same, while the problems are not. The reason why partnerships face different problems is simply that the factors causing various problems differ among localities in their presence and strength. The main task for a partnership should be to *adapt* a general theory of crime causation to the particularities of the local community rather than attempting to create such a framework. To be able to transform a general theory of crime causation into a local strategy and action plan the partnership, as a rule, needs adequate education and training and/or external support.

The Problem of Crime Causation Has to be Put at the Top of the Crime Prevention Agenda

This is not the time and place (nor is the space available) to discuss the problem of crime causation in detail. I have done that elsewhere (Wikström, 2004, 2005, 2006; Wikström and Sampson, 2003). I will just offer a few general observations that I believe are important if we wish to improve the effectiveness of current crime prevention.

The problem of crime causation has to be put at the top of the crime prevention agenda. *Adequate resources need to be allocated to programs of research into the causes of crime and a national centre of true excellence needs to be created to assist (advise and educate) policy-makers and practitioners to make the best use of the knowledge produced.* In addressing the problem of crime prevention we will never be able to escape the question of crime causation because to be able to prevent something requires that it has causes, and that the causes can be manipulated in a way that the effect does not occur.[17] If there are no causes (or no way to influence them), prevention is impossible. If we believe in crime prevention, we have to believe in crime causation. If we believe in crime prevention, we should make every effort to improve our knowledge about the causes of crime.

One of the reviewers of this paper questioned whether we have to understand the causes to be able to prevent crime: "we do not need to know why rain falls in order to keep dry with an umbrella" (anonymous reviewer). Let's consider in some detail this quite common type of objection against the value of a "cause-oriented approach" in crime prevention.

I agree with the reviewer that we do not need to know why rain falls in order to know how to prevent us from being wet when it rains. However, what causes a rainfall is not what causes us to be wet. It is the rainfall that causes us to be wet. The rainfall is the cause and being wet the effect, one possible intervention to stop the rainfall causing us to be wet is the use of an umbrella. It is precisely because the anonymous reviewer knows that the rainfall causes him or her to be wet that he or she can effectively intervene by using his or her umbrella (if he or she didn't know that it was the rain that caused him or her to get wet it would only be an act of pure chance that could prevent him or her from getting wet when it rains).

The question about what causes rainfall is, so to speak, a question about the *causes of the cause* (of being wet) rather than a question about the *cause* (of being wet). In other words, I would argue that the reviewer's complaint, in fact, is not that we do not need to know the cause to be able to prevent something; instead, the complaint is that we do not need to know what causes the cause to be able to prevent it (which I believe is a correct observation). However, one could argue (as I would do) that the perhaps most effective way to stop people from getting wet from rainfall would be the ability to manipulate the causes of rainfall so it doesn't rain[18] (then there would be no need to use umbrellas or take shelter or to develop any other means to protect us from being wet by rainfall). In other words, and applying this argument to the problem of crime, addressing more fundamental causes of crime (the causes of the causes) may often be a more effective and lasting way of prevention than addressing the immediate causes.[19]

I submit that criminological research has produced a lot of important knowledge about crime (non-random patterns), but that this knowledge is rather poorly organised and not always adequately analysed in terms of crime causation. This point is well illustrated by the *risk-factor approach* (and its application in risk-focused prevention). Farrington has pointed out that, "a major problem with the risk factor paradigm is to determine which risk factors are causes and which are merely markers or correlated with causes" (Farrington, 2000, p. 7). He also observed, "there is no shortage of factors that are significantly correlated with offending and antisocial behavior; indeed, literally *thousands* of variables differentiate significantly between official offenders and nonoffenders or correlate significantly with self-reported offending" (Farrington, 1992, p. 256, my emphasis). To base crime prevention on a strategy that aims to minimise as many as possible of the vast number of suggested risk factors (where often their status as causes at best are unclear) may not be the most economical and successful way to address the problem of crime prevention.

I argue that, in order to advance knowledge about crime causation (and to improve the knowledge-base for crime prevention) *we need to move from the current focus on a risk-factor approach (and its application in risk-focused prevention) to an explanatory approach (with its application in cause-oriented prevention).* That is, we need to move from the current focus on mapping out non-random patterns of correlation and making predictions (a risk-factor approach) – where prevention aims to minimise risk factors – to concentrating more on the task of establishing causation and providing explanation (an explanatory approach), where prevention aims to affect key social, developmental and situational mechanisms that influence individuals' crime involvement (see further, Wikström, 2006).

Rutter has pointed out: "the histories of biology and medicine indicate that it is usually possible to reduce complex multifactorial causation to a much more limited set of causal mechanisms" (2003, p. 19). I submit that the extent to which this can be accomplished for crime causation, and adapted in a form that is useful to policy-makers and practitioners,[20] is the degree to which we can create a more rational basis for the (national and local) organisation and delivery of effective crime prevention. This would help us to focus our strategy and action plans on targeting a smaller number of fundamental causes (rather than a large number of markers and symptoms) and to focus our time and resources on developing (by trial and error) the most effective interventions possible in addressing the fundamental causes of the problem.

CONCLUSION

Preventing crime is not an easy task. It needs to be taken seriously to be successful. To make a difference, strategies for crime prevention and action plans need to be knowledge-based, and where possible, also evidence-based, to target key causal processes, and to be supported by an organisational and funding structure that allows crime prevention to be long-term in its goals, sustained and monitored in its activities, and continuously evaluated and modified in response to what is learnt. Patchy strategies of quick fixes should not be expected to yield significant and lasting results and may just waste time and money.

All this may seem obvious but, as I have tried to illustrate at some length, even a casual observation of the organisation and activities of local crime prevention partnerships (and national crime prevention actors, for that matter) in the U.K., Sweden and elsewhere shows that they often suffer from many of the pitfalls discussed. I have argued that a main reason for this is the common lack of guidance by a shared knowledge-base when devising strategy and action plans. A well-developed and knowledge-based strategy (founded on an empirically-grounded theory of crime causation) would make it possible for policy-makers and practitioners to better focus their attention on the social, developmental and situational processes in which intervention can make the greatest impact in preventing or reducing crime and disorder. Moreover, this may also help in creating a more relevant and comprehensive evidence-base by promoting a concentration of scientific evaluations of the kind of interventions that are the most likely to affect key social, developmental and situational processes in crime causation. In short, to advance crime prevention beyond its current state of common pitfalls we need a stronger emphasis on knowing (what to do) rather than just keep on doing without knowing.

Address correspondence to: Prof. Per-Olof Wikström, University of Cambridge, Institute of Criminology, Sidgwick Site, Cambridge CB3 9DT, UK; e-mail: POW20@cam.ac.uk

NOTES

1. What really characterises Ken's amazing contribution to crime prevention, besides being one of the nicest people and the most aspiring golfer in the field, as well as one of the most stimulating thinkers and innovative crime prevention scholars around, is his burning urge to make academic research relevant, accessible and used by policy-makers and practioneers. In this respect, he *is* the benchmark to which all of us should aspire.

2. While is undoubtedly true that defining and describing a problem may give us some ideas about where to look for potential causes, it is equally true that defining and describing a problem does not automatically tell us what causes the problem and how it can be prevented.

3. Space limitations only allow me to briefly touch upon this important topic.

4. For example, short-term situational measures dominate among the interventions that have been evaluated.

5. As a rule, no evaluation is better than a poor evaluation because in the latter case one risks drawing the wrong conclusions about the effectiveness of a particular type of intervention.

6. For example, Welsh and Farrington (2006, p. 1) rightly ask, "How can a program that has produced no discernible evidence, as shown through numerous evaluations, be considered for implementation?" and they go on to observe that, "unfortunately, this happens all the time."

7. To avoid any misunderstandings, I am fully supportive of the value of grounding action on evidence and the importance of building a strong evidence-base (important work in building the evidence-base is currently being carried out, for example, as part of the activities of the Campbell Collaborations Crime and Justice Group – see, e.g., Welsh and Farrington, 2006). The problem I try to identify and discuss is the one caused by the general lack of a guiding knowledge framework about the causes of crime that can help local crime prevention partnerships (and national crime prevention actors, for that matter) to better focus their activities on the most important areas that need to be addressed to achieve the most effective crime prevention.

8. An observation that may have had something to do with the fact that a lot of them were drug users and that sustained drug use does not help physical appearance.

9. Apart from my own (and others') personal experiences, this view is, for example, also supported by a review of community safety partnerships' strategy documents available on the crimereduction. gov.uk web site.

10. At the other extreme, there is the view that reactions and interventions are best kept at a minimum (generally based on the idea that labelling people always make the situation worse). Here the problem is not one of acting too quickly, but rather one of being too passive. It is not uncommon that a main partnership "battlefield" is between those who wants to act instantly and those who do not want to act at all.

11. A different but related problem is that sometime funding considerations fuel the demand for immediate action. I have been present in partnership meetings where it bluntly has been stated that the most important goal is to spend the money (so not to lose the funding), not to make a difference. A typical situation is that money is left over towards the end of a funding period and that one has to quickly find projects (any projects) to spend the money on.

12. The effectiveness of which as a preventative tool is highly questionable.

13. There is no particular reason why police officers, local politicians or head teachers should have any in-depth knowledge about crime causation or about the effectiveness of particular interventions.

14. However, just to organisationally create a "centre of excellence" does not mean that it actually become a centre of excellence. This also requires that one is able to motivate and recruit the best expertise available to work for such an enterprise. In fact, creating "a centre of excellence" without any excellence may just make things worse.

15. I do not argue that "treating symptoms" always is ineffective, just that if one can target the underlying causes the effects are more likely to be of greater and lasting significance.

16. As I see it, the greatest value of a problem-oriented approach is in the *implementation* of a crime prevention strategy, that is, when the knowledge- and evidence-base are applied to deal with the particular profile of local problems.

17. This is not to say that it is impossible to prevent crime without knowing its causes (in our actions we can of course be lucky and by pure chance influence a cause). It is just to say that the better we know the causes, the more likely we are to spend our time and money

on interventions that have the prospect of being effective (rather than wasting time and money in capitalising on the odd chance that some of our actions may be successful).

18. There are obviously many reasons why we wouldn't like to stop rainfall, but this is not of immediate importance for the general point I make about the relative effectiveness of addressing fundamental and immediate causes in prevention.

19. Although I would argue that it is necessary to understand the immediate causes to be able to develop an understanding of the "causes of the causes" (see further, Wikström, 2006).

20. The importance of the task of organising knowledge about crime causation in a form that makes it useful to policy-makers and practitioners in thinking about devising crime prevention strategies has been helpfully identified and addressed by Ekblom (2000, 2002). See also, Wikström and Torstensson (1999).

REFERENCES

Bullock, K., & Tilley, N. (2003). From strategy to action: The development and implementation of problem-oriented projects. In K. Bullock & N. Tilley (Eds.), *Crime reduction and problem-oriented policing*. Cullompton, UK: Willan Publishing.

Byrne, S., & Pease, K. (2003). Crime reduction and community safety. In T. Newburn (Ed.), *Handbook of policing*. Cullompton, UK: Willan Publishing.

Community safety partnership audits and strategies in the UK. See: crimereduction. gov.uk website.

Ekblom, P. (2000). The Conjunction of Opportunity – A tool for clear, joined-up thinking about community safety and crime reduction." In S. Ballantyne, K. Pease & V. McLaren (Eds.), *Secure foundations: Issues in crime prevention, crime reduction and community safety*. London: Institute for Public Policy Research.

Ekblom, P. (2002). From the source to the mainstream is uphill: The challenge of transferring knowledge of crime prevention through replication, innovation and anticipation. In N. Tilley (Ed.), *Analysis for crime prevention*. Crime Prevention Studies, vol. 13. Monsey. NY: Criminal Justice Press.

Farrington, D. P. (1992). Explaining the beginning, progress and ending of antisocial behavior from birth to adulthood. In J. McCord (Ed.), *Facts, frameworks, and forecasts: Advances in criminological theory*, vol. 3. New Brunswick, NJ: Transaction.

Farrington, D. P. (2000). Explaining and preventing crime: The globalization of knowledge – the American Society of Criminology 1999 Presidential Address. *Criminology, 38*(1), 1-24.

Farrington, D. P., & Welsh, B. C. (2006). *Preventing crime. What works for children, offenders, victims and places*. Dordrecht, NETH: Springer Verlag.

Home Office (1991). *Safer communities: The local delivery of crime prevention through the partnership approach* (Morgan Report). London: Standing Conference on Crime Prevention.

Liddle, A. M., & Gelsthorpe, L. (1994a). *Inter-agency crime prevention: Organising local delivery*. Crime Prevention Unit Series paper 52. London: Home Office.

Liddle, A. M. & Gelsthorpe, L. (1994b). *Crime prevention and inter-agency co-operation*. Crime Prevention Unit Series paper 53. London: Home Office.

Phillips, C. et al. (2000). *A review of audits and strategies produced by Crime and Disorder Partnerships in 1999*. Home Office Briefing Note 8/00. London: Home Office.

Reiss, A., Jr. (1992). Research as the core technology in crime prevention. In *Crime control: Past, present and future*. Seoul: Korean Institute of Criminology.

Reiss, A., Jr. (1995). The role of the police in crime prevention. In P-O Wikström, R. V. G. Clarke & J. McCord (Eds.), *Integrating crime prevention strategies: Propensity and opportunity*. BRÅ-report 1995:5. Stockholm: Fritzes.

Rutter, M. (2003). Crucial paths from risk indicator to causal mechanism. In B. B. Lahey, T. E. Moffitt, & A. Caspi (Eds.), *Causes of conduct disorder and juvenile delinquency*. New York: Guilford Press

Savolainen, J. (2005). Think nationally, act locally: The municipal-level effects of the National Crime Prevention Program in Finland. *European Journal on Criminal Policy and Research 11*, 175-191.

Sherman L. W., Farrington D. P., Welsh B. C., & Layton MacKenzie, D. (2002). *Evidence-based crime prevention*. London: Routledge.

Tilley N. (2003). Community policing, problem-oriented policing and intelligence-led policing. In T. Newburn (Ed.), *Handbook of policing*. Cullompton, UK: Willan Publishing.

Walters R. (1996). The "dream" of multi-agency crime prevention: Pitfalls in policy and practice. In R. Homel (Ed.), *The politics and practice of situational crime prevention*. Crime Prevention Studies, vol. 5. Monsey, NY: Criminal Justice Press.

Wikström, P-O. (2004). Crime as alternative. Towards a cross-level situational action theory of crime causation. In J. McCord (Ed.), *Beyond empiricism: Institutions and intentions in the study of crime*. Advances in Criminological Theory, vol. 13. New Brunswick, NJ: Transaction.

Wikström, P-O. (2005). The social origins of pathways in crime. Towards a Developmental Ecological Action Theory of crime involvement and its changes. In D. P. Farrington. (Ed.), *Integrated developmental and life course theories of offending*. Advances in Criminological Theory, vol. 14. New Brunswick, NJ: Transaction.

Wikström, P-O. (2006). Linking individual, setting and acts of crime. Situational mechanisms and the explanation of crime. In P-O. Wikström & R. J. Sampson (Eds.), *The explanation of crime: Contexts, mechanisms and development*. Cambridge, UK: Cambridge University Press.

Wikström, P-O., Clarke, R. V. and McCord, J. (1995). *Integrating crime prevention strategies: Propensity and opportunity*. BRÅ-report 1995:5. Stockholm: Fritzes.

Wikström, P-O., & Torstensson, M. (1999). Local crime prevention and its national support: Organisation and direction. *European Journal of Criminal Policy and Research*, 7, 459-481.

Wikström, P-O., & Sampson, R. J. (2003). Social mechanisms of community influences on crime and pathways in criminality. In B. B. Lahey, T. E. Moffitt & A. Caspi (Eds.), *Causes of conduct disorder and juvenile delinquency*. New York: Guilford Press.

Sustainability versus Safety: Confusion, Conflict and Contradiction in Designing Out Crime

by

Rachel Armitage
The Applied Criminology Centre, The University of Huddersfield

Abstract: *This chapter highlights the confusing and contradictory policy and guidance within the field of designing out crime within the built environment and challenges policy makers to address an issue which, as yet, has remained unresolved. Whilst it is accepted that conflicting research will always exist, the current debate surrounding the criminogenic features of permeable design has diverted practitioners' attention from the immediate task of reducing crime. Having highlighted the current conflict within the U.K. planning system, the chapter concludes with a detailed analysis of the specific environmental factors which increase a property's vulnerability to victimisation. This is presented as a simple, usable risk assessment mechanism to be used by crime reduction practitioners as a means of identifying which properties will become vulnerable to crime if built (therefore allowing them to challenge planning applications) or, in the case of properties already developed, allowing resources to be directed towards properties at most risk.*

Crime Prevention Studies, volume 21 (2007), pp. 81–110.

INTRODUCTION

This chapter presents a culmination of research conducted between 1998 and 2004 on the subject of crime and the built environment. My introduction to this field began in 1998 when I was asked by Ken Pease to conduct an evaluation of the Secured by Design (SBD) scheme, which I later published in 2000 (Armitage, 2000). At the commencement of the project, although research had shown that the individual principles upon which the SBD scheme was based each worked to reduce crime and disorder, it was unclear whether the initiative as a package was acting as an effective crime reduction measure. The U.K. Crime and Disorder Act (1998) had just been introduced, requiring multi-agency partners to work together to reduce crime and disorder. The Home Office had launched their £250 million Crime Reduction Programme, and an increasing emphasis was being placed upon the identification and implementation of what works in reducing crime. The ensuing two years saw publications from several authors (Brown, 1999; Pascoe, 1999; Armitage, 2000), each concluding that SBD confers a crime reduction advantage. The future was bright. A scheme had been developed which required the input of multi-agency partners as diverse as planning officers, police, registered social landlords, architects and private housing developers. The principles upon which it was based had each revealed crime reduction advantages, and the scheme as a package had stood up to rigorous independent evaluation. The stage was set for a harmonious, multi-agency approach towards crime reduction, and as Ken summarised at the academic debate at New Scotland Yard in February 2000, "there is now enough evidence to say that Secured by Design confers a crime reduction advantage" (Hodge, 2000, p. 24).

Unfortunately, Ken's conclusion, although logical, was overly optimistic. Rather than accepting and implementing the findings of available evidence, the ensuing years have seen an abundance of confusing and contradictory policy and guidance which have diverted practitioners' and policy makers' attention from the immediate task of reducing crime. Although key agencies within the field of designing out crime have now recognised that the crime implications of design must be considered, this acceptance is futile unless those involved can agree on which environmental factors are criminogenic. The current climate in this field of designing out residential crime is littered with frustrating contradictions. It is hard to believe that such a conflicting set of principles, policies and guidance would have been ignored for so long within a more appealing or glamorous criminological subject. It is hoped that the findings presented throughout this chapter will challenge those within the field to confront – as opposed to avoiding – the contentious issues surrounding housing layout and crime reduction, and will go some way towards clarifying many of the conflicting issues.

THE ARGUMENT

The main area of conflict within the field of designing out crime has been the issue of permeability or through movement of people and vehicles. This debate (which has rather simplistically been presented as one of *culs-de-sac* versus through roads) has dominated much of the discussion surrounding SBD over the last five years, with headlines such as "End of the Road for the *Cul-de-Sac*" (Fairs, 1998, p. 1), "*Culs-de-Sac* Hit the Skids" (Stungo, 1998, p. 2) and "How Brookside Boom Helped the Burglars" (Summerskill, 2000, p. 16). Those in favour of limiting through-movement generally argue that a residential area which encourages movement (be it vehicular or pedestrian) gives offenders an opportunity to attach that area to their awareness space. If a property is located on a through road which is used as part of an individual's route to work, school or leisure facilities, that individual will become familiar with who lives where, what time they leave for work and what car they drive, and will generally feel less conspicuous within that neighbourhood. Those who argue in favour of permeable housing believe that residential areas should encourage movement and thus allow passersby to create an informal surveillance or act as guardians for that area. Much support for the issue of permeable housing estates emerged following the Rio Earth Summit of 1992 (United Nations Conference on Environment and Development, 1992) and its product document Agenda 21, which encourages sustainability – getting people out of their cars and onto their feet and bicycles.

As was mentioned within the opening paragraph, the last two decades have seen a major change in the perception of how a reduction in crime in England and Wales is to be achieved. This change can be characterised as having two primary facets, which are closely linked. The first is the advance of situational crime prevention (SCP), following the demonstration that crime trends are more readily understood in terms of the supply of crime opportunities than the distribution of criminal propensity across the population (Mayhew et al., 1976; Felson, 1998; Felson and Clarke, 1998). This insight has been reinforced by the demonstration that the regulation of opportunities will impact on rates of crime (Clarke, 1992).

The second facet of the change in the perception of crime reduction flows from the first, but in fact developed alongside it, with its first expression being found in the Morgan Report of 1991 (Home Office, 1991). This is the recognition that the supply of crime opportunities is under the control of agencies other than the police, such that the historic reliance upon the police as the primary crime reduction functionaries was misguided, and certainly unfair. The Introduction of the Crime and Disorder Act (1998) represented the culmination of the process begun by the Morgan Report, and it has gone some way towards addressing the mismatch between control over crime opportunities and the responsibility for crime reduction. In particular Section 17 places a responsibility upon "relevant authorities" to consider the crime and disorder implications of every decision that they make, and sections 5 and 6 (amended by the Police Reform Act 2002) place a duty upon agencies such as local authorities, police, primary care trusts, police authorities and fire authorities to develop strategic partnerships to tackle crime and disorder within their areas. The claim that this act has only gone some way towards achieving its aims relates to the confusion which remains, not least the exclusion of both central Government and the private sector from the provisions of the Act (an omission which Ken has vowed to rectify before he retires!). The specific problems regarding the separation of responsibilities in the planning process are identified by Moss (2001), who highlights the legal loophole which has left government bodies such as the Planning Inspectorate exempt from the provisions of this Act. In cases such as *Aquarium Entertainments Ltd. v Brighton and Hove Council*, this loophole in the legislation has allowed developers, after they are denied planning permission on the grounds of crime prevention, with the opportunity to appeal to the Planning Inspectorate who, exempt from Section 17 considerations, grant permission for the original development.

In the criminological arena of designing out crime within the built environment, the task of partnership working has become needlessly complex. Take for example the commonplace proposal to a local authority by a private developer to build 30 new properties. The local authority for this area are bound by Section 17 of the Crime and Disorder Act (1998), which states that "it shall be the duty of each authority . . . to exercise its various functions with due regard to the likely effect of those functions on . . . crime and disorder in its area" (Great Britain, 1998a). The local authority are also bound by Section 6 of the Human Rights Act (1998), which states that it is unlawful for a public authority to act in a way which is incompatible with a convention right. Three convention rights (Schedule 1 – Part 1, Articles 5 and 8 and Article 1 of the First Protocol, Part 2) relate to safety and security. Therefore, it is in the interest of the local authority to ensure that the proposed properties are designed in a manner which will reduce their vulnerability to crime and disorder. Looking towards criminological research as an indication of how to design out crime would suggest that as a means of reducing crime opportunities, properties should be designed with minimum access/egress and limited permeability (Brantingham and Brantingham, 1975, 1993, 2000; Bevis and Nutter, 1977; Brantingham et al., 1977; Brown and Altman, 1983; Newlands, 1983; Greenberg and Rohe, 1984; Beavon, 1984; Taylor and Gottfredson, 1987; Cromwell et al., 1991; Poyner and Webb, 1991; Rengert and Wasilchick, 2000; Wiles and Costello, 2000). As well as seeking guidance from criminological research, a local authority concerned with the reduction of crime may also look for guidance from the police, in particular Architectural Liaison Officers (ALOs) or Crime Prevention Design Advisors (CPDAs). Again, this advice would suggest limiting footpaths and through movement.

> It is recognised that too many footpaths and through roads in developments help to make crime easier to commit. They provide choice of alternative escape routes from the scene of the crime, rather than obliging the offender to return by the way he came. The opportunity to take a different route gives him the anonymity and safety he seeks, as opposed to the dangers of returning the same way, where he may have already been noticed. The more alternative routes there are, the more confident the wrongdoer feels, and the easier it is to commit crime. (Standards and Testing, 2004)

In contrast, the sources of guidance for planning departments (who are still part of the local authority bound by the Crime and Disorder Act and the Human Rights Act), whose task it is to make decisions regarding the design and layout of residential housing, offer very different advice regarding permeability and accessibility. "Places, Streets and Movement: A Companion guide to Design Bulletin 32 – Residential roads and footpaths" (Department of the Environment, Transport and the Regions, 1998, p. 39) states that: "The principle of the walkable neighbourhood is the key to creating a sociable, sustainable community." Towards an Urban Renaissance (Department of the Environment, Transport and the Regions, 1999) also makes contradictory suggestions relating to housing layout.

> A user friendly public realm should make walking and cycling easy, pleasant and convenient by keeping the size of urban blocks small,

with frequent pedestrian cut-throughs to make a new development permeable and accessible to the existing neighbourhoods. (Department of the Environment, Transport and the Regions, 1999, p. 71)

Academic research – in particular work published by Rudlin and Falk (1995), Hillier and Shu (1998) and Shu (2000) – also supports the notion that through movement and permeability are preferable to limited access when attempting to reduce crime. However, later work by Hillier (2004), whilst maintaining that through routes are preferable to enclaves, recognises the simplistic interpretation of his findings by journalists who preferred to present the case of *culs-de-sac* versus through roads, whilst ignoring the "difficult bits" (p. 9). In this paper, Hillier's findings bear many similarities to those presented below. Rather than it being a simplistic presentation of through roads versus *culs-de-sac*, Hillier suggests that it is "leaky" *culs-de-sac* as opposed to *culs-de-sac* in general, which present security problems, and that even integrated streets (through roads), if designed with a system of back alleys, will also be vulnerable to crime.

Unfortunately, recent opportunities to address this confusion have been wasted. Planning Circular 5/94 (Department of the Environment, 1994), placed the consultation between police ALO/CPDAs and planning departments on a more formal footing as well as recognising the link between design and crime. Although the circular did not make consultation between police and planners mandatory, it encouraged it as best practice and urged planning authorities to consider crime prevention in their development plans. The Urban Policy White Paper (Office of the Deputy Prime Minister, 2000) proposed that circular 5/94 should be reviewed, and in 2004 *Safer Places: The Planning System and Crime Prevention* (Office of the Deputy Prime Minister and Home Office, 2004) was published. Although this guide highlights the importance of crime reduction considerations in planning and design, its seven attributes of safer places have not addressed the confusion surrounding access and movement, and the message conveyed still remains unclear. For example, the guide highlights how safer places will have "well-defined routes, spaces and entrances that provide for convenient movement without compromising security" (p. 16). Yet the following paragraph highlights how crime and anti-social behaviour are more likely to occur if "there are several ways into and out of an area – providing potential escape routes for criminal activity" (p. 16). The answer, according to this guide, is that "too few connections can undermine vitality, too many – and especially too many under-used or poorly thought out connections – can increase the opportunity to commit crime" (p. 16).

Unfortunately, this lack of clarity does not help practitioners who are faced with the task of reducing crime.

Many agencies are required under current legislation to do all that they reasonably can to prevent crime and disorder within their area. In the case of the design of residential housing this is not an easy task. That the current government places an emphasis upon evidence-led practice is a positive step. The fact that this evidence is producing contradictory findings and guidance has led to confusion amongst many key agencies involved in the design, development and ultimately the granting of permission for residential housing. If it were as straightforward as Schneider and Kitchen (2002) suggest, the issue of designing out crime would be in that state of harmonious multi-agency working alluded to within the opening paragraph.

> Indeed, the notion of sustainability – defined as "development that meets the needs of the present without compromising the ability of future generations to meet their own needs" (UN Commission on Environment and Development, 1987) is highly compatible with place-crime prevention planning. (Schneider and Kitchen, 2002, p. 16)

Indeed the differences could not be greater. These opposing views are manifested in the SBD scheme, whose principles include maximising surveillance, minimising access and maximising defensible space; and New Urbanism, whose principles include encouraging walkable neighbourhoods, mixed land use, using rear access alleys, hiding garages and eliminating *culs de sac* in favour of permeable street networks. It is hoped that a brief synopsis of the two will help to explain the opposing principles.

SBD is an award scheme, established in 1989, which aims to encourage housing developers to design out crime at the planning stage. The scheme is managed by the Association of Chief Police Officers (ACPO) and supported by the Home Office. The scheme sets standards for compliance (drawn up in consultation with the Department of Transport, Local Government and the Regions – now the Office for the Deputy Prime Minister, as well as trade, industry and standards organisations), which are based largely upon the principles of maximising surveillance, minimising access and egress, maximising territoriality and defensible space and ensuring that properties and their boundaries are physically secure. Whilst the number of studies evaluating the crime reduction benefits of the scheme as a whole are limited in number (Brown, 1999; Pascoe, 1999; Armitage, 2000), there exists an abundance of literature supporting the individual crime reduction principles upon which it is based. These include mini-mising access (Brantingham and Brantingham, 1975, 1993, 2000; Bevis and Nutter, 1977; Brantingham et al., 1977; Brown and Altman, 1983; Newlands, 1983; Greenberg and Rohe, 1984; Beavon, 1984; Taylor and Gottfredson, 1987; Cromwell et al., 1991; Poyner and Webb, 1991; Mir-lees-Black et al., 1998; Rengert and Wasilchick, 2000; Wiles and Costello, 2000), maximising surveillance (Reppetto, 1974; Cromwell et al., 1991; Brown and Bentley, 1993; Rengert and Wasilchick, 2000), increasing physi-cal security (Brown and Altman, 1983; Cromwell et al., 1991), and increas-ing territoriality (Newman, 1973, 1995; Brown and Altman, 1983; Brown and Bentley, 1993).

The emergence of New Urbanism, as Town and O'Toole (2005) highlight, can be traced to 1961 and the work of Jane Jacobs, who advocated busy, vibrant streets as a means of maximising surveillance (eyes on the street). Unfortunately, these principles, which are being used as the basis for small developments within towns and villages, were never intended to be translated to the suburbs. As Jacobs (1961, p. 26) states: "I hope no reader will try to transfer my observations into guides as to what goes on in towns, or little cities, or in suburbs which still are suburban." New Urbanism combined two movements in the architecture-urban planning community. The first, sometimes referred to as neotraditionalism, focused upon using urban design to give people a sense of community. Neotradi-tionalists recommended design features such as sidewalks, front porches, parks, community centres, and other common areas, all aimed at getting people to interact with one another. The second movement focused upon the relationship between land use and transportation. Modern suburbs had made people auto-dependent, which led to pollution, obesity, and other social ills. To remedy this, planners recommended higher-density compact cities that mixed housing with retail and commercial uses so that people could walk to the grocery store or places of employment. The communitar-ian neotraditionalists were not concerned about transportation issues, while the anti-auto compact-cities advocates did not especially care about front porches or community centres. Yet their prescriptions overlapped in many ways, especially in their desires for higher densities and mixed uses. In 1991, leaders of both movements met at Yosemite Park's Ahwahnee Hotel and wrote the Ahwahnee Principles, which became the foundation for New Urbanism. New Urbanism's guiding principles are based upon walkability, connectivity, mixed use and diversity, mixed housing, quality architecture and urban design, traditional neighbourhood structure, increased density, smart transportation, sustainability and quality of life. Contrary to the abundance of literature supporting the principles of SBD, the benefits which New Urbanism asserts in terms of crime reduction, in particular in its third and fifth principles under "the block, the street and the building" (Charter of the New Urbanism, undated) appear to be presented without supporting evidence. To the contrary, recent research suggests that the cost of policing New Urbanist developments will be approximately three times that of policing a SBD development. If both under-reporting and the true economic cost of crime are taken into account (as opposed to simply policing costs), this figure increases from three to just over five (Knowles, undated). Although Schneider and Kitchen (2002) made initial claims regarding the crime reduction impact of the New Urbanist redevelopment of Hulme, Manchester, the ten year review of the Hulme development process conducted by the Centre for Urban and Regional Futures (SURF) at the University of Salford (SURF Centre, 2002), revealed less positive findings regarding crime and the fear of crime within this area. Whilst reporting that there had been a regeneration effect in the early years of the redevelopment, it showed that crime (in particular burglary and theft from a vehicle) had risen at a greater rate for the regeneration area of Hulme than for the city of Manchester as a whole. In support of these findings, Crime Pattern Analysis revealed that between 2002/2003 and 2003/2004, the burglary rate for the Hulme regeneration area was three and a half times the national average – 70 and 68 burglaries per 1,000 households in comparison to 19 (Town, 2004).

THE EVIDENCE

Having identified the current conflict within the U.K. planning system, the remainder of this chapter presents the findings of a detailed analysis of the specific environmental factors which increase a property's vulnerability to victimisation. It is hoped that the findings will go some way towards clarifying the confusion surrounding the issues of permeability and through movement.

The sample for this study included the 25 SBD and 25 Non-SBD housing estates which had been used in the original evaluation of the Secured by Design scheme (Armitage, 2000) and which covered 1,058 properties located throughout the West Yorkshire region. The collection of data involved conducting an assessment of each of these 1,058 houses using a checklist developed specifically for this project (available below at the Appendix). The checklist was developed using previous indices of risk as well as the literature relating to environmental risk factors that has been discussed throughout this paper. The checklist was split into the seven categories of road network, access, property within awareness space of others, surveillance, parking, social climate and traces.

The final version of the checklist was produced following several validation exercises to ensure that the statements/questions were not ambiguous or open to misinterpretation. The criticism to which this methodology is most vulnerable concerns inter-rater reliability. Since it was not possible for the author to be unaware of an estate's SBD status, the rating had to be as objective as possible. Seeking to ensure this objectivity involved conducting a small pilot scheme at an estate not utilised within the final analysis. Two individuals scored the same properties without consultation. If there were discrepancies between their findings, these statements/questions were re-worded to improve clarity. The process was repeated until both individuals were reaching the same conclusions for each question/statement. A second validation exercise involved consultation with several ALOs to ensure that the questions/statements covered all relevant debates surrounding the scheme.

Data collection involved certain conventions which should be made explicit. The intention behind the collection of these data was to assess a property's vulnerability to crime as viewed by an outsider, i.e., a potential offender. Therefore, when assessing whether there was evidence of factors such as a neighbourhood watch scheme, the objective was not to analyse the intensity of that scheme or even whether it actually existed, but purely to measure evidence of its existence as seen by an outsider. If there was a neighbourhood watch scheme in an area, but no overt signs of the scheme, it would be categorised as "no." On the other hand, if there was no "working" scheme in an area, but signs of a scheme were present, it would be categorised as "yes." Following the collection of these data, the fieldwork was concluded with another small pilot exercise whereby two individuals scored the original pilot sample to ensure that there was still consistency between findings. To this end, it is suggested that the scores for each property are as reliable as possible.

Which Environmental Factors Were Linked with Crime Risk?

To recapitulate, by this stage of the study evidence had been acquired about a range of environmental factors for each of the 1,058 properties and an indication of whether that property had been subjected to crime victimisation (using West Yorkshire Police's recorded crime data). Each of the 33 environmental factors was cross-tabulated against prior victimisation to reveal which factors were most associated with crime-prone homes. The results revealed that of the 33 environmental factors, 13 were associated with the risk of burglary (at a statistically significant level of 0.1). These environmental factors are presented in Table 1 below.

The remaining factors were not associated with burglary at a statistically significant level. For only those variables which exhibited a statistically reliable association with burglary victimisation at the 0.1 level, Table 2 presents the odds-ratios of the burglary probability of each named attribute of a property relative to the absence of that attribute. Thus, for example, heavy traffic is associated with 1.84 times the burglary risk of homes passed by only light traffic.

In terms of total crime as opposed to burglary alone, 17 of the 33 factors were associated with the risk of victimisation. These are displayed in Table 3.

The remaining factors were not associated with total crime at a statistically significant level. As with the burglary analysis, Table 4 presents, only for the variables which exhibited a statistically reliable association with victimisation at the level of 0.1, the odds-ratio of victimisation risk. This table presents each environmental factor and the risk which its presence produces. For example, being located on a through road is linked to a risk of victimisation 1.2 times that of living on a leaky *cul de sac* and 1.27 times that of living on a "true" *cul-de-sac*. A property which shows signs of much disrepair is 1.74 times more likely to be victimised than a property which shows no signs of disrepair.

Designing a Practitioners' Risk Assessment Mechanism

The purpose of this chapter is to highlight, and go some way towards clarifying, the confusion relating to the environmental factors which influence crime risk. But it appears appropriate to introduce, however briefly, a risk assessment mechanism designed using the previous data which it is hoped can be utilised by crime reduction practitioners as a means of identifying which properties will become vulnerable to crime if built (therefore allowing them to challenge planning applications) or, in the case of properties already developed, allowing resources to be directed towards properties at most risk.

Table 1: Environmental Factors Associated with Burglary

Environmental Factors	Percentage of Sample Victims of Burglary			Average Burglary Risk for Sample of 1,058 Properties	Statistical Significance
Is the property adjacent to open space?	Yes = 19.2%	No = 15.3%	-	16.1%	*
Road Network	True Cul-de-Sac = 14.1%	Leaky Cul-de-Sac = 18.4%	Through Road = 17.8%	16.1%	*
Presence of Real/Symbolic Barrier	Yes = 14%	No = 17.9%	-	16.1%	*
Does Estate have a footpath leading to local shops?	Yes = 26.3%	No = 15.5%	-	16.1%	**
Does Estate have a footpath leading to a maze of other footpaths?	Yes = 26.5%	No = 14.5%	-	16.1%	**
Does Estate have a footpath leading to another residential area?	Yes = 17.9%	No = 14.8%	-	16.1%	*
Volume of traffic at nearby road junction	Light = 12.3%	Moderate = 23.3%	Heavy = 22.6%	16.1%	**
Volume of pedestrian traffic in front of property	Light = 15.7%	Moderate = 25.6%	-	16.1%	**
Signs of Neighbourhood Watch scheme?	Yes = 11.1%	No = 17.1%	-	16.1%	**
Evidence that property has a burglar alarm?	Yes = 22.6%	No = 12%	-	16.1%	**
Is there a gate leading from footpath into rear garden?	Yes = 35.7%	No = 15.8%	-	16.1%	*
Are there signs of brief desertion?	Yes = 41.7%	No = 15.8%	-	16.1%	**
Are there signs of long-term desertion?	45.5%	15.8%	-	16.1%	**

* denotes significance at level of <0.1 (using Chi-Square)
**denotes significance at level of <0.05 (using Chi-Square)

Table 2: Environmental Factors Associated with Burglary Risks (odds-ratio)

Environmental Factor	Odds-Ratio
Footpath to other residential area	1.21
Adjacency to open space	1.25
Absence of real/symbolic barrier	1.28
Through road (vs closed *cul-de-sac*)	1.30
No evidence of neighbourhood watch scheme	1.54
Footpath to local shops	1.70
Footpath to other footpaths	1.83
Heavy traffic (vs light)	1.84
Evidence of burglar alarm	1.88
Moderate traffic (vs light)	1.89
Gate from rear path into garden	2.26
Signs of brief desertion	2.64
Signs of lengthy desertion	2.88

Having established the environmental variables which should feature in any prioritisation of crime reduction effort, the next step was to turn these into a simple, usable scale for risk assessment. The method to give effect to this was selected on the grounds of its simplicity and robustness rather than statistical sophistication. It was based upon the Burgess points system described in Simon (1971, p. 31), who refers to it as "one of the simplest prediction methods," with an application in a criminological context described in Nuttal et al. (1977), who commend it as robust and simple. It does not address the problems of multicollinearity as more sophisticated models do, and it is open to criticisms of shrinkage (in that it is a more powerful predictor of the sample on which it was constructed than any other sample), but has the crucial advantage of transparency of rationale and construction. It can be used without sophisticated software (or even a computer!) and is therefore more likely to appeal to the practitioners to whom it was designed for. Essentially, a score is derived from the difference between the mean rate of crime suffered generally, and the rate of crime suffered by homes with a particular characteristic. The process

Table 3: Environmental Factors Associated with Victimisation

Environmental Factors	Percentage of Sample Victims of Crime				Average Crime Risk for Sample of 1,058 Properties	Statistical Significance
Road Network	True Cul-de-Sac = 37.1%	Leaky Cul-de-Sac = 44.7%	Through Road = 47.3%	-	41%	**
How close is the property located to a footpath?	0 houses away from footpath = 47.2%	1-5 = 39.3%	6-10 = 50.4%	More than 10 = 38.2%	41%	**
Does Estate have a footpath leading to local shops?	Yes = 52.6%	No = 40.4%	-	-	41%	*
Does Estate have a footpath leading to a maze of other footpaths?	Yes = 52.9%	No = 39.3%	-	-	41%	**
Is there a gate leading from footpath into rear garden?	Yes = 92.9%	No = 40.3%	-	-	41%	**
Is the property visible from a nearby footpath?	Yes = 47.3%	No = 40%	-	-	41%	*
How heavy is the volume of traffic at the nearest road junction?	Light = 36.8%	Moderate = 52.6%	Heavy = 54.7%	-	41%	**
How heavy is the flow of pedestrian traffic in front of property?	Light = 40.1%	Moderate = 62.8%	-	-	41%	**
Does the property have signs of litter/graffiti?	None = 38.1%	Some = 50.7%	Heavy = 57.7%	-	41%	**

Table 3 *(continued)*

Environmental Factors	Percentage of Sample Victims of Crime				Average Crime Risk for Sample of 1,058 Properties	Statistical Significance
Does the property show signs of disrepair?	No signs = 39.8%	Some signs = 50%	Many signs = 69.2%	-	41%	▲▲
Signs of dog	Yes = 66.7%	No = 40.7%	-	-	41%	**
Signs of a burglar alarm	Yes = 52.7%	No = 33.8%	-	-	41%	**
Does property have a window open/door ajar?	Yes = 45.8%	No = 40.1%	-	-	41%	*
Is property located on the nearest main road?	Yes = 60%	No = 40.7%	-	-	41%	*
The house is not overlooked at the front	Yes = 46.7%	No = 39.4%	-	-	41%	**
Are there signs of brief desertion?	Yes = 75%	No = 40.6%	-	-	41%	▲▲
Are there signs of long-term desertion?	81.8%	40.6%	-	-	41%	**

* denotes significance at level of <0.1 (using Chi-Square)
** denotes significance at level of <0.05 (using Chi-Square)

of applying the Burgess method of analysis to this study involved the following steps:

a) The analysis detailed in Tables 1 and 3 (plus their accompanying text) was utilised to identify the environmental factors which showed a statistically significant association with crime risk.

b) For each of those factors, the average risk of burglary/total crime for the whole sample was subtracted from the percentage risk associated with that variable.

Table 4: Environmental Factors Associated with All Crime Risks (odds-ratio)

Environmental Factors	Odds-Ratio
Window open/ajar	1.14
Property visible from footpath	1.18
Not overlooked at front	1.19
Through road (vs 'leaky' *cul-de-sac*)	1.20
Adjacent to footpath (vs 10+ doors away)	1.24
Some disrepair (vs none)	1.26
Through road (vs closed *cul-de-sac*)	1.27
Footpath to local shops	1.30
Some graffiti (vs none)	1.33
Footpath to other footpaths	1.35
Moderate traffic (vs light)	1.43
Located on main road	1.47
Heavy traffic (vs light)	1.49
Heavy graffiti/litter (vs none)	1.51
Evidence of burglar alarm	1.56
Moderate pedestrian traffic (vs light)	1.57
Evidence of dog	1.64
Much disrepair (vs none)	1.74
Signs of brief desertion	1.85
Signs of lengthy desertion	2.01
Visible from traffic lights	2.15
Gate from rear path into garden	2.31

c) A score was awarded to each environmental factor. This score was the figure derived from this calculation.

d) Each property within the sample was awarded a total score based upon the environmental factors which it possessed.

e) All properties within the sample were banded into risk deciles. The mean incidence and prevalence of crime for each decile was established to ensure that the lowest decile (that which had the lowest score) did experience the lowest level of crime, and that the highest decile (that with the highest environmental risk score) had the highest levels of crime.

In the simplest case, if the rate of victimisation of homes in an area is 10%, the rate for homes with window locks is 5% and for homes without window locks is 15%, then the "window locks" factor is scored thus: +5 = no window locks, -5 = window locks fitted. The process described is repeated for all the attributes which attained statistical significance in the exploratory stage described above. Each home thus receives a total Burgess score. These scores are meaningless until converted into the rate of crime suffered by groups of homes sharing a Burgess score. To do this, as noted above, homes were divided into the 10% with highest Burgess scores, the 10% with next highest and so on down to the 10% with the lowest scores. The rate of crime suffered by each such band was then calculated. The mean incidence and prevalence of crime for each decile was established to ensure that the lowest decile experienced the lowest level of crime, and the highest decile experienced the highest levels of crime.

The analysis was conducted for burglary as a separate crime type as well as total crime. The results displayed in Tables 5 and 6 show the scores for each environmental factor. For example, being located next to open land scores 3.1, being situated on a through road scores 1.7. The higher the score, the greater the chance of being victimised.

The data presented in Tables 1 and 3 introduced the apparent increased risk associated with a property possessing a burglar alarm, a finding which appears counterintuitive. Although evidence of a burglar alarm was associated with the risk of burglary at a statistically significant level, and would have scored 6.5 for present and -4.1 for not present, the fact that the crime data for this study were collected retrospectively leaves the author unable to ascertain with any certainty whether the presence of the burglar alarm preceded the burglary, or (a more likely scenario) whether it was installed as a result of the offence. For this reason, it was felt appropriate (without further research) to remove this factor from the checklist.

As with the checklist for burglary, a decision was made to remove both presence/absence of a burglar alarm and presence/absence of a dog from the Burgess checklist for all crimes. Evidence of a dog would have added 28.2 to a property's score (absence of a dog subtracting 0.3). In a similar vein, presence of a burglar alarm would have added 11.7 to a property's Burgess score (absence subtracting 7.2). Due to the inability

Table 5: Burgess Checklist – Risk of Burglary

Environmental Factor	Burgess Score
Proximity to open land	Located next to open land – *score +3.1* Not located next to open land – *score -0.8*
Road Layout	Situated on a *cul-de-sac* without a linked pathway (true *cul-de-sac*) – *score -2* Situated on a *cul-de-sac* with a linked pathway (leaky *cul-de-sac*) – *score +2.3* Situated on a through road – *score +1.7*
Barriers	Situated on an estate with a real or symbolic barrier – *score -2.1* Situated on an estate without a real or symbolic barrier – *score +1.8*
Footpaths	Situated on an estate which contains a footpath leading to local shops – *score +10.2* Situated on an estate which does not have a footpath leading to local shops – *score -0.6* Situated on an estate with a footpath leading to a maze of other footpaths – *score +10.4* Situated on an estate which does not have a footpath leading to a maze of other footpaths – *score -1.6* Situated on an estate which has a footpath leading to another residential area – *score +1.8* Situated on an estate which does not have a footpath leading to another residential area – *score -1.3* A gate leading from a rear footpath into the rear garden – *score +19.6* No gate leading from a rear path into rear garden – *score -0.3*
Pedestrian Movement	0-5 pedestrians pass in front of the property in five minutes – *score -0.4* 6+ pedestrians pass in front of the property in five minutes – *score +9.5*
Neighbourhood Watch	Situated on an estate with evidence of Neighbourhood Watch – *score -5* Situated on an estate without evidence of Neighbourhood Watch – *score +1*
Desertion	Property shows signs of brief desertion – *score +25.6* Property does not show signs of brief desertion – *score -0.3* Property shows signs of lengthy desertion – *score +29.4* Property does not show signs of lengthy desertion – *score -0.3*
Total Score =	

Table 6: Burgess Checklist – Risk of All Crimes

Environmental Factor	Burgess Score
Road Layout	Situated on a *cul-de-sac* without a linked pathway (true *cul-de-sac*) – *score -3.9*
	Situated on a *cul-de-sac* with a linked pathway (leaky *cul-de-sac*) – *score +3.7*
	Situated on a through road – *score +6.3*
Footpaths	Situated 0 properties away from a footpath – *score +6.2*
	Situated 1-5 properties away from a footpath – *score -1.7*
	Situated 6-10 properties away from a footpath – *score +9.4*
	Situated more than 10 properties away from a footpath – *score -2.8*
	Situated on an estate which contains a footpath leading to local shops – *score +11.6*
	Situated on an estate which does not have a footpath leading to local shops – *score -0.6*
	Situated on an estate with a footpath leading to a maze of other footpaths – *score +11.9*
	Situated on an estate which does not have a footpath leading to a maze of other footpaths – *score -1.7*
	A gate leading from a rear footpath into the rear garden – *score +51.9*
	No gate leading from a rear path into rear garden – *score -0.7*
	Property visible from footpath – *score +6.3*
	Property not visible from a footpath – *score -1*
Traces	Window open/door ajar – *score +4.8*
	Window not open/door not ajar – *score -0.9*
Pedestrian Movement	0-5 pedestrians pass in front of the property in five minutes – *score -0.9*
	6+ pedestrians pass in front of the property in five minutes – *score +21.8*
Awareness Space	Situated within viewing distance of traffic lights – *score +46.5*
	Not situated within viewing distance of traffic lights – *score -0.3*
	Located on the nearest main road – *score +19*
	Not located on the nearest main road – *score -0.3*

(continued)

Table 6 *(continued)*

Environmental Factor	Burgess Score
Surveillance	Not overlooked at the front – *score +5.7*
	Overlooked at the front – *score -1.6*
Management and Maintenance	Property shows signs of no litter/graffiti – *score -2.9*
	Property shows signs of some litter/graffiti – *score +9.7*
	Property shows signs of heavy litter/graffiti – *score +16.7*
	Property shows signs of no disrepair – *score -1.2*
	Property shows signs of some disrepair – *score +9*
	Property shows many signs of disrepair – *score +28.2*
Desertion	Property shows signs of brief desertion – *score +34*
	Property does not show signs of brief desertion – *score -0.4*
	Property shows signs of lengthy desertion – *score +40.8*
	Property does not show signs of lengthy desertion – *score -0.4*
Total Score =	

(using the present data alone) to ascertain whether these factors preceded or were installed as a result of the offence, it was felt that they should not be included in the checklist.

As was referred to within the description of the methodology, the two checklists for burglary and total crime were validated to ensure that the properties with the highest Burgess scores actually experienced the highest incidence and prevalence of crime, and the properties with the lowest Burgess scores experienced the lowest levels of crime. This validation proved successful, with the positive correlations between Burgess Score and crime experienced displayed in Table 7.

Table 7: Correlation between Burgess Score and Victimisation

Relationship	Correlation Coefficient
Burgess Score and All Crime Incidence	+0.7749
Burgess Score and All Crime Prevalence	+0.8621
Burgess Score and Burglary Incidence	+0.6418
Burgess Score and Burglary Prevalence	+0.7978

What does this analysis show us? The exploratory phase set out at the opening to this section of the chapter identified the particular environmental factors which were associated with the risk of victimisation. These are the factors which, when present, increase a property's vulnerability to victimisation. The Burgess method of analysis involved converting these factors into scores, allowing each environmental factor to be awarded a number which represents its influence upon crime (the higher the number, the greater the risk of crime when that factor is present). Finally, this process was validated by awarding a total Burgess Score to each of the 1058 properties based upon the environmental factors which they possessed, and then testing the relationship between the Burgess Score and the crime incidence, prevalence and concentration experienced by properties to ensure that those with the highest scores experienced the highest levels of crime, and those with the lowest scores experienced the lowest levels of crime. The results were positive, suggesting that this method would be a valid tool for identifying risk amongst residential properties.

CONCLUSION

The original justification for this chapter lay with the need to clarify the debate surrounding housing layout and crime reduction, in particular the issue of permeability. The research findings presented largely support the premise that properties positioned within permeable estates are more vulnerable to victimisation. The environmental factors which emerge as associated with elevated crime (and burglary) levels suggest that higher levels of movement past the home are generally associated with higher levels of risk. Thus, in the somewhat heated debate about the role of permeability in enabling crime, the general thrust of the data suggests that high permeability (as proxied by the property's proximity to a footpath, whether that footpath leads to shops/other residential areas/a maze of other footpaths, and the level of pedestrian and vehicular movement through the estate) is indeed associated with higher levels of crime. In fact, 8 of the 13 environmental factors which were associated with risk of burglary at a statistically significant level of 0.1, and 10 of the 17 factors which were associated with total crime at a statistically significant level of 0.1, were related to permeability and access.

Improvement Perspective

Although the subject warrants an entirely separate chapter, it behoves the author to highlight a concern raised and expanded upon in Armitage

(2004). For the results presented throughout this chapter, the sample has been collapsed and uses both SBD and Non-SBD estates (primarily as a means of increasing the sample size). Somewhat surprisingly, when the SBD and Non-SBD samples are separated, the results reveal that the SBD sample had consistently higher Burgess Scores than the Non-SBD sample. For all crime categories, the mean Burgess Score for the SBD sample was +4.8, for the Non-SBD sample it was -4.4. When burglary alone was analysed, the results revealed again that the SBD sample had a higher Burgess Score (+3.3) than the Non-SBD sample (-4.9). Although the SBD sample experienced lower levels of crime, and properties with higher Burgess Scores experienced higher levels of crime, SBD properties possessed had higher Burgess Scores. This finding suggests that the SBD scheme has been swimming against the tide – reducing crime whilst estates possess a greater presence of the environmental factors which are associated with the risk of victimisation. A more rigorous implementation of its own principles would act to further reduce the crime levels amongst SBD estates.

The Way Forward

The last two decades have seen increasing recognition of the contribution which the design of products and services can make to crime reduction. This has nowhere been more true than in the design of buildings and the spaces between them. From the initial work of Jacobs (1961) and Newman (1973, 1995) in the U.S.A., and Poyner alone (1983, 1988) and with Webb (1991) in the U.K., has grown a clearer understanding of the crime-reductive design of homes. Its most significant practical manifestation in the U.K. has been the SBD award scheme which seeks to encourage developers to design out crime at the planning stage. Set within a current climate in which agencies previously excluded from the crime reduction agenda, as well as those traditionally considered to be responsible for its management, have been tasked with demonstrating their ability to work together to reduce crime and disorder, the SBD scheme has the potential to flourish. It not only approaches the crime problem from a holistic perspective – removing suitable targets, introducing capable guardians and removing likely offenders – it also requires the commitment and the co-operation of a variety of multi-agency partners. Yet, this potential has been stifled by the production of conflicting, contradictory and confusing research, policy and guidance. Whilst it is accepted that conflicting research will always exist, the current debate surrounding the criminogenic features of permeable design has diverted practitioners' and policy makers' attention from the immediate task of reducing crime.

Before concluding, it behoves the author to stress the real life implications of a debate which on paper appears simply interesting or challenging. A paper presented by Brooke (2004) demonstrated the impact of New Urbanist principles in Bradford, West Yorkshire. Built in 1992, estate A consisted of 5 blocks of apartments (each block containing 6 properties), 100% owner-occupied and located within an estate (estate B) which is predominantly local authority-owned (although some of the properties had been purchased from the local authority). Whilst estate B features a traditional suburban layout with fully private rear gardens which abut each other and clearly defined semi-private front gardens, estate A was designed according to the New Urbanist principles of walkable, public and permeable neighbourhoods – the development is completely permeable, access is unrestricted and the only private or defensible space is inside the apartment behind each resident's door.

Unfortunately, the reality of inappropriate design is that whilst the design of estate B may be "nothing remarkable, it could be taken from many of our cities" (Brooke, 2004), its burglary rate remains almost identical to the national average (19 in 1,000 properties for 2003/2004). In contrast, estate A (whose design may have been considered more innovative than that of estate B when it was built in 1992) has a burglary rate of 366 in 1000 properties (2003/2004), 19.7 times the national average. In the 12 years since its development, estate A has gone from 100% owner-occupied to 13% owner-occupied and only 37% of the apartments are occupied at all! Whilst this may appear overstated, it is simply one example from one city within the U.K. The challenge now is for those working within the field of designing out crime to ensure that future policy and guidance is clear, aligned and based upon what works.

Address correspondence to: Dr. Rachel Armitage, Senior Research Fellow, The Applied Criminology Centre, The University of Huddersfield, Queensgate, HD1 3DH, UK; e-mail: r.a.armitage@hud.ac.uk

Acknowledgments: The author would like to thank both Stephen Town and Michael Brooke (Architectural Liaison Officers, Bradford District), who provided much of the inspiration for this chapter.

REFERENCES

Aquarium Entertainments Limited versus Brighton and Hove Council. Appeal Ref: T/APP/Q1445/A/99/1025514/P2, 15-18 and 22 February 2000.

Armitage, R. (2000). *An evaluation of Secured by Design Housing within West Yorkshire – Briefing Note 7/00.* London: Home Office.

Armitage, R. (2004). *Secured By Design – An investigation of its history, development and future role in crime reduction.* Unpublished PhD Thesis, The University of Huddersfield, Huddersfield, West Yorkshire, UK.

Beavon, D. J. K. (1984). *Crime and the environmental opportunity structure: The influence of street networks on the patterning of property offences.* Unpublished M.A. Thesis, Simon Fraser University, Burnaby, British Columbia.

Bevis, C., & Nutter, J. B. (1977). *Changing street layouts to reduce residential burglary.* Paper presented to the American Society of Criminology annual meeting in Atlanta.

Brantingham, P. L., & Brantingham, P. J. (1975). Residential burglary and urban form. *Urban Studies, 12,* 273-284.

Brantingham, P. L., & Brantingham, P. J (1993). Environmental routine and situation: Towards a pattern theory of crime. *Advances in Criminological Theory, 5,* 259-294.

Brantingham, P. L., & Brantingham, P. J. (2000). *A conceptual model for anticipating crime displacement.* Paper presented at the American Society of Criminology Conference, San Francisco.

Brantingham, P. L., Brantingham, P. J., & Molumby, T. (1977). Perceptions of crime in a dreadful enclosure. *Ohio Journal of Science, 77,* 256-261.

Brooke, M. (2004). *Mallard Court, Bradford: A paper presented at the ALO Conference.* Leeds, UK.

Brown, J. (1999). *An evaluation of the Secured by Design Initiative in Gwent, South Wales.* Unpublished MSc. dissertation, Scarman Centre for the Study of Public Order, Leicester, UK.

Brown, B. B., & Altman, I. (1983). Territoriality, defensible space and residential burglary: An environmental analysis. *Journal of Environmental Psychology, 3,* 203-220.

Brown, B., & Bentley, D. (1993). Residential burglars judge risk: The role of territoriality. *Journal of Environmental Psychology, 13,* 51-61.

Charter of the New Urbanism. (undated). Retrieved 30 December 2004 from: http://www.newurbanism.org/pages/532096/index.htm

Clarke, R. V. (1992). Introduction. In R. V. Clarke (Ed.), *Situational crime prevention – Successful case studies* (pp. 3-36). New York: Harrow and Heston.

Cromwell, P. F., & Olson, J. N. (1991). *Breaking and entering: An ethnographic analysis of burglary.* Newbury Park, CA: Sage.

Department of the Environment. (1994). *Planning out Crime – Circular No. 5.* London, Department of the Environment.

Department of Environment, Transport and the Regions. (1998). *Places, Streets and Movement – A Companion Guide to Design Bulletin 32 Residential Roads and Footpaths.* London, Department of Environment, Transport and the Regions.

Department of Environment, Transport and the Regions. (1999). *Towards an Urban Renaissance – Final Report of the Urban Task Force.* London, Department of Environment, Transport and the Regions.

Fairs, M. (1998). End of road for *Cul-de-Sac. Building Design,* 1373, 1.

Felson, M. (1998). *Crime and everyday life* (2nd ed.). Thousand Oaks, CA: Pine-Forge Press.

Felson, M., & Clarke, R. V. (1998). *Opportunity makes the thief: Practical theory for crime prevention.* Police Research Paper 98. London: Home Office.

Great Britain. (1998a). *Crime and Disorder Act 1998. Chapter 37.* London: Her Majesty's Stationery Office (HMSO).

Great Britain. (1998b). *Human Rights Act 1998. Chapter 42.* London: HMSO.

Great Britain. (2002). *Police Reform Act 2002. Chapter 30.* London: HMSO.

Greenberg, S., & Rohe, W. (1984). Neighbourhood design and crime: A tale of two perspectives. *Journal of American Planning Association,* 50(1), 48-61.

Hillier, B., & Shu, S. (1998). *Crime and urban layout: The need for evidence.* Easingwold: Home Office Crime Prevention College.

Hillier, B. (2004). Can streets by made safer? *Urban Design International,* 9, 31-45.

Hodge, M. (2000). Secured by Design confers a crime reduction advantage – Report on an academic debate at New Scotland Yard. *Digest,* April, 2000.

Home Office. (1991). *Safer communities: The local delivery of crime prevention through the partnership approach.* Standing Conference on Crime Prevention (The Morgan Report). London: Home Office.

Jacobs, J. (1961). *The death and life of great American cities.* New York: Random House.

Knowles, P. (undated). *Designing out Crime – The cost of policing new urbanism.* Retrieved 30 December 2004 from: http://www.operationscorpion.org.uk/design_out_crime/policing_urbanism.htm

Mayhew, P., Clarke, R. V. G., Burrows, J., & Winchester, S. (1976). *Crime as opportunity.* Home Office Research Study No. 34. London: Home Office.

Mirlees-Black, C., Budd, T., Partridge, S., & Mayhew, P. (1998). *The 1998 British Crime Survey – England and Wales.* London: Home Office.

Moss, K. (2001). Crime Prevention v Planning: Section 17 of the Crime and Disorder Act 1998. Is it a Material Consideration? *Crime Prevention and Community Safety: An International Journal,* 3(2), 43-48.

Newlands, M. (1983). *Residential burglary patterns in a Vancouver neighbourhood.* Unpublished honors thesis, Simon Fraser University, Burnaby, BC, Canada.

Nuttall, C. P., Barnard, E. F., Fowles, A. J., Frost, A., Hammond, W. H., Mayhew, P., Pease, K., Tarling, R., & Weatheritt, M. J. (1977). *Parole in England and Wales, Home Office Research Study No. 38.* London: Home Office.

Office of the Deputy Prime Minister. (2000). *Our towns and cities: The future.* London: HMSO.

Office of the Deputy Prime Minister and Home Office. (2004). *Safer places – The planning system and crime prevention.* London: HMSO.

Newman, O. (1973). *Defensible space: People and design in the violent city.* London: Architectural Press.

Newman, O. (1995). Defensible space: A new physical planning tool for urban revitalization. *American Planning Association Journal,* 61(2), 149-155.

Pascoe, T. (1999). *Evaluation of Secured by Design in public sector housing – Final report*. Watford: Building Research Establishment.

Poyner, B. (1983). *Design against crime: Beyond defensible space*. London: Butterworth.

Poyner, B. (1988). Video cameras and bus vandalism. *Security Administration, 11*, 44-51.

Poyner, B., & Webb, B. (1991). *Crime free housing*. Oxford: Butterworth.

Rengert, G. F., & Wasilchick, J. (2000). *Suburban burglary: A tale of two suburbs* (2nd ed.). Springfield, IL: Charles C Thomas Publishers.

Reppetto, T. A. (1974). *Residential crime*. Cambridge, MA: Ballinger.

Schneider, R. H., & Kitchen, T. (2002). *Planning for crime prevention – A transatlantic perspective*. London: Routledge.

Shu, S. (2000). Housing layout and crime vulnerability. *Urban Design International, 5*, 177-188.

Simon, F. H. (1971). *Prediction methods in criminology – including a prediction study of young men on probation*. Home Office Research Study 7. London: Home Office.

Standards and Testing. (2004). Retrieved 19 September 2004 from: http://www.securedbydesign.com/standards/index.asp

Stungo, N. (1998). Culs-de-sac hit the Skids. *Building Design, 1377*, 2.

Summerskill, B. (2000, July 16). How Brookside boom helped the burglars. *Observer*, p. 16.

SURF Centre. (2002). *Hulme, ten years on*. Salford: University of Salford.

Taylor, R., & Gottfredson, S. D. (1987). Environmental design, crime and prevention: An examination of community dynamics. *Crime and Justice: An Annual Review of the Research, 8*, 387-416.

Town, S. (10 May, 2004). *New urbanism and crime*. Available through e-mail to (ST138@westyorkshire.pnn.police.uk).

Town, S., & O'Toole, R. (2005). Crime-friendly neighbourhoods. *Reason, 36*(9), 30-36.

United Nations Conference on Environment and Development. (1992). *Agenda 21*. Rio De Janeiro, Brazil.

Wiles, P., & Costello, A. (2000). *The 'road to nowhere': The evidence for travelling criminals*. Home Office Research Study 207. London: Home Office.

Appendix: Other Environmental Risk Factors Checklist

Address:

Day:

Date:

Time:

Observed by Resident (i.e. twitching curtains etc.): yes/no

Questioned/Confronted by Resident: yes/no

Road Network	Yes	No	Other
1) *Cul de sac* without linked pathway			
2) *Cul de sac* with linked pathway			
3) Through road			
4) Entrance to estate is marked by symbolic/ real barrier i.e. change in road colour/ texture, pillars, gate etc.			

Access *footpath is any pedestrian thoroughfare that is NOT a pavement/sidewalk	Yes	No	Other
5) Number of properties away from footpath*			
a) 0 (i.e. adjacent)			
b) 1-5 (properties)			
c) 6-10 (properties)			
6) Footpath leads to:			
a) Shops			
b) Open land			
c) Maze of other footpaths			
d) Other residential area			
7) Footpath runs at rear of house			
8) Gate leading from footpath into rear garden			
9) Property is visible from footpath			

(continued)

Appendix *(continued)*

Access *footpath is any pedestrian thoroughfare that is NOT a pavement/sidewalk	Yes	No	Other

10) Boundary of property is marked by
   a) Wall
   b) Solid Fence
   c) Post and Rail Fence i.e. see through
   d) Thorny foliage
   e) Fence/wall topped with trellis
   f) Nothing

Property within 'Awareness Space' of Others?	Yes	No	Other

11) Within viewing distance of 'Stop' sign
12) Volume of Traffic at 'stop sign'
   a) Light (0-5 vehicles stop within 3 minutes)
   b) Moderate (6-10 vehicles stop within 3 minutes)
   c) Heavy (10+ vehicles stop within 3 minutes)
13) Within viewing distance of traffic lights
14) Volume of Traffic at traffic lights
   a) Light (0-5 vehicles stop within 3 minutes)
   b) Moderate (6-10 vehicles stop within 3 minutes)
   c) Heavy (10+ vehicles stop within 3 minutes)
15) Within viewing distance of road junction
16) Volume of traffic at road junction
   a) Light (0-5 vehicles stop within 3 minutes)
   b) Moderate (6-10 vehicles stop within 3 minutes)
   c) Heavy (10+ vehicles stop within 3 minutes)

Appendix *(continued)*

Property within 'Awareness Space' of Others?	Yes	No	Other
17) Average speed of traffic in front of residence			
18) Volume of traffic in front of residence			
a) Light (0-5 vehicles pass in 3 minutes)			
b) Moderate (6-10 vehicles pass in 3 minutes)			
c) Heavy (10+ vehicles pass in 3 minutes)			
19) Volume of pedestrian traffic in front of residence			
a) Light (0-5 pedestrians pass in 3 minutes)			
b) Moderate (6-10 pedestrians pass in 3 minutes)			
c) Heavy (10+ pedestrians pass in 3 minutes)			
20) People 'hanging around' within vicinity of property			

Surveillance	Yes	No	Other
21) Front door facing street			

Parking	Yes	No	Other
22) Driveway			
23) Garage			
24) Communal Parking			
25) Street parking			

Social Climate	Yes	No	Other
26) Evidence of Neighbourhood Watch Scheme			

(continued)

Appendix *(continued)*

Social Climate	Yes	No	Other
27) Evidence of Litter/Graffiti within vicinity of property			
a) None			
b) Some			
c) Heavy			
28) General upkeep of Property			
a) No signs of disrepair			
b) Some sign of disrepair			
c) Many signs of disrepair			
29) Signs of short term desertion: e.g. milk bottles left outside			
30) Signs of long term desertion e.g. untended garden, piles of letters/ newspapers, property boarded up			

Traces	Yes	No	Other
31) Evidence of dog			
32) Evidence of burglar alarm			
33) Window open/door ajar			

Designing Out Crime: Has Section 17 of the U.K.'s Crime and Disorder Act 1998 Been Effective?

by

Steve Everson

and

Peter F. Woodhouse
Design Out Crime Limited,
West Yorkshire, UK

Abstract: *This study reports on U.K. efforts to stimulate designing out crime via national legislation. Section 17 of the U.K.'s Crime and Disorder Act 1998 obliged police, fire, health, local authorities and other agencies to cooperate in the prevention of crime and disorder. The legislation is sufficiently important that its impact and assessment warrants the attention of an international audience. This study presents findings from surveys of the impact upon the workings of police and local government authority personnel plus two in-depth area case studies. As what we believe to be the first published study of its type, it is hoped that the study contributes to the assessment of this type of legislation for crime reduction, and to knowledge relating to practices to promote designing out crime. The study concludes with recommendations for practice.*

Crime Prevention Studies, volume 21 (2007), pp. 111–131.

INTRODUCTION

> "A criticism [of previous practice] has been that housing, shopping areas, schools, and the like were designed in ways that a moment's thought would have shown to be criminogenic, but such thought was never given until the work had been done and the crime started." (Ken Pease, 1997, pp. 972-973)

Designing out crime is but one of the areas addressed in the work of Ken Pease. This article presents findings from a U.K. study of legislation to promote inter-agency efforts in designing out crime. The study, commissioned by the Government Office for the East Midlands (GOEM), sought to examine the implementation of Section 17 of the Crime and Disorder Act 1998 (CDA 1998). The aims of the study were twofold: to develop a snapshot of the regional situation, and to proffer recommendations for future action.

There are many examples of agency partnerships working to reduce crime and disorder. These include youth offending, drugs, road safety and repeat victimisation programmes. However, these typically are not focused upon environmental design. The CDA 1998 placed an obligation upon police, fire, health services, local authorities and other organisations to co-operate in developing and implementing strategies to tackle crime and disorder. Section 17 of the Act states:

> Without prejudice to any other obligation imposed on it, it shall be the duty of each authority to which this section applies to exercise its various functions with due regard to the likely effect of the exercise of those functions on, and the need to do all that it reasonably can to prevent, crime and disorder in its area.

Section 17 of the CDA 1998 specified that failure to consider the crime consequences of their action could render these agencies liable to scrutiny and sanction from the Audit Commission, H.M. Inspectorate of Constabulary, or other appropriate review bodies. Ken Pease and Kate Moss recognised that CDA 1988 was potentially one of the most powerful pieces of crime prevention legislation of recent times. They termed it a "wolf in sheep's clothing," as it paved the way for legal challenges to agency action, or inaction, through judicial review (Moss and Pease, 1999). Although the CDA included a range of organisations, bodies and individuals in the process of tackling crime and disorder, in practice the police and local authorities bore the brunt of expectation, and these are the focus of the present study. The scope of the legislative change introduced by Section 17 of the CDA 1998 is such that we believe its development and impact warrants bring brought to the attention of an international audience.

Designing Out Crime

Crime Prevention through Environmental Design or CPTED (Jeffrey, 1971) is the concept that buildings and other aspects of the physical environment should minimise the risk of crime and disorder to occupants, users and visitors. Defensible space theory (Newman, 1972) and the work of Jane Jacobs (1961) are key related areas. The field is hereafter referred to as designing out crime (DOC). Jacobs was blunt on the crime-design relationship:

> [To] build city districts that are custom made for easy crime is idiotic.
> Yet that is what we do. (Jacobs, 1961, p. 31)

The relationship between design and crime has been refined over time, in particular by Crowe (1991) and by Ian Colquhoun (2004), who provides an excellent recent review. Colquhoun described CPTED as based on:

> [O]ne simple idea that crime results partly from the opportunities presented by the physical environment. This being the case, it should be possible to alter the physical environment so that crime is less likely to occur. (Colquhoun, 2004, p. 56)

Aspects of DOC have been evaluated. Secured by Design (SbD) is the award scheme sponsored by the Association of Chief Police Officers (ACPO) and is the most recognised manifestation of DOC in the United Kingdom. SbD was launched in 1989 and is managed by ACPO Crime Prevention Initiatives Limited (ACPO CPI), and evaluations suggest it is extremely effective (Armitage, 1999, 2000; Pascoe, 1999; Pascoe and Brown, 1999). Commenting upon SbD and Armitage's evaluation, Ken Pease noted:

> [B]urglary levels in homes built to the standard are 30% lower than in non-SBD homes. The effect of uprating homes to SBD standards is even more dramatic. The best estimate is that the extra cost of building to SBD standards (currently around £440) will be saved in reduced burglaries over six years (a brief span compared to the life of a house), to say nothing of savings in distress and in the cost of police and victim time spent dealing with the offence. (Pease, 2001, p. 15)

A sister scheme to SbD, the Secured Car Parks (SCP) award scheme, is also sponsored by ACPO and managed on a day-to-day basis by the British Parking Association.

> The Association of Chief Police Officers (ACPO), launched the Secured Car Parks scheme in 1992 as part of their Secured by Design initiative to encourage those responsible for car parks to improve security standards as a means of reducing criminal activity, the fear of crime and the perception of crime in all car parks and vehicle retention areas. (ACPO, ACPOS and ACPO CPI, 2004, p. 4)

At the time of writing in late 2004, the scheme was being replaced by the ParkMark™ Safer Parking Award (PMSPA). PMSPA is intended to be more responsive to local needs and thereby encourage participation by car park operators.

The Role of Local Partnerships

Despite the all-embracing nature of the CDA 1998, in practice the local government authorities and the police service are the key players in local DOC partnerships. Local authorities are typically represented by local planning officers, and the police service by Architectural Liaison Officers or ALOs (known as Crime Prevention Design Advisors or CPDAs in some areas).

Police and local authority representatives typically discuss proposed developments with building developers. This generally takes the form of a negotiation, which can be tricky if there are conflicting interests. For example, fire-safety standards can conflict with crime-safety standards (on issues such as door and window security), or the latter have significant cost implications for developers. The key to the success of the process is early and effective consultation, preferably prior to the application for planning permission. The primary incentive for a developer to co-operate is to remove potential objections to planning permission. Whilst a police objection to a development plan would not automatically result in failure of the application, the risk of that outcome and the consequential delay and cost in appealing the decision does provide some leverage. Generally speaking, the later in the process that any changes are made to plans, the more costly the changes. In addition to re-drafting costs there can be, *inter alia*, implications for utility providers and delays to pre-construction work on site. Amendments agreed after planning permission has been granted tend to be minor, as there is less incentive for developers to change existing plans.

Development occurs across the U.K. In the East Midlands, East of England and South East regions, the Milton Keynes and South Midlands Growth Area alone has been estimated as having the potential to provide 300,000 jobs and 360,000 homes by 2031 (Tym et al., 2002, para 8.3). While such potentially large crime generators would ideally be planned to be crime-free, this is far from the natural way of thinking about urban development. Ken Pease pleaded for more creative thinking in this area:

> Some of the most remarkable social changes of the last decades have occurred by a semi-mysterious process where things take on a momentum of their own once issues are recognised. . . . With crime, there is not the problem of convincing ourselves that the problem exists. The issues are clear. All we have to recognise are new, more creative solutions. Designing out crime is one solution to which government, business and consumers can subscribe. We don't have to change the world. We just have to change the way we think. (Pease, 2001, p. 35)

THE EAST MIDLANDS' STUDY

This study reported here used the DOC process as a vehicle to examine the effectiveness of the implementation of Section 17 of the CDA 1998 within the East Midlands region. The research was designed as a "scoping study" to:

a. examine the extent and nature of links between the local government's Crime and Disorder Reduction Partnerships (CDRPs) and their local ALOs, and determine whether they cooperate with Local Strategic Partnerships (LSPs) in the process of DOC;
b. establish the current position, barriers and potential for improvement;
c. identify good practice within and without the East Midlands region; and,
d. conduct the work from a partnership perspective with a broad regional focus, but with particular reference to a comparative study of Nottingham city and Ashfield (two contrasting areas in Nottinghamshire).

The research involved consultation between the research team and the Government Office of the East Midlands (GOEM). The consultation sought to identify relevant projects or programmes. Following this, the study had four key components.

1. a national survey of police ALOs in England and Wales. The survey questionnaire examined the working relationships between ALOs and local government planning departments, good practice exemplars and features that enhanced or acted as barriers to an effective DOC process. The version of the survey that was distributed in the East Midlands region was slightly longer and carried more in-depth questions on some topics;

2. a survey of local government planning departments in the East Midlands region;

3. a survey of Crime and Disorder Reduction Partnerships (CDRPs) and Planning Departments in the East Midlands region; and,

4. two in-depth case studies were developed in two very different areas of Nottinghamshire (Nottingham City and the Ashfield District). The case studies approached local government planners and police ALOs as the main starting points.

Components 2 and 3, the surveys of local planners and CDRPs, were designed to examine their working relationships and their work with police ALOs in relation to designing out crime. The findings from the component are detailed sequentially below.

1. The National Survey of Police Architectural Liaison Officers

Survey questionnaires were sent to all ALOs in the U.K. At the time of the research there were 43 area police forces in the U.K., 38 of which were outside the East Midlands region. Responses were received from 28 of these forces, and from a total of 83 ALOs within them. Whilst accurate figures for the number of officers working in DOC are not available, our informed estimate is that this probably represents slightly more than half. In the East Midlands' survey, completed questionnaires were received from all 25 ALOs representing all five police forces: Derbyshire Constabulary, Leicestershire Constabulary, Lincolnshire Police, Northamptonshire Police and Nottinghamshire Police. The region's higher response rate probably reflects the involvement of the East Midlands regional government and the potential for change in the region as a result of the study.

In what follows, findings for the East Midlands region are compared to findings for the remainder of England and Wales. There was no reason to suspect that the survey responses were unrepresentative of ALOs across England and Wales. However, it is important to note that the East Midlands region is not necessarily representative of England and Wales. While it is therefore informative to compare national and regional pictures, we acknowledge the difficulty in drawing strong conclusions.

Police ALOs across the U.K. were asked if their work tasks carried responsibilities in addition to designing out crime. All ALOs in the East Midlands had additional responsibilities, compared to only three-quarters elsewhere (Table 1). The additional responsibilities of East Midlands' ALOs were evident to varying degrees in relation to closed-circuit television (CCTV), intruder alarms and Neighbourhood Watch. East Midlands' ALOs reported having worked on DOC issues for a slightly longer post-DOC-training period than their national counterparts (Table 1). However, East Midlands' ALOs were less likely to be involved with SbD and Secured Car Parks (SCP) projects, possibly due to their more extensive non-DOC commitments. Eight percent of East Midlands' ALOs and 13% of other ALOs reported having a desk located within the planning department. These similarly low rates are important in the context of the finding that ALOs believed having a desk within the planning department was one of the most important factors in maintaining quality collaboration.

Table 1: Experience and Responsibilities of Police Architectural Liaison Officers

	National % (n=83)	East Midlands % (n=25)
Experience[a]	62	74
Any additional responsibilities beyond DOC[b]	78	100
CCTV responsibilities	53	60
Neighbourhood Watch responsibilities	24	48
Priority alarm responsibilities	42	60
General crime prevention responsibilities	67	96
% DOC[c]	53	23

Notes:
  a. Experience is measured in months of working since officer undertook initial training in DOC issues at the Home Office Crime Reduction Centre.
  b. Figures in the table relate to % of such officers with the particular additional responsibilities.
  c. % DOC indicates the average percentage of time such officers worked on DOC issues.

Only 12% of East Midlands' ALOs had received training on DOC, compared to around a third of ALOs elsewhere (Table 2). This finding is worth emphasising: *the majority of police officers with statutory responsibility for designing out crime had not received any relevant training.* In addition, according to ALOs, 40% (slightly less in the East Midlands) of their counterpart local planning officer(s) had received DOC training. This suggests that a higher proportion of local authority planning officers were DOC-trained than ALOs. From the additional questions asked of East Midlands' ALOs it was determined that only one in eight of them reported that local planning committee members had received any training or information about DOC issues.

Close to two-thirds of East Midlands' ALOs reported involvement with local CDRPs, compared to slightly over half of ALOs elsewhere. This could reflect the additional (non-DOC) tasks of East Midlands' ALOs if such work brought them into more frequent contact with CDRPs. However, the additional questions asked of East Midlands' ALOs suggested that only around half of officers with CDRP involvement considered their contact to be frequent and consistent.

The majority of ALOs reported either that their workload remained the same as the previous year or had increased between 2003 and 2004 (58% nationally, 47% in the East Midlands). Only eight percent of officers in the national survey, and none of the East Midlands' respondents, reported a DOC-workload decrease. A third of ALOs nationally (34%) and half of East Midlands' ALOs (53%) reported an increase in their workload between 2003 and 2004.

The workload of ALOs depended upon receiving information about applications for development permission. ALOs were asked whether they received planning applications from the local planning department without having specifically requested the applications. Around a quarter of "unsolicited applications" were for major developments and most of the remainder were for a mixture of major and minor developments (Table 2). Nationally, at least a third, and possibly up to two-thirds of referrals arrived due to a existing agreement or protocol for the transfer of information from the local authority planning office (Table 2).

Part of the national survey asked open-ended questions examining factors that assisted or hindered the effectiveness of police ALOs. Seventy-three percent reported that liaison with other ALOs was extremely beneficial to their work, and that a good working relationship with local planners was essential. Officers with a desk in the planning office felt it was particularly advantageous in building a professional understanding with local

Table 2: The Practices and Views of Police Architectural Liaison Officers

Item	National % (n=83)	East Midlands % (n=25)
Partnerships		
ALO involved with local Crime and Disorder Reduction Partnerships (% Yes)	55	64
DOC Training		
for Local Authority Planners (% Yes)	40	36
for ALOs (% Yes)	33	12
ALO Workload Change 2003-2004		
Increase	34	53
Decrease	8	0
Same	58	47
Workload subtotal	*100*	*100*
Nature of Unsolicited Applications to ALOs		
Major Developments	23	25
Minor Developments	8	0
Mixture	69	75
Unsolicited applications subtotal	*100*	*100*
Were Unsolicited Applications from Planners Sent Due to a Prior Agreement?		
Yes	32	44
No	36	25
Some	32	31
Prior agreement subtotal	*100*	*100*
Senior Police Management Knowledge of, and Approach to, Designing Out Crime (according to ALOs)		
DOC Ignored	Not asked	16
DOC Not Understood and not Encouraged	Not asked	44
DOC Not Understood but Encouraged	Not asked	28
DOC Understood but not Encouraged	Not asked	8
DOC Understood and Encouraged	Not asked	4
Senior Police subtotal		*100*

authority planners. Where liaison and communication between planners and police was poor, ALOs reported it was difficult to work effectively. Workload was cited as a barrier to success, particularly where ALOs had significant non-DOC responsibilities. Time targets placed upon planners to deal with applications were also cited as a barrier to effective working. This was because DOC was often perceived as slowing down or even hindering the planning process.

Police ALOs reported that DOC received little support from central government, ACPO, police forces and local authorities. In particular, ALOs reported that police senior management was pre-occupied with short-term targets and failed to understand the medium and long-term benefits of DOC. The East Midlands' version of the survey contained additional quantitative questions on this issue. Fully 88% of East Midlands' ALOs reported that, in their view, senior police management either ignored or did not understand DOC work, even though around a third of those who did not understand it were felt to encourage it. Only 4% of senior management were felt to both understand and encourage DOC work (Table 2).

2. The Survey of Planning Departments

This questionnaire survey was briefer than the one administered to police ALOs, and administered only with planning departments in the East Midlands region. Completed surveys were received from 15 of the 46 planning departments. This provides a small sample size, and so caution should be exercised when reading results presented as percentages below. However, the results are still informative and there is no reason to believe they are not indicative of broader experience.

Sixty percent of planners reported that time targets for the processing of planning applications served to reduce the effectiveness of the planning process. Twenty-seven percent felt that time-targets made no difference to effectiveness, and only 13% felt that they improved the planning process (Table 3).

Self-assessment of knowledge is not necessarily a valid indicator of actual knowledge because it is difficult to "test" knowledge in a self-completion survey administered by mail. However, it provides an indicator of what planners believed they knew, and there is no reason to believe they had any particular interest in providing inaccurate responses (they were assured that all respondents were anonymous). Eighty percent of

Table 3: The Practices and Views of Local Authority Planning Officers (n=15)

Item	Percent of planners
Government Time Targets for Processing Planning Applications	
Improved effectiveness of planners	13
Made no difference	27
Reduced effectiveness of planners	60
Subtotal	*100*
Knowledge of Planners (% reporting good or reasonable knowledge)	
Secured by Design awards scheme	80
Section 17 of the 1998 Crime and Disorder Act	80
Crime prevention can be a material consideration	93
Training (% receiving training)	
DOC training for planners	27
DOC training for planning committee members	27

planners stated that they had a good or reasonable working knowledge of the SbD award scheme. Eighty percent also reported a good or reasonable knowledge of Section 17 of the CDA 1998, while 93% stated that they were aware that crime prevention could be a material consideration in the planning process (as detailed by Moss and Seddon, 2001, p. 25). However, 73% of planners had not received any training in DOC issues, and there was an identical response in relation to the training of planning committee members in such matters (Table 3). This finding is worth emphasising: *three-quarters of local government planners with statutory responsibility for designing out crime as defined by the CDA 1998 had not undergone any relevant training.*

Forty percent of planners expressed concern about the workload implications of crime prevention and DOC issues. This response, coupled with that for the time targets, illustrates the pressures placed upon planners and their understandable reluctance to "further complicate" an already difficult situation. It may be such pressures that led a fifth of planners to respond that they felt that it was possible to build "sustainable communities" without any reference to DOC.

3. The Survey of Crime and Disorder Reduction Partnerships

This survey was only conducted in the East Midlands region. Completed questionnaires were received from 18 of the 42 CDRPs in the region. The questionnaires were generally completed by the Community Safety Manager/Officers within the CDRP.

Seventy-eight percent of respondents (n=14) stated that they were conversant with DOC. However, 67% stated that members of their CDRP would benefit from training on such issues. All but one of the respondents stated that they had an ALO with DOC responsibilities who worked within their CDRP area. The other respondent did not know of the local ALO. Fifty-six percent of respondents (n=10) stated that the ALO was utilised by their CDRP to assess the DOC possibilities of all the crime and disorder issues addressed by the partnership. This response from CDRPs was broadly in line with that of the ALOs in the region.

Half of CDRP respondents stated that their CDRP utilised a member of the local planning department in addressing DOC issues. Thirty-nine percent of the CDRP respondents (n=7) stated that there was a protocol in place to ensure full and timely consultation between planners and the ALO in relation to new local developments.

4. The Two In-depth Local Case Studies

Two case studies were undertaken in the East Midlands region, to facilitate the identification of more specific aspects DOC work. The aim was to examine the mechanisms by which DOC operated and to gain some insight into the variation in operations between areas. The case studies involved visits to the two areas, in-depth interviews with ALOs and planners, plus examination of relevant documentation.

Area 1 was the city of Nottingham, a vibrant city centre containing two universities and a thriving commercial centre with a multitude of licensed premises, nightclubs and other late night entertainment. It was arguably striving to be a "24 hour" city. Like many cities it had "problem" areas, with some reputation for inner-city alcohol-related disorder as well as some problematic residential areas on its outskirts.

Area 2, Ashfield, was a semi-rural area, formerly the hub of the now defunct Nottinghamshire coalfields. Other than some "commuter home developments" in the Sutton-in-Ashfield and Hucknall areas, there was little recent investment and regeneration. With the decline of the U.K. coal industry, the area suffered from a relatively high level of unemployment at the time of the research.

Case 1: Nottingham

Nottingham had a design guide for both "Community Safety in Residential Areas" and for "Industrial, Commercial and Retail Development." Both contained guidance on incorporating crime reduction measures into the development process. The documents were to be incorporated in the new local plan anticipated for 2004. A list of planning applications was sent on a weekly basis to the police ALO, who could also access them on the planning department website. There was a monthly meeting at the planning department with the ALO to review planning applications, where particular concerns could be discussed with the case officer. The ALO was involved in ongoing consultations with developers and planners on a number of major developments in the city centre, including the tram system and the linked Park and Ride facilities. Details of all developments involving the County Council, such as schools, libraries, social services and highways, were sent to the appropriate crime reduction manager for that area, all of whom had received ALO training.

There was evident tension between the city's efforts to provide 24-hour commercial entertainment and the perception of the subsequent negative consequences for personal safety and order maintenance. The proliferation of licensed premises and other developments primarily aimed at 18-30 year olds could, it seemed, possibly result in the city centre becoming a "no-go" area for other residents and visitors outside that age group, particularly from late evening onwards. The analogy between epidemics and the proliferation of crime and disorder issues has been well made (Gladwell, 2001). The perception of crime and disorder could also stem the expansion of residential occupation in the city centre.

The researchers concluded that the appropriate application of the terms of the Licensing Act 2003 might assist in relieving the tensions between commerce and safety in the city. The proliferation of liquor-licensed establishments to achieve the "24 hour town/city" aspirations of councils seemed to exacerbate the crime and disorder problems of those areas. It is all too common for the resolution of potential development problems to fall between the two stools of planning and liquor-licensing regulation despite the best efforts of ALOs and senior police management. It is to be hoped that the further implementation of the CDA 1998 would assist in resolving such problems. The level of development within the city centre appeared to easily justify the employment of a full-time ALO to work in the city planning office.

Case 2: Ashfield

The level and pace of development in Ashfield was much lower than in the city of Nottingham. Unlike the city, Ashfield did not have design guides in place. A weekly list of planning applications was sent to the police ALO, who then let the planner, who *de facto* acted as police liaison, know which applications were of particular interest. A monthly meeting was attended by either the ALO or the local crime reduction manager (who had also undergone ALO training) where DOC-planning issues were discussed.

There had never been any training for the planning committee members in Ashfield. Having noted that, it was also true that the ALO and planner had not encountered any problems or resistance from the committee on DOC issues. This was perhaps because very few applications came before the committee, and these tended to be for major developments. All other applications were dealt with under "devolved powers," whereby senior planning officers supervised and managed the planning process. Their decisions could be subject to the planning appeal process if there was an irreconcilable dispute.

Despite the fact that there were no "design guides" incorporating DOC issues, the development briefs for recent major developments tended to be in a standard format. Briefs typically stressed the need for the development to be designed in such a way as "to limit the potential for crime," and urged the provision of natural supervision whereby locations were readily overlooked and therefore informally supervised by residents and passers-by.

Summary of Key Findings

Some of the key findings of the study are summarised below, based on both the survey and the researchers' in-depth investigation into the issues.

- Few ALOs and planners received training on DOC.
- Few ALOs actively communicated or worked with their counterpart CDRPs.
- ALOs were relatively isolated in their work, often being obliged to reinvent the wheel.

- ALOs with many responsibilities in addition to DOC may, due to the additional workload, not be as effective in conducting their DOC duties.

- ALOs and DOC in general appeared to receive relatively little support from either central government or senior police management.

- Few local government planners or planning committee members received DOC training.

- DOC issues are improperly perceived as "holding up" planning applications, perhaps because of pressure for rapid processing of such applications.

- Senior police management tend to be ignorant of DOC issues and its effectiveness in crime reduction.

- Senior management in CDRPs show little interest in, or knowledge of, DOC issues and its crime reduction effectiveness.

- Most DOC effort is concentrated upon public rather than private housing developments. Developers of private housing often fail to incorporate DOC, and evidence found elsewhere suggests they give fallacious reasons for its omission (see Armitage and Everson, 2003).

- Most police targets and performance indicators are short term. This contrast with the manner in which DOC works to prevent crime.

The research also sheds light upon national-level issues and politics. In particular, the researchers hope the longstanding contradiction between DOC advice from the Home Office and the "New Urbanism" agenda of the Office of the Deputy Prime Minister will be overcome by the Planning Out Crime Guidelines, "Safer Places," the update of Circular 5/94 (Office of the Deputy Prime Minister and Home Office, 2004). In addition, lack of co-ordination on planning and licensing issues can become major crime and disorder problems, particularly in major towns and cities. The crime and disorder aspects of the Licensing Act 2003, when in effect (most likely from 2005), coupled with the fact that both licensing and planning will then both be local authority functions and subject to S. 17, should enable those problems to be minimised.

PROMISING PRACTICES

The study allowed the researchers to gather a broad array of information on national and regional practices in the area of designing out crime. This section briefly gives an overview of additional efforts that were perceived to be some of the better practices encountered and that are not detailed above. While therefore somewhat subjective, this section complements the other areas of the study and is appropriate insofar as the issues discussed here are generally under-researched. In the opinion of the present writers, the examples detailed here warrant further examination and evaluation.

1. Street-level DOC Audits

The London Borough of Camden ran a project named Crime Opportunity Profile of Streets (COPS). An appropriately trained individual walked down a street and noted features that could encourage crime or disorderly behaviour. A report was submitted to the local partnership with suggestions for addressing the problems. Where the property or premises concerned was privately owned, the problem was explained to the owner along with practical advice for its redress. The issues addressed by this project included drug dealing, drug taking, theft from the person, robbery, begging, fly posting (unauthorized/illegal pasting of advertisements, particularly on external walls of buildings, windows and street furniture), littering, footway obstruction, graffiti and criminal damage, rough sleeping and loitering for illicit purposes. The local authority departments that benefited from such reports included planning, building control, highways, licensing and street environment. The project was primarily aimed at city/urban areas but could be adapted for a rural setting. The project benefited from generous funding from the European Economic Community over a two-year period to enable the surveys and reports to be completed and action taken.

2. Community Regeneration

In Bradford, West Yorkshire, the Royds Community Association was formed in 1995 following a successful Single Regeneration Fund bid for £31 million for a seven-year programme. This level of funding rose to £108 million when the contributions from other agencies and partners were included. This was an example of community involvement in regeneration. The project encompassed three large social housing estates in Bradford, namely Buttershaw, Woodside and Delph Hill. The estates were originally built approximately 50 years ago, and they were characterised by poor housing, lack of facilities, unemployment, high crime, drug abuse and rising levels of anti-social behaviour. There were approximately 3,500 dwellings incorporated in the project housing 12,000 residents. The project was managed by a board of 22 directors: 12 local residents, 3 elected members of the local authority and 7 Institutional Directors representing local institutions and other partners. These included a housing association, the police, the Primary Care Trust, a private construction company and local church representatives. One of the features of the project was that SbD principles had been adopted in each phase of the development.

The result had been a much more vibrant and cohesive community, the support of one hundred community groups and 40 voluntary organisations, and the creation of 9 new sports facilities, 7 play areas, 3 community centres and 2 community shops. By the end of 2004, there had been no forced entry burglaries to the dwellings in the project. The levels of vandalism and graffiti on the estates were much lower than experienced prior to the project. There was also a feeling of ownership of the estate by the community.

3. Effective Inter-agency Collaboration

In October 1999 a police ALO was appointed in Wakefield, West Yorkshire to work within the planning department of the local district council. The resulting co-operative effort between that officer and the development control officers showed noted benefits (Moss and Seddon, 2001, p. 28). In this particular instance the costs were met by the local police commander's office. However, there have been similar instances where the police and local authority shared the costs. The proximal working of the ALO with the planners allowed immediate and informal access to advice and discussion, and the building of a professional working relationship in a relatively short time period. Whilst the system of integrated ALO/Planner working has now been replicated in some other areas, this was, to the authors' knowledge, its first application.

4. Regional ALO Meetings

In both the North East and South East regions of the U.K. there are long-established meetings among police ALOs. In the North East these meetings take place as a sub-group of the regional crime prevention group meetings of the Association of Chief Police Officers. The primary benefit is the transfer of information among ALOs, who were thereby no longer working in isolation (a problem expressed by others in the survey). However, a key secondary benefit of being an ACPO-subgroup was that it raised the profile of ALOs and brought their work to the attention of senior police officers.

5. Residential Design Guides

West Yorkshire Police published a residential design guide written in consultation with the West Yorkshire Planning Authorities (West Yorkshire Police, 2003). The document brought a variety of benefits. It provided a simple and easy-to-use guide for all professionals involved in the development process. It acted as a "minimum" standard for any district within the police force area that had not already incorporated design guides into their local plans. It raised the profile of DOC and, having been accepted by the constituent planning authorities, it eliminated the need to reiterate the arguments on every planning application. It encouraged developers to incorporate such features at the earliest opportunity, which in the perfect world is before the application is submitted. This, in turn, works to ensure that the resulting development is more resistant to crime and disorder.

Northamptonshire police introduced their Supplementary Planning Guidance (SPG) "Planning Out Crime in Northamptonshire" (Northamptonshire Police et al., 2004). This document provides comprehensive guidance on planning out crime and was adopted by all of the planning authorities in Northamptonshire, in conjunction with Northamptonshire Police. The SPG document has been further strengthened by the adoption, by all of the parties, of a protocol that has set out the detail of the working arrangements in relation to the SPG.

The five areas of promising practice are all relatively straightforward. Resource implications are not, for the most part, extensive. In research terms, the Camden street-level observational audit has particular possibilities for evaluation. It is also an area in which the development of observational checklists could be particularly important, and a coordinated effort at their development and dissemination might be appropriate.

CONCLUSIONS

This study sought to empirically examine working relationships and practices in a key area where statutory crime prevention responsibilities have changed significantly in recent years. The findings of the study suggest several recommendations, particularly for training:

- There is a need for more extensive training and information on DOC. Police ALOs require an understanding of the planning system, its terminology and the constraints upon planners.

- Planners, planning committee members and CDRP managers would benefit from understanding DOC issues, the crime reduction benefits, and information about how to further address their responsibilities under Section 17 of the CDA 1998.

- Senior police officers need to understand the benefits of DOC if they are to commit further resources to this area of work. The Home Office might usefully promote change in this area.

- Some consideration should be given to police performance indicators that reflect the longer-term crime reduction outcomes from DOC. Most extant performance indicators are short-term, failing to reflect the mechanism by which DOC works to prevent crime.

One possible catalyst to assist in creating a greater awareness and appreciation of DOC activity might be the development of an evaluation package for the work carried out by ALOs. Support from senior police management for DOC issues is unlikely without an appreciation of its impact.

Generally speaking, ALOs work in relative isolation from other ALOs as well as most other police officers. They are often re-inventing the wheel, encountering situations and problems with which they are unfamiliar but which have been addressed by colleagues elsewhere. Some effort to encourage communication among peers may overcome this problem. Possibilities include regional liaison meetings, membership of organisations such as the Designing Out Crime Association (DOCA), alongside Internet-based police ALO forums or a Listserve.

It is one thing to create a physical environment that is designed to reduce crime and the fear of crime. The safety of that environment should be sustainable to enable the benefits to continue over time. The encouragement of community involvement in such developments is an already accepted way of bringing this about. Saville and Cleveland describe "second generation CPTED" which:

> . . . views the design of the built environment as only the first step to creating healthy, sustainable communities. What really counts is creating a sense of community through a holistic approach to physical, social and economic development. (Saville and Cleveland, undated, cited in Colquhoun, 2004, pp. 61-62)

Referring again to Saville and Cleveland's work, Colquhoun reports that the second generation CPTED not only utilises "traditional CPTED design principles" but that it is considered:

> . . . necessary to expand efforts into the realm of residents' responsibility, residents' participation, youth activities, urban meeting places and human scale neighbourhoods. (Colquhoun, 2004, p. 63)

Whilst the principal focus of the present study was one U.K. region, it is likely that many of the conclusions drawn are more broadly applicable. As what we believe to be the first large-scale multi-faceted study of its type, it is hoped that it also makes a broader methodological contribution to the study of the spread of DOC practices and the assessment of the effectiveness of Section 17 of the 1998 Crime and Disorder Act. We have been present when Ken Pease has described situational crime prevention as the potential grit in the oyster from which the pearl of community spirit and cohesion can emerge. The possibility that healthy communities might evolve from designing out crime efforts, driven by statutory responsibility among agencies to ensure that safe practices are integral to building developments, is a vision that warrants our time and attention.

Address correspondence to: Dr. Steve Everson, Design Out Crime Limited, 129 High Street, Thornhill, Dewsbury, West Yorkshire, WF12 OPR, UK; www.designoutcrime.com

REFERENCES

ACPO, ACPOS and ACPO CPI. (2004). *ParkMark™ Safer parking: General Introduction Assessment Guidelines.* Haywards Heath: British Parking Association.

Armitage, R. (1999). *An Evaluation of Secured by Design Housing Schemes throughout the West Yorkshire Area.* Unpublished research paper by the Applied Criminology Group, University of Huddersfield. Wakefield: West Yorkshire Police.

Armitage, R. (2000). *An evaluation of Secured by Design in housing in West Yorkshire.* Briefing Note No. 7/00. London: Home Office.

Armitage, R., & Everson, S. (2003). Building for burglars? *Crime Prevention and Community Safety: An International Journal,* 5(4), 15-25.

Brown, J. (1999). *An evaluation of the Secured by Design Initiative in Gwent, South Wales.* Unpublished M.Sc. thesis, Scarman Centre, University of Leicester.

Colquhoun, I. (2004). *Design out crime: Creating safe and sustainable communities.* Oxford: Architectural Press.

Crowe, T. (1991). *Crime prevention through environmental design: Applications of architectural design and space management concepts.* Boston, MA: Butterworth-Heinemann.

Ekblom, P. (1997). Gearing up against crime: A dynamic framework to help designers keep up with the adaptive criminal in a changing world. *International Journal of Risk Security and Crime Prevention, 2*(4), 249-265.

Gladwell, M. (2001). *The tipping point: How little things can make a big difference.* London: Abacus.

Jacobs, J. (1961). *The death and life of great American cities* (2000 reprint ed.). London: Pimlico.

Jeffrey, C. R. (1971). *Crime prevention through environmental design.* Beverly Hills, CA: Sage.

Moss, K., & Pease, K. (1999). Crime and Disorder Act 1998: Section 17 A Wolf in Sheep's Clothing? *Crime Prevention and Community Safety: An International Journal, 1*(4), 15-19.

Moss, K., & Seddon, M. (2001). Crime prevention and planning: Searching for common sense in disorder legislation. *Crime Prevention and Community Safety: An International Journal, 3*(4), 25-31.

Northamptonshire Police, Northamptonshire County Council, Corby Borough Council, Daventry District Council, East Northamptonshire Council, Kettering Borough Council, Northampton Borough Council, South Northamptonshire Council and Borough Council of Wellingborough. (2004). *Planning out crime in Northamptonshire: Supplementary planning guidance.* Northampton, UK: Northamptonshire County Council and Northamptonshire Police.

Office of the Deputy Prime Minister (ODPM) and Home Office. (2004). *Safer places: The planning system and crime prevention.* London: The Stationery Office.

Pascoe, T. (1999). *Evaluation of Secured by Design in public sector housing.* London: Building Research Establishment and Department of Environment, Transportation and the Regions.

Pease, K. (1997). Crime prevention. In M. Maguire, R. Morgan and R. Reiner (Eds.), *The Oxford handbook of criminology* (2nd ed.). Oxford, UK: Oxford University Press.

Pease, K. (2001). *Cracking crime through design.* London: Design Council.

Saville, G., & Cleveland, G. (undated). *2nd generation CPTED: An antidote to the social Y2K virus of urban design* (http://www.e-doca.net/Resources/Articles/2nd_generation_cpted.pdf).

Schneider, R. H., & Kitchen, T. (2002). *Planning for crime prevention: A transatlantic perspective.* London: Routledge.

Tym, R., & Partners et al. (2002). *Milton Keynes and South Midlands Study.* Available online at: http://www.emra.gov.uk/publications/documents/mksms-ch8.pdf (accessed 24 July 2005).

West Yorkshire Police (2003). *Design for community safety: A residential guide.* Wakefield: West Yorkshire.

The Nottingham Burglary Risk Index (BRIx)

by

Kate Moss-Brookes

Midlands Centre for Criminology & Criminal Justice, Loughborough University

and

Jenny Ardley
De Montfort University

Introduction

Abstract: *This chapter illustrates a crime prevention technique based upon the permissible exchange of data as allowed under the U.K.'s Crime and Disorder Act 1998. Specifically it proposes an approach which minimises formal data sharing whilst maximising relevance to crime reduction through the development of a risk index for domestic burglary. It owes much to Professor Ken Pease who, at the time of the study was engaged in parallel work for Nottingham City Council and whose imaginative ideas and advice are much in evidence in this paper.*

The background to this project can be found in two previous papers. Moss and Pease (2004, p. 10) contended that:

> ... information which should be available across agencies is essentially information about *research estimated risk to individual people, households and locations, but not the components of that risk.* Information

about prior victimisation, lone parent status and recent criminal history, all demonstrated by research to elevate crime risk, should be combined into a single risk index whose contributing components remain invisible to each other . . .

and asked how this desirable outcome might be achieved.

Second, in a report (Moss, 2003) commissioned by the Government Office for the East Midlands (GOEM), which sought to evaluate information sharing to reduce crime within the region, the need for a more strategic and evidence-led approach to information sharing to reduce crime was illustrated. Alongside this, GOEM also felt that there was a need to encourage Crime and Disorder Reduction Partnerships (CDRPs) to have a greater involvement in and ownership of the strategic development of specific crime reductive projects and a need to determine what data, over and above that which was currently available, should be obtained as a matter of urgency, to inform an evidence-led response to particular crime problems in Nottingham. To provide an empirical underpinning for a more strategic approach, the report recommended that there should be greater focus on the gathering of specific data in an effort to target specific problems, rather than in populating systems with data with little ultimate effect because of lack of clarity about their implications. The project further suggested that such an approach could initially be taken in relation to the problem of domestic burglary within the city of Nottingham for a number of reasons:

- Domestic burglary had been identified as a key priority.

- Notwithstanding national demonstrations, there was a need to establish "proof-of-concept" (empirical evidence of local risk factors) for risk-based crime reduction locally.

- There was a need to determine what sort of data, over and above that which may currently be available, should be routinely gathered, to inform an evidence-led response to domestic burglary in Nottingham.

The Nottingham Burglary Risk Index, or BRIx project as it became known, suggested that two residential pilot areas should be chosen wherein to develop a risk index for domestic burglary. Data gathered from different agencies would be brought together to inform this approach, supplemented by information gathered for the purpose of the project. In the event, the latter consisted of surveys of locations and victims within the two areas in question.

Scope of the Project

The intention of the project was to draw up a risk assessment instrument based upon accepted and proven risks, rather than those that could best be described as anecdotal or experiential. In this case the bases for this were three individual pieces of academic research, namely Budd's (1999) work on domestic burglary, research on repeat victimisation by Farrell and Pease (2001), and the Winchester and Jackson (1982) Environmental Risk Index. Combining these elements in a manner which informed the gathering of specific data and which also formed the basis of empirical survey work that was later carried out, was to be the foundation of the burglary risk assessment instrument. In order to achieve this, it was necessary to collect data specific to identified risks previously highlighted by the cited and other work.

Because of confusion evident in discussions with practitioners in community safety, it seems important to distinguish between the informing spirit of BRIx and that of prospective mapping, as pioneered by Kate Bowers and Shane Johnson (see, for example, Bowers, Johnson and Pease, 2004). The two are complementary. BRIx seeks to establish relatively enduring risks, so that partner agencies can take remedial action in advance of crime. Prospective mapping has as its starting point the observation that "hot spots" are "slippery" (i.e., that areas of high crime are changeable; see Townsley and Pease, 2002), and that crime events in the recent past should shape police deployment and other short-term preventive action. In the conventional jargon of criminology, BRIx addresses risk heterogeneity (i.e., the non-uniformity or multifariousness of risk), and prospective mapping considers the causes of future crime events (see Pease, 1998; Tseloni and Pease, 2004). Since there is only so much risk to go round (thank goodness), in areas and epochs when prospective mapping is most important, BRIx-type approaches will be least important – and vice versa. However, experience suggests that there will be few circumstances where either approach is of only trivial importance.

Developing a Schedule of Contingent Actions

The title of this sub-section derives from a proposal of Moss and Pease (2004) addressed to the principles and practice of data sharing. This proposal contended that hitherto data sharing had been attempted for reasons of goodwill and had not been explicitly linked to crime risk, and hence not limited on a need-to-know basis. The argument of the paper ran as follows:

1. Risk factors should be identified.

2. Those partners which have stewardship over particular factors should make an undertaking to address those risk factors in a group identified as being at enduring high risk.

3. Information combining risk factors should be delegated to one partner or a trusted third party.

4. The X% of households at greatest risk should be identified on the basis of combined data by the delegated partner or trusted third party, which should communicate to individual partners *only* those households where risk factors in the control of that agency were implicated.

The merits of this approach (readers are referred to the original article for a fuller account of the mechanics) are as follows:

1. Each partner will only ever have information about those high risk households in which factors which it can influence contribute to that risk. Thus all shared information is empirically based and shared only on a need-to-know basis, thus clarifying the data sharing process.

2. Each partner will have made in advance an undertaking to address its "owned" factors when a household is identified as being at high risk.

Apparently condemned to be misunderstood, community safety practitioners in discussion have sought to refer to the schedule of contingent actions as an action plan. It is not. The schedule of contingent actions is the initial undertaking by partners to "own" certain risk factors and to remedy these factors, without knowing at the time of the undertaking which households they will be called upon to assist, or what other factors contribute to the high risk experienced by these households.

Although one of the benefits of this approach was that all information at the point of use had the personal elements deleted and was therefore entirely anonymous, it was felt that a protocol should be agreed. This was easily arranged through the data protection manager for Nottingham City Council and was subsequently signed by representatives of the police, the city council and the Home Office to enable the project to move ahead.

Before describing the results from the analysis of the data that was collected by the BRIx project, it is relevant to set this project within the context of the domestic burglary position as it stood in Nottingham City at the time of the study.

The Context of Burglary in Nottingham

The Nottingham burglary trend had been downward and more markedly so in late 2003 and early 2004. This trend had no doubt been occasioned by the urgent police action that was taken at that time. Certain initiatives which were in place at that time had no doubt supplemented enforcement action and were maintaining these results with the possibility of improving upon them. These initiatives included:

- The Nottingham Act, which has great potential for impacting the market in stolen goods. The Act's main provision gives the local authorities and the police the power to search the premises of second-hand goods dealers and requires such dealers to be licensed;

- The successful deployment of Smartwater, which is a forensic coding product combined with microdot technology. It is designed to be applied to household property and thus assigns that household a unique forensic code. Although invisible to the naked eye, stolen items treated with Smartwater can be identified with a UV light tracer; and,

- Targeting of prolific offenders through Project Sherwood, an approach taken by Nottingham City Police which sought to engage all Crime and Disorder Reduction partners in the management of prolific offenders through effective identification, intervention and rehabilitation.

It was felt that these successes could be further built upon in a number of ways. One of these was to emphasise the potential for clearer designation of responsibility for burglary reduction actions which could be elucidated by the BRIx project. This also has the potential to support stronger linkage with the National Intelligence Model (NIM). This model seeks to align priorities in relation to intelligence, prevention and enforcement within one control strategy. Experience to date suggests that most focus (by the police) relates to enforcement priorities. The opportunity is present to designate responsibility for prevention to the local authority (supported by the police and other partners), retaining responsibility for enforcement by the police (supported by other partners) but with intelligence remaining the responsibility of both (police and local authorities supported by partners).

It is relevant at this point to give an overview of trends of domestic burglary over the period stated.

Figure 1 shows the trends for the city as a whole from February 1998 to August 2003 smoothed by centred three-point moving averages.

As we know, underlying trends can be obscured by seasonal trends so we needed to take account of this. Figure 2 therefore shows seasonal variation for the same period.

For the purposes of this study it was really the last 12 months that was of greatest interest, so in Figure 3 the author has taken the period from February 2003 to January 2004 and has adjusted the figures to discount seasonal trends by using mean burglary rates for the period from 1998, and weighting 03-04 data accordingly.

The general downward trend in the year to January 04 seems to have accelerated, (relative to experience in previous years) over the last three months of that year.

The trend for the city as a whole is reflected in each of the six sub-areas. In the interests of avoiding tedium, these analyses have been omitted from this paper but are available from the author on request.

This data presents the trend in burglary for the city at the time of the BRIx. To summarise, it was possible to say two positive things:

Figure 1: Smoothed Domestic Burglary Trends

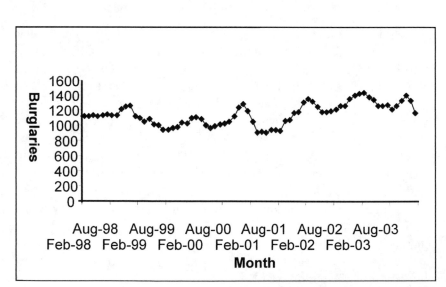

Figure 2: Seasonal Variation in Burglary

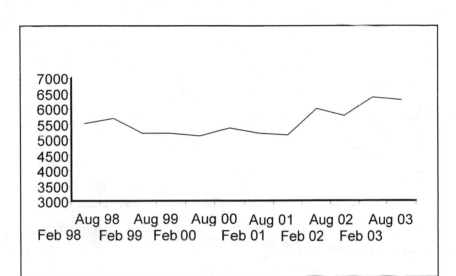

1. The slope throughout the most recent year was downwards everywhere; and,

2. For the total and all but one of the sub areas, the last month or few months of the period even outperformed that downward trend.

There was reason for optimism therefore, but whilst the trend was gratifyingly downward, it was not steeply so. It remained important to understand the nature of the residual problem. Furthermore, the reason for the decline was and remains opaque. The general view was that the decline was driven by the targeting of offenders. However, the detection rate did not increase. If it were security driven, the proportion of attempts should have increased, but did not. There is some suggestion that miscoding as between domestic and other burglaries increased over the period, and that there was an increase in burglaries through bodily force, but this scarcely clarifies the picture.

The Development of a Consolidated Risk Index

The BRIx Project set out to establish the factors which contribute to burglary risk. The intention then was to identify the homes at greatest

Figure 3: Domestic Burglary Feb 2003 to Jan 2004 (seasonally adjusted)

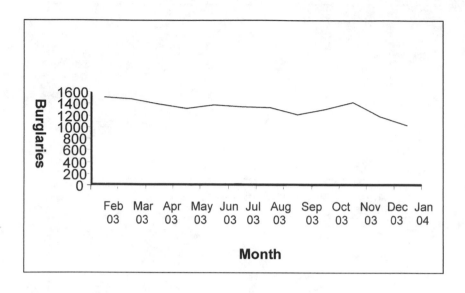

risk of burglary and the agencies best placed to diminish that risk. An underlying theme of the work is that data sharing should not be routinely undertaken, rather that partnership working is advanced by tasking agencies to take remedial action with homes at elevated risk.

The data contributing to this analysis comes from the Sneinton and Top Valley areas of Nottingham and from three sources:

1. a house-to-house resident survey;

2. a survey of home attributes (the location survey); and,

3. police data identifying burgled homes.

The total number of homes from which at least some data was available was 1,286, and the total number of burglary events captured was 418, covering events between November 1, 2000 and the end of October 2003, and including multiple events against the same household.

The first step was to detail all the associations between, on the one hand, victim and location information, and on the other burglary victimization. The variables which were usable (in terms of tolerable levels of missing data and factor clarity and which showed a statistically reliable association with burglary risk) were noted and weighted by the strength of the association. These factors and weightings are set out in Table 1 below. The means of combining them was the Burgess method, as being simple, robust, and capable of easy revision in the light of practitioner experience (see Armitage, 2004). In short, the difference in percentage burgled for the risk group in question relative to the average risk for all cases (where data were available; i.e., cases with missing information on a variable were omitted from the calculation of average risk for that variable). Thus, for example, householders aged 16-24 had a victimization rate 9% above the average, so the variable was scored +9 as a contributor to risk. Likewise, householders over 50 had a 9% lower than average rate of burglary, so being in that age group was scored as -9.

The full list of factors contributing to points scores is supplied in Table 1.

The point scores from each factor applying to each individual household were aggregated, yielding a consolidated risk score for every household. The 10% of homes with the highest point scores had a probability four times the rate of homes in the lowest scoring 10% of experiencing one or more burglaries across the period for which data was available. This is perhaps the safest way of expressing the results, given that the amount of missing data makes the middle of the points range difficult to interpret. Since the intended use of the BRIx Index was to identify households at high risk, this is not a severe limitation.

DISCUSSION AND RECOMMENDATIONS

The points system described here affords a good first attempt at allocating risk scores to individual homes on the basis of characteristics of both the home and those who live there. Since the factors which confer the risk are transparent, and since these differ for different high risk homes, the partner with the primary responsibility for reducing risk will differ. This was the intention of the BRIx project, but its usefulness as a burglary reduction tool is incumbent upon the relevant agencies a) having responsibility for this risk subsequently getting around the table and being prepared to act upon the information given to them, and b) undertaking routinely to collect the information which the research shows empirically to be associated with burglary risk. Before discussing what it might be appropriate to do, one should consider the trade-off in value of using local rather than national data.

Table 1: Factors Contributing to Burglary Risk

Dwelling characteristics	Points
Length of occupation	
< one year	+9
1-5 years	-5
> 5 years	-3
Dwelling type	
Terraced	-1
Semi-detached	+10
Front door observable from street	
Yes	+3
No	-1
Open land adjacent	
Yes	+2
No	-1
On main road	
Yes	+9
No	-3
Home occupied	
Yes	0
No	+7

Neighbourhood disorder (litter, graffiti, etc.)	
Yes	+9
No	0

Victim ethnicity	
Asian	+12
Black	-11
White	-1

Victim employment status	
Employed	+1
Retired	-9
Unemployed	-3

Victim age	
16-24	+9
> 24-35	+3
> 35-50	+3
> 50	-9

The BRIx risk assessment device set out above has the advantage of being local to Nottingham. It has in consequence the disadvantage of using limited data. There seems to be a degree of parochialism in crime and disorder reduction partnerships (as was ever the case in the local administration of justice). This probably means that local risk indices will generally be preferred to national ones. If that is the case for Nottingham, then the BRIx index is probably the best available. Insofar as there are areal variations in housing stock, demography and land use, there is much to be said for the local emphasis. For example, Rachel Armitage (2004) found that the Winchester and Jackson risk index, constructed on Kent households, did not discriminate well in West Yorkshire, probably because of differences in housing stock. (She went on to produce a fine burglary predictor for West Yorkshire.) However, there is a case for using national data to yield a template risk index. The British Crime Survey routinely contains information which could form the basis of a good risk index of national application, which could be tweaked locally. (See Budd, 1999 for the best available presentation of national burglary data from the BCS.) In short, the writer is making two recommendations:

1. that the Home Office conducts or contracts out the modest amount of research necessary to construct a national burglary risk index and make it available for local use (possibly after local refinement); and,

2. that Nottingham uses BRIx as it stands to pilot the implementation of a risk index, thus gaining experience which would be valuable in the event of a national risk index becoming available.

Much could be written about how the Home Office could, through its BCS researchers, aid local CDRPs in specifying local factors which could helpfully be incorporated in a national index, to avoid the Armitage revelation of local variation in the relative predictive power of individual risk factors.

Readers may at this point wish to eschew the risk index approach and champion one or other of the areal classification systems (ACORN or MOSAIC), where area types are identified which unquestionably do vary in domestic burglary, as other crime types. (ACORN is a geodemographic tool to identify and understand the U.K. population by using 125 demographic statistics and 287 lifestyle variables. MOSAIC is a generic area-based classification system which is used in both the public and private sectors in the U.K. It contains over 400 data variables to classify households in the U.K. to 1 of 61 types and 11 groups.) This, in the writers' view is not a preferred route, although such classification may be useful for other resource allocation purposes. This is because area classification is somewhat remote from manipulable factors. To say that a particular area type is prone to crime directs attention away from specific area characteristics which may be changeable. For example, in BRIx (as demonstrated elsewhere), people who have recently moved in have higher vulnerability to burglary. This suggests that a relevant local official (perhaps an appropriately trained community support officer) could engage with recent arrivals to help with security, property marking, recruitment into Neighbourhood Watch schemes, and so on. The link between litter and burglary risk invites action by the relevant local authority service. Thus the risk factors identified in BRIx, (while not necessarily causal and not to be acted upon without thought) at least focus upon specific area characteristics rather than the less helpful general area type.

Whatever route towards a risk index is taken, both Armitage (2004) and the present writer place great importance on using a scale construction method which is transparent, i.e. which allows local partnerships to understand and modify. Extreme technical sophistication sits uneasily with swift local revision of a risk index.

Address correspondence to: Dr. Kate Moss-Brookes, Midlands Centre for Criminology & Criminal Justice, Loughborough University, Leicestershire, LE11 3TU, UK; e-mail: k.r.brookes@lboro.ac.uk

REFERENCES

Armitage, R. (2000). *An evaluation of Secured by Design Housing within West Yorkshire.* Briefing Note 7/00, London: Home Office.

Armitage, R. (2004). *Secured by design – An investigation of its history, development and future role in crime reduction.* Unpublished PhD thesis, University of Huddersfield, Huddersfield, West Yorkshire, UK.

Bowers, K. J., Johnson, S., & Pease, K. (2004). Prospective hot spotting: The future of crime mapping? *British Journal of Criminology, 4,* 641-658.

Budd, T. (1999). *Burglary of domestic dwellings: Findings from the British Crime Survey.* Statistical Bulletin No. 4/99. London: Home Office.

Farrell, G., & Pease, K. (2001). *Repeat victimization.* Crime Prevention Studies, vol. 12. Monsey, NY: Criminal Justice Press.

Moss, K. (2003). *Project Jupiter: Evaluation, penetration, need and provision. A report on the strategic research and recommendations in relation to the Data Exchange Initiative piloted by Government Office for the East Midlands.* Unpublished report, University of Loughborough, Leicestershire, UK (March).

Moss, K., & Pease, K. (1998). Section 17 Crime and Disorder Act 1998: A wolf in sheep's clothing? *International Journal of Crime Prevention and Community Safety, 1,* 15-19.

Moss, K., & Pease, K. (2004). Data sharing in crime prevention: Why and how. *Crime Prevention and Community Safety: An International Journal, 6,* 7-12.

Pease, K. (1998). *Repeat victimisation: Taking stock.* Home Office Research and Planning Unit Paper 90. London: Home Office.

Townsley, M., & Pease, K. (2002). Hot spots and cold comfort: The importance of having a working thermometer. In N. Tilley (Ed.), *Analysis for crime prevention.* Crime Prevention Studies, vol. 13. Monsey, NY: Criminal Justice Press.

Tseloni, A., & Pease, K. (2004). Repeat personal victimisation: Random effects, event dependence and unexplained heterogeneity. *British Journal of Criminology, 44,* 931-945.

Winchester, S., & Jackson, H. (1982). *Residential burglary: The limits of prevention.* Home Office Research Study Number 74. London: Her Majesty's Stationery Office.

Kings and Castles,
Cavemen and Caves:
The Impact of Crime
on Male Victims

by

Mandy Shaw
Nottingham Trent University

and

Sylvia Chenery
Applied Criminology Associates

Abstract: *"Big boys don't cry . . . ," or so it has been said in a variety of places in popular culture, including the 1993 film of the same name and a song by the popular music group Extreme. There are also reminders in the academic literature (Goodey, 1997; Sparks, 1996). There is a presumption that the most traumatised victims of crime are females. But what happens, for example, when men feel unable to protect their family and home from repeated burglaries, when they have been socialised into the role of being a protector? How does this affect the role of the "keeper of the castle?" What sort of psychological impact does this have? Recent research has shown that men often suffer high levels of stress and anxiety in the aftermath of crime, but find difficulty in admitting they need help. This chapter provides examples of male experiences of crime, explores the impacts and discusses the potential for future provision of victim services.*

Crime Prevention Studies, volume 21 (2007), pp. 147–161.

INTRODUCTION

Research on fear of crime has been growing steadily during the last four decades (Sundeen and Mathieu, 1976; Garofalo, 1982; Hanmer and Saunders, 1984; Smith, 1986; Stanko, 1987; Box et al., 1988; Hale, 1996; Semmens et al., 2002; Gabriel and Greve, 2003; Dodd et al., 2004). The single most commonly recognised factor influencing fear of crime has consistently been found to be gender. In a plethora of studies, and over a long period of time, women have been found to display characteristics associated with fear more commonly than men (e.g., Hanmer and Saunders, 1984; Home Office, 2002). Feminist criminologists (e.g., Stanko, 1987) have argued that women's fear is related to the fear for personal safety, particularly their fear of sexual offences. Paradoxically, evidence indicates that, despite their increased risk of victimisation, men are less likely to experience fear. It has been argued that this may in part be due to methodological reasons, such as "a failure to distinguish between risk evaluation, worry and fear" (Hale, 1996, p. 84). Linked with this, others have suggested that, "men may be constrained by their machismo from willingly admitting feelings of anxiety" (Hale, 1996, p. 96). Stanko and Hobdell (1993, p. 400) also suggest that "criminology's failure to explore men's particular experiences of violence is often attributed to men's reluctance to report 'weakness.' "

More recently, the impact of victimisation on the fear of crime has begun to be recognised. The focus has echoed the fear of crime literature, with the impact of inter-personal crimes such as sexual assault and rape being represented in the literature more than property crimes such as burglary, although there has been increasing recognition of the emotional impact of burglary (Mawby, 2001; Donaldson, 2003).

In addition, there has been a growing body of literature on the nature and impact of sexual violence against men, for example on male rape (Gregory and Lees, 1999; Allen, 2002) and on female-on-male domestic violence (Grady, 2002). Some attention has also been paid to the victimisation of men in contexts where they are statistically at greatest risk (Tomsen, 1997; Stanko and Hobdell, 1993). In a "criminal justice system (which) remains far from being victim-friendly" (Newburn and Stanko, 1994, p. 152), though, there is still a neglect of male victims. This is surprising given the higher prevalence of male victimisation compared with crime victimisation of females. It is also a matter of concern given the related neglect in service provision for male victims. Furthermore, it serves to perpetuate the notion of a hegemonic masculinity where men apparently do not experience suffering in the aftermath of victimisation.

Just as in many feminist studies, where women have been represented as a homogeneous group to the detriment of the understanding of the variety of different experiences of women, so too have men largely been represented as one homogeneous group in the literature. In addition, the impact of victimisation, particularly repeat victimisation, has been neglected (Shaw, 2001). Stanko and Hobdell (1993) acknowledge that men are not encouraged to speak about their fears. There are methodological implications here: the use of the word "fear," in research such as the British Crime Survey (BCS), and by policy makers and the police, has not encouraged men to speak of their experiences, this being bound up in questions of masculinity. Writing on childhood sexual abuse, Holmes et al. (1997) suggest that men deny the impact of these crimes on them as a coping strategy. In a separate study, Gadd et al. (2002, p. 45) found that male victims of domestic abuse found reporting their victimisation "embarrassing and humiliating." Whilst not wishing to diminish the impact of the traumatic experience of child abuse or domestic abuse, there is evidence to suggest that some men also deny the impact of burglary on them. Research has suggested that when men do admit that crime has impacted upon them, that impact is significant in many cases (Shaw, 2001). These are the subjects addressed in this chapter.

Specifically, only scant attention has been paid to the male victims of burglary, which seems surprising given the priority by major organisations such as police, local authorities, Home Office and Victim Support to the crime of burglary. The limited research evidence on the impact of burglary on men, though, finds that not surprisingly men do articulate a response to victimisation. For example, Maguire (1982, cited in Stanko and Hobdell, 1993, p. 400) found that "men were more likely to express anger than distress or shock in response to burglary." Responses other than anger have not been addressed widely, however.

RESEARCH ON MALE VICTIMS

Studies of the fear of crime and the impact of inter-personal crimes have contributed to the presentation of men's and women's experiences as being dichotomous. The authors of this chapter have more than 20 years' experience in the field between them, and have spent a substantial amount of that time talking at length to both male and female victims. Quantitative studies of the impact of victimisation have previously not been sensitive to male victims and their perception of victimisation. In this chapter, the opportunity is taken to focus on the neglected area of the impact of burglary on men. The evidence also shows that the separation of personal and property crime is a false one, as is illustrated in considering the impact of property crime and burglary on their victims. Published and previously unpublished material is used, inspired directly and indirectly by working with Ken Pease. In so doing, we represent what Ken often refers to as the "hearts and flowers" of the subject – the personal stories which say so much. The impact of burglary on men is significant, from research evidence presented, and there is all too little awareness of the phenomena in policy-making circles. Men *are* affected by burglary victimisation, they simply show the impact differently. As the title of the chapter suggests, the inclination of many men is to try and solve the problem of burglary by securing the castle that is their home. When the crime is repeated, though, this presents an altogether new dynamic over which men have no control. When the security of the home is in question the impact of victimisation is compounded, with related victim support implications.

The Nature and Cost of the Burglary Event

This chapter examines the diversity of impacts of a range of criminal acts, in particular burglary. The 1998 BCS estimated that "less than half of crimes were reported to the police" (Mirrlees-Black et al., 1998), and that only about half the number of these reported crimes actually were recorded onto police crime information systems.

There are a number of reasons why victims fail to report crime, but two common answers from repeat burglary victims are: a perception that no action will be taken by the police; and a lack of necessity because the household is not covered by insurance (Anderson et al., 1994). These are not the only reasons for the differences, but a constant theme emerging from research is a lack of confidence by victims in the criminal justice system.

It is known that the true cost of crime to society is enormous. It breaks down social cohesion, it fuels fears and anxieties and creates demands on existing over-stretched resources. But is the emotional and physical impact of crime regarded as priority by the criminal justice system? To answer this question, consider the Brand and Price (2000, p. viii) estimate of the cost of an average burglary (reproduced in Table 1).

The "anticipated" domain is associated with costs that can be predicted and planned for, i.e., the costs of preventing burglary. The "consequential" domain relates to the outcome of a burglary.

Table 1: Brand and Price (2000) Estimate of the Social and Economic Costs of an Average Residential Burglary

Domains	Specific types of costs	Cost (£)
Anticipated	Security	330
	Insurance	100
Consequential	Property stolen	830
	Lost outputs	40
	Emotional and physical impact on victims	**550**
	Costs of victim services	**4**
Response	Criminal justice costs	490
Total		2300

It may be surprising to learn that roughly one-quarter of the cost of a burglary arises from the emotional and physical impact of victims. Although it is recognized that there are significant difficulties in estimating these costs, the amount is in stark contrast to the mere £4 of victim support.

Due to the reasons already given, the overall costs of crime are notoriously difficult to calculate and much is based upon estimates. It seems we are still some way from accurately quantifying the real costs of crime. However, the Home Office update (Duboung and Hamed, 2005) focuses on issues such as crime against individuals and households, giving more comprehensive information than had previously been available. Improvements include changes to the way the emotional and physical costs of violent crime against individuals are valued.

The Impact of Repeat Victimisation

In some studies on the impact of victimisation on fear it has been suggested that, "a victim's fear of crime depends mainly, but not entirely on the severity of the victimisation" (Kury and Ferdinand, 1998, p. 97). Although Kury and Ferdinand (1998, p. 97) acknowledge that, relative to victims of crime, "more non-victims believe that their living place will be broken into within the next year," the particular plight of repeat victims needs to be raised. Although the task is to reduce fear of crime, which is shared by victims and non-victims alike, by looking at the impact on repeat victims we can suggest better ways of measuring fear of crime. Kury and Ferdinand did not consider repeat victimisation and how the extent of victimisation may impact upon fear of crime qualitatively differently than a single severe victimisation (see Shaw, 2001).

Shaw (2001) assessed the impact of victimisation on a sample of male and female repeat victims. By analysing fear of crime related to episodic incidents, a temporal rhythm of fear was identified that was manifested differently in men and women. Among other things, this study highlighted that repeat victims do not become desensitised to repeated attacks but continue to express a fear reaction with each successive victimisation – this being particularly pertinent for male victimisation, where it is sometimes seemingly impossible to solve the problem of victimisation happening again and again.

For the first time, Shaw (2001) paralleled the experience of repeat victims to the process of bereavement. For both the male and female victims in the research, levels of victimisation-related trauma were such that they resembled the human grief responses of numbness, anger and isolation, depression and acceptance, identified originally by such influential writers as Kubler-Ross (1969) and Parkes (1970). For operational purposes, Shaw developed a typology based on the extent of fear (high, medium and low). The male responses to repeat victimisation were equivalent to the women's responses. Some of the male victims' responses are outlined below; all had suffered at least two burglary victimisations.

There had been a suggestion in earlier research that men's responses to victimisation may resemble bereavement, although the direct link was not made at the time. Stanko and Hobdell's (1993, p. 406) research on male victims of assault on a night out found that "the men's accounts of the effects of assault ranged from the immediate, within hours of the assault, to those lingering over weeks and months, and even extending over years . . . the impact was generally one of shock, fear, anger, and/or disbelief." Shaw's research thus consolidated underlying themes in the literature and explicitly used a bereavement model.

MALE RESPONSES TO BURGLARY AND IMPACT ON MASCULINITY

In presenting the following personal accounts of male repeat victims, we allow their stories to speak for themselves. Parts of these accounts can also be found in Anderson et al. (1994), Chenery et al. (1997) and Shaw (2001).

Tom (aged 35-40) was a repeat victim and had experienced a number of crimes, including a burglary. When speaking specifically about the burglary, he commented that:

> ... you fear it can always happen and you know it's beyond your control and so if it's beyond your control the fears always there and it doesn't go away. (Shaw, 2001)

Another male repeat victim, Lewis (aged 45-49), experienced a greater fear at night:

> ... we never got broke into at night ... but we always worried about the night time, even though we never got broken into at night. (Shaw, 2001)

One interviewee in his seventies had lost all confidence in his own ability to care for himself following a particularly violent burglary:

> ... I used to be a boxer in the army, and have always kept myself fit ... now I don't feel I can take care of myself ... (Chenery et al., 1997)

In a recent interview with a Victim Support worker, an account was given of a male burglary victim who initially sought practical security advice. He was described as *"a big, burly bloke,"* but once he started to talk about his feelings he broke into tears stating:

> ... I can't help my wife and family ... I feel helpless. ... (Shaw, 2001)

Stanko and Hobdell (1993) offered one of the first insights into the impact of assault victimisation on men, particularly in relation to its impact on feelings of masculinity. Their research found that "the men interviewed located their emotional, physical, and social responses to their victimisation in relation to "being men." The frame of masculinity was quite apparent. ... " In Shaw (2001), the impact of burglary on men's identity was also evident. Tom, already referred to above, described the impact of the burglary and the other crimes he had experienced. Without prompting, he referred to circumstances when his identity as a man was threatened by his experiences. Although he talked mainly about his fear of personal attack, here, it was the index crime of burglary which had contributed to these feelings. There were also fears of racially-motivated crimes, Tom being of half-Chinese origin. Part of this excerpt can also be found in Shaw (2001).

> I mean, some boys are strongly built, you know, and they can, you know, ... react ... all this fear of being hurt, you know, the fear of

being attacked and the fear of the unknown, you know, the fear of dying prematurely, you know . . . but I know it does affect your consciousness and your thinking – your attitude towards people . . . because what happened to me . . . I don't feel towards people I know but towards people I don't know. . . .

Anger is a strong element within victims, particularly males. In the interview with Lewis, although he suffered physical injury following a robbery, it was a burglary shortly after that which had the greatest emotional effect on him.

. . . and I think that was my real turning point: I thought, there's nobody gonna drive me from here . . . I'll let them kill me in the house . . . that made me even more angry and more determined there was no way I'd move. (Shaw, 2001)

Lifestyle Impact

The adoption of safety measures can reflect the extent of concern of a victim following victimisation. For some victims this can amount to significant changes to everyday routines. Lewis's obsession with everyday checks on his property (see Shaw, 2001), illustrated in the following quotation, developed as a result of the long period of repeated victimisation. Despite the ending of the victimisation some months prior to the interview, and the perpetrators having moved out of the area, Lewis still went to extraordinary lengths to protect his property.

. . . even though they've gone we still never let it go . . . first in the morning I go out the back – check the car and check the shed . . . Every morning . . . I still check everything. (Shaw, 2001)

Anderson et al. (1994) found the extent to which those repeatedly burgled can be affected. Husbands felt inadequate in their ability to care for their families, and social and personal life patterns changed.

. . . we don't go out together as a family any more . . . someone always has to stay in the house. . . .

. . . I used to go to the local Social Club with my partner, but we don't go there any more, who knows it might be one of the people there who've burgled us. . . .

Fear of further crimes may not only force a man to "withdraw into his cave," but can make him change his daily routine. For example, one male assault victim refused to continue to take his daily walks near his home. He therefore drove five miles out of the area to take his "daily consti-tutional."

The House as the Castle

Many people, male or female, will be able to identify with the concept of the home as a " . . . safe haven from crime" (McConnell, 1989, cited in Kury and Ferdinand, 1998, p. 97). Tom is again referred to here. Part of this excerpt can also be found in Shaw (2001, p. 176).

> MS: . . . you mentioned that (after) the burglaries . . . you felt so insecure you likened it to being raped?
>
> Tom: Yeah . . . well, I don't know anything about rape, right, it can happen to men nowadays but . . . the initial drama is just inexplicable, you know . . . because your house is like your castle, you know, and all the things you ever worked for, you know, it's all there – it's all personal to you and people only come by invitation, right, and here were some assholes who came through, by force, and helped themselves to things that you hold dearly to . . . very intimate I think . . . and you feel like your privacy, you know, being taken away, being invaded, you know, being taken away. It's like . . . so because your flat, your house is part of your . . . an extension of your personhood you feel it's an attack on you, so the nearest knowledge I could draw is like being raped because it's not . . . nowhere as near as being raped but it's about the closest thing I could experience . . . it was very painful, you know.

High-profile Cases

There have been a number of high-profile cases in the United Kingdom in recent years where male victims of burglary have sought to protect their property during a burglary incident, thereby risking their own personal safety. These cases serve to strengthen the view that the separation of property and personal crimes is a mistake in trying to understand men's reaction to burglary. This is because the identity of many people is tied up in their property. For men, the house is the symbol of many things, to varying degrees including status, security, belonging, and independence. This is not necessarily different for women. The key difference is the conventional view of the male being the provider, breadwinner and protec-tor of the home.

The first high-profile case was that of Tony Martin, a *chronic* victim, from Norfolk, England, who shot and killed a burglar, Fred Barras. Martin served a prison sentence for shooting Barras as he tried to escape from Martin's house. The case received huge press attention, and debates followed about whether Martin was a victim or a criminal, re-igniting debates about the extent to which force can be used by householders to protect their property. Many commentators (e.g., Aaronovitch, 2003, p. 1) have suggested that there is potentially a "Tony Martin in all of us." Martin was released from prison in July 2003 after serving two-thirds of a five-year sentence.

Teacher Robert Symons was tragically killed when a burglar broke into his house in west London in October 2004 (BBC news, 22/10/04). He had been disturbed from his sleep when he heard a noise in a downstairs room and had gone to investigate. Unlike Tony Martin, there was no sign that Mr. Symons had tried to challenge the burglar. This man simply did what many men would do to protect his family and home – investigate a noise in the middle of the night.

In November 2004, rock star Ozzy Osbourne's Buckinghamshire country house was broken into. The rock star's response to the burglary was reported widely in the media. *The Guardian* newspaper reported that:

> Ozzy got up at 4 am to go to the lavatory and ran into the burglar making off with his haul. Ozzy then got him in a headlock and "thought of snapping his neck," but reconsidered and let him go. (Chancellor, 2004, p. 1)

The point here is that a burglary is an invasion of the castle which it has not been possible to defend. When a repeat occurs, as the examples from our research and the Tony Martin case shows, the responses can be extreme.

SUPPORT NEEDS

Stanko and Hobdell (1993, p. 143) state: " . . . [i]t appears that male victims of assault view their victimisation through a male frame, the essence of which sees victimisation as 'weak and helpless.'" This creates difficulties for men in expressing feelings, leaving them isolated and unable to ask for support. It is this barrier which has led some men to take matters into their own hands. As has been shown, this can have important impacts upon people's reactions to crime and hence it is important that policy is tailored to recognise this and attempts be made to minimise extreme reactions to crime that can lead to serious consequences.

What should also be recognised, but which has not been sufficiently researched to date, is that in general men talk less than women when they are suffering stress, such as the impact of victimisation. However, there is evidence that men do want to talk, particularly if the opportunity to talk is couched in practical, problem-solving terms. The ability to take up help is usually gendered, but anecdotal evidence suggest that local Victim Support agencies have seen a significant increase in the number of queries from men, in particular young males who are particularly fearful of violent crime. They found older male victims to be more reluctant to seek help, often putting on a "macho" front, declaring that counselling is not for them. Interestingly, Hodgson (2003) found it was the more mature males who suffered from psychological breakdowns.

Men will often make initial contact with support agencies in order to gain information regarding access to practical advice, for example security advice following a burglary incident. However, when given the opportunity to talk, they are often confused by their own feelings – the simple question of "are you ok?" from a professional support worker can sometimes open the floodgates.

Men often see accessing help for health-related issues as a weakness. Medical journals commonly report that significantly fewer men than women seek advice (Banks, 2001; White and Johnson, 2000). As discussed earlier, it is often much later, after the event, when men attempt to return to normal life patterns, that the impact shows and the powerful psychological trauma affects work, home and personal relationships.

Identifying the needs of male victims may, in the future, avoid the serious consequences described earlier. The categories of need identified by Maguire (1985) for victims in general are useful to consider here: informational needs; practical needs; and emotional needs. Men are more likely to respond to practical help than if "emotional" help is offered by itself. If the opportunity to be supported emotionally is provided alongside information and practical needs, more men may take the opportunity to be helped. Hodgson's report (2003) found that many of the victims interviewed received little support outside of their immediate family or friends. They commonly complained of lack of personal contact with the police, and lack of advice and information.

Anger is a response which has been recognised in the literature. Providing an outlet for the release of this anger, for example through greater awareness in victim support training, might help men deal with a crime such as burglary, particularly when it is repeated.

There is evidence to show that the cumulative impact of victimisation can cause stress levels to increase, even for incidents regarded as more trivial than domestic burglary. There is also now evidence to show that there is an impact on the physical and mental health of victims (Shaw and Pease, 2002). Therefore, should the level of resources directed towards victims be considered far too insignificant when its cost is calculated at only £4?

The BCS (Home Office, 2000) revealed that the majority of victims experienced some degree of emotional upset after victimisation, and research undertaken by Anderson et al. (1994) and Hodgson (2005) discovered that a significant number of men interviewed had suffered some degree of physiological trauma, in some cases leading to complete mental breakdowns.

However, the less visible emotional and psychological effects often go unnoticed and unattended by the authorities, families and friends. Nevertheless, the emotional impact of crime has been referred to as the most devastating component of victimisation, and it is often more serious and damaging than any physical or financial injury sustained (Zehr, 1990; Achilles and Zehr, 2001) and thus warrants appropriate attention.

CONCLUSION

The evidence we have presented here suggests that men experience significant feelings of anxiety after burglary. Goodey (1997, p. 401) argues that from an early age "boys don't cry," and refers to Mac an Ghaill's influential work which suggests two consistent themes: "first, that there was no safe place in which boys felt they could talk about their feelings of vulnerability and, secondly, boys suffered from the absence of an emotional language for expression of such feelings (Mac an Ghaill [1994], cited in Goodey, 1997, p. 416). Evidence in the present chapter suggests that some men do find that they can articulate their feelings in research interviews and that emotional language is often used to articulate these experiences. The challenge now to be faced is how to promote and develop a provision of support services that are sensitive to men's issues, eliciting their true reactions to crime, providing appropriate support and recognizing the heterogeneity of the male (and female) population and their multifaceted reactions to crime.

Address correspondence to: Mandy Shaw, Senior Lecturer in Criminology, Nottingham Trent University, Burton Street, Nottingham, NG1 4BU, UK; e-mail: mandy.shaw@ntu.ac.uk

REFERENCES

Aaronovitch, D. (2003). The Tony Martin in all of us. *The Guardian*, 29.7.03. Accessed 16.12.03 from: http://www.guardian.co.uk/g2/-story/0,,1007712,00. html

Achilles, M., & Zehr, H. (2001). Restorative justice for crime victims: The promise, the challenge. In G. Bazemore & M. Schiff (Eds.), *Restorative community justice: Repairing harm and transforming communities*. Cincinnati: Anderson Publishing.

Allen, S. (2002). Male victims of rape: Responses to a perceived threat to masculinity. In C. Hoyle & R. Young (Eds.), *New visions of crime victims*. Portland, UK: Hart.

Anderson, D., Chenery, S., & Pease, K. (1994). *"Biting back": Tackling repeat burglary and car crime*. Crime Detection and Prevention Paper 58. London: Home Office.

Banks, I. (2001). No man's land: Men, illness and the NHS. *British Medical Journal*, *323*, 1058-1060.

Box, S., Hale, C., & Andrews, G. (1988). Explaining fear of crime. *British Journal of Criminology*, *28*, 340-356.

Brand, S., & Price, R. (2000). *The economic and social costs of crime*. Home Office Research Study 217. London: Home Office.

Chancellor, A. (2004). Guide to age. *The Guardian*, 4.12.04. Available from: http://www.guardian.co.uk/print/0,3858,5076869-103425,00.html

Chenery, S., Holt, J., & Pease, K. (1997). *'Biting back II': Reducing repeat victimisation in Huddersfield*. Home Office Crime Detection and Prevention Paper 82. London: Home Office.

Dodd, T., Nicholas, S., Povey, D., & Walker, A. (2004). *Crime in England and Wales 2003/04*. London: Home Office.

Donaldson, R. (2003) *Experience of older burglary victims*. Development and Practice Report 11. London: Home Office.

Duboung, R., & Hamed, J. (2005). *The economic and social costs of crime against individuals and households 2003/04*. London: Home Office.

Gabriel, U., & Greve, W. (2003). The psychology of fear of crime: Conceptual and methodological perspectives. *British Journal of Criminology*, *43*(3), 600-614.

Gadd, D., Farrall, S., Dallimore, D., & Lombard, N. (2002). *Domestic abuse against men in Scotland*. Edinburgh: Scottish Executive.

Garofalo, J. (1981). Fear of crime: Causes and consequences. *Journal of Criminal Law and Criminology*, *72*, 839-859.

Goodey, J. (1997). Boys don't cry. *British Journal of Criminology*, *37*(3), 401-418.

Grady, A. (2002). Female-on-male domestic violence: Uncommon or ignored? In C. Hoyle & R. Young (Eds.), *New visions of crime victims*. Portland, UK: Hart.

Gregory, J., & Lees, S. (1999). *Policing sexual violence* (chap. 5). London: Routledge.

Hale, C. (1996). Fear of crime: A review of the literature. *International Review of Victimology, 4*, 79-150.

Hanmer, J., & Saunders, S. (1984). *Well-founded fear: A community study of violence to women*. London: Hutchinson.

Hodgson, B. (2005). Impact of crime on victims. *British Journal of Community Justice*, 3(3).

Holmes, G. R., Ofeen, L., & Waller, G. (1997). See no evil, hear no evil, speak no evil: Why do relatively few male victims of childhood sexual abuse receive help for abuse-related issues in childhood?" *Clinical Psychology Review, 17*(1), 69-88.

Home Office. (2000). *The 2000 British Crime Survey: England and Wales*. London: Her Majesty's Stationery Office.

Home Office. (2002). *Crime in England and Wales 2001/02*. London: Home Office.

Kubler-Ross, E. (1969). *On death and dying*. London, UK: Tavistock.

Kury, H., & Ferdinand, T. (1998). The victim's experience and fear of crime. *International Review of Victimology, 5*, 93-140.

Maguire, M. (1985). Victims' needs and victim services: Indications from research. *Victimology: An International Journal, 10*(1-4), 539-559.

Mawby, R. I. (2001). The impact of repeat victimisation on burglary victims in East and West Europe. In G. Farrell & K. Pease (Eds.), *Repeat victimisation* (pp. 69-82). Crime Prevention Studies, vol. 12. Monsey, NY: Criminal Justice Press.

Mirrlees-Black, C., Budd, T., Partridge, S., & Mayhew, P. (1998). *The 1998 British Crime Survey*. Home Office Statistical Bulletin 21/98. London: Home Office.

Newburn, T., & Stanko, E. (1994). *Just boys doing business? Men, masculinities and crime* (chap. 9). London: Routledge.

Parkes, C. M. (1970). The first year of bereavement: A longitudinal study of the reaction of London widows to the death of their husbands. *Psychiatry*, 4, 444-467.

Semmens, N., Dillane, J., & Ditton, J. (2002). Preliminary findings on seasonality and the fear of crime: A research note. *British Journal of Criminology, 42*(4), 798-806.

Shaw, M. (2001). Time heals all wounds? In G. Farrell & K. Pease (Eds.), *Repeat victimisation* (pp. 165-197). Crime Prevention Studies, vol. 12. Monsey, NY: Criminal Justice Press.

Shaw, M., & Pease, K. (2002). Minor crimes, trivial incidents: The cumulative impact of offending. *Issues in Forensic Psychology, 3*, 41-48.

Smith, S. (1986). *Crime, space and society*. Cambridge: Cambridge University Press.

Sparks, R. (1996). Masculinity and heroism in the hollywood "blockbuster": The culture industry and contemporary images of crime and law enforcement. *British Journal of Criminology, 36*(3), 348-360.

Stanko, E. (1987). Typical violence, normal precaution: Men, women and interpersonal violence in England, Wales, Scotland and the USA. In J. Hanmer and M. Maynard (Eds.), *Women, violence and social control* (pp. 122-134). London: Home Office.

Stanko, E. A., & Hobdell, K. (1993). Assaults on men: Masculinity and male violence. *British Journal of Criminology, 33*(3), 400-415.

Sundeen, R., & Mathieu, J. (1976). The fear of crime and its consequences among the elderly in three urban communities. *Gerontologist, 16*, 211-219.

Tomsen, S. (1997). A top night: Social protest, masculinity and the culture of drinking violence. *British Journal of Criminology, 37*(1), 90-102.

White, A., & Johnson, M. (2000). Men making sense of their chest pain – niggles, doubts and denials. *Journal of Clinical Nursing, 9*, 534-541.

Zehr, H. (1990). *Changing lenses: A new focus for crime and justice.* Scottsdale, PA: Herald Press.

Fear of Crime, Perceived Disorders and Property Crime: A Multivariate Analysis at the Area Level

by

Andromachi Tseloni
Nottingham Trent University

Abstract: *This work estimates associated models of areas' fear of crime, perceived disorders and property crime rates over area characteristics and region of England and Wales via multivariate (multilevel) modelling. This statistical model, which draws upon data from the 2000 British Crime Survey and the 1991 (U.K.) Census at the postcode sector-level, allows for the estimation of any interdependence among the three dependent variables. The study shows that the effects of area characteristics and region on fear of crime, disorders and property crime rates are not uniform. Roughly half of the between-areas covariance of property crime rates, fear of crime and perceived disorders is explained by the areas' characteristics and regional dummy variables. The estimated multivariate models of this work, apart from expanding theoretical knowledge, may assist crime prevention efforts via identifying the most efficient measure for a set of targets as well as any diffusion or displacement effects between crime reduction and public reassurance initiatives.*

Crime Prevention Studies, volume 21 (2007), pp. 163–185.

1. INTRODUCTION

The relationship between crime rates and crime perceptions is not straight-forward, while previous empirical research, fruitful as it may be, is far from conclusive (Jackson, 2004; for an overview see Hale, 1996). The consensus so far is that fear of crime relates to perceived economic, social and physical vulnerability, both local and individual, as well as public attitudes towards crime (Taylor and Hale, 1986; Jackson, 2004). Perceived disorders – namely graffiti, unsupervised teenagers, racial harassment, and drug use or dealing in one's own neighbourhood – have been found to affect fear of crime via informal community cues on crime rates (i.e., Taylor and Hale, 1986; Spelman, 2004). Past victimisation more than doubles the odds ratio of perceiving high anti-social behaviour in one's neighbourhood (Wood, 2004) while it nearly doubles[1] the odds ratio of fear of crime (Hale et al., 1994; Tseloni, 2002).

In previous literature on fear of crime or disorders, crime rates or victimisation are an extra explanatory variable in single-equation models, while in its turn, fear has been used to explain perceived disorders (see, for instance, Spelman, 2004) and vice versa (Taylor and Hale, 1986). Thus each variable has in turn assumed the role of predictor in models of fear of crime or disorders. Since all three measures are endogenous, whereby they occur simultaneously and are affected by more or less the same area and individual characteristics, analysis of their relationship via single-equation modelling produces biased and inconsistent estimates (Judge et al., 1988).

This study attempts to estimate the interdependence of crime rates, fear of crime, and perceived incivilities or disorders at the area level, controlling for areas' demographic and socio-economic characteristics or regional idiosyncrasy. It thus estimates the proportion of this interdependence which can be explained by the area's profile and region. To this end, multivariate (multilevel) models which draw upon social disorganisation theory (Shaw and McKay, 1942) are estimated. Multivariate or joint multilevel regression models which have just appeared in non-criminological social policy research – for instance, health (Griffiths et al., 2004), education (Yang et al., 2002), etc. – are methodologically the next step to Professor Pease's long history of joint empirical work on victimisation (e.g., Tricket et al., 1992), with Ken's name legendarily coming last or not appearing at all on his insistence! Ken recently employed multilevel methodology to investigate "boosts" and "flags" of repeat personal crimes (Tseloni and Pease, 2004), and had he contributed to the present chapter, the social

– 164 –

policy implications of the model below and its results (among other missed improvements) would have been more fully investigated. The following analysis is based on aggregate data at the postcode sector geographical unit, which represents "area" or "community" throughout this discussion (see Lynn and Elliot, [2000] for its appropriateness).

Social disorganisation theory asserts that crime is associated with community (in)efficacy (Shaw and McKay, 1942; Sampson and Groves, 1989). Its proponents contend that the ability of a community to supervise teenage peer groups, develop local friendship networks and stimulate residents' participation in local organisations depends on community characteristics. Social disorganisation and resulting crime and delinquency rates depend on the neighbourhood's *socio-economic status, residential mobility, ethnic heterogeneity, family disruption* and *urbanisation.* Social disorganisation theory could encompass fear of crime and perceived disorders, although it was primarily developed to explain crime rates. Theory on fear of crime has been empirically driven (Hale, 1996), while published research on perceived disorders or incivilities (an equivalent term used in the 80's) is sparse (see end note #22). From what little is known, socially disadvantaged communities tend to register high levels of perceived disorder (Budd and Sims, 2001). Their residents also register high levels of fear of crime, not only due to the areas' actual crime rates but also due to their economic and social vulnerability (Hale, 1996). Community demographic and socio-economic attributes make up the set of covariates of the later crime rates and perceptions models. Crime refers here to property or household crimes.

The effects of area characteristics and region on fear of crime, perceived disorders and property crime rates are *jointly* estimated here via multivariate (multilevel)[2] modelling (Goldstein, 1995; Snijders and Bosker, 1999). Multivariate multilevel (henceforth MvMl) models account for the (residual) covariance between the response or dependent variables (here, for instance, property crime rates and each crime perception, namely fear and disorders), which are taken from the same unit of analysis (in this case, postcode sector: see, Goldstein, 1995; Snijders and Bosker, 1999). Apart from estimating the between-response variables covariances, MvMl modelling produces more efficient estimates than single equation models of each response or dependent variable and more powerful statistical tests of the estimated fixed and random effects (Snijders and Bosker, 1999, pp. 200-201). It also allows for comparisons and joint significance tests of the fixed effects of the same explanatory variable on more than one response variable (Snijders and Bosker, 1999, pp. 200-201).

Two crime prevention uses of MvMl models of crime rates and perceptions are immediately apparent. First, crime policy initiatives informed by such models may focus on one or multiple targets by affecting the most influential predictor, respectively. This is because the models can inform on the relative importance of each area characteristic for each dependent variable – i.e., crime, fear of crime or disorder – as well as all three jointly. Resource allocation would be more efficient if it focuses on different area characteristics depending on whether there are single or multiple policy outcomes (see also concluding section). For instance, if poverty was greatly associated with crime rates but had little to do with fear of crime, whereas population density was significant for both targets, then policies which aim at reducing both fear of crime and crime rates would be most effective when resources are allocated according to population density. Given this fictitious empirical result and policy targeting, resource allocation based on poverty could only affect fear of crime via its (residual) covariance with crime rates but not in a direct manner. As long as each area characteristic displays similar direction of associations with all three dependent variables, the choice of policy "measure" affects its efficiency without unpredicted harm. Second, crime prevention or public reassurance initiatives informed by estimated MvMl models allow for the prediction of externalities or in criminological terminology displacement or diffusion effects (Pease, 1998). If the measure affects the set of response variables or target(s) with (same) opposite signs, the (latter) former effect would occur.[3] In the above example, use of poverty instead of population density, while affecting fear of crime at a minimum, did not increase it. Imagine now that poverty was negatively associated with fear of crime. Then, even if fear of crime was not on the agenda, crime reduction policies based on areas' poverty would adversely affect fear of crime. In other words (uninformed) policies may reduce one social problem at the expense of intensifying another.

The models for crime rates and perceptions of this study are estimated over area characteristics and region with postcode sector being essentially the only unit of analysis. Regionally, England and Wales is divided into Wales and the nine Government Office Regions of England. Sampling points are nested within regions which identify a higher-level of aggregation beyond postcode sector. The number of regions, however, is not large enough to provide any significant "between-regions" random variation (Browne and Draper, 2000). Individual attributes which apart from area characteristics significantly affect victimisation, fear of crime and perceived disorders (see, for instance, Kennedy and Forde, 1990; Hale, 1996; Wood,

2004, respectively) could have offered a lower-level of analysis. They are however by design ignored in this study in order to facilitate area-level predictions and, consequently, crime prevention and/or public reassurance initiatives.

The next section presents the variables, responses and covariates, which are employed in this study. The statistical methodology and the results of the estimated MvMl models are given thereafter. A concluding section summarises the results in the light of their implications for theory and puts forward how they may assist crime prevention and public reassurance initiatives.

2. THE DATA

2.1. Fear of Crime, Perceived Disorders and Property Crime

Property crime rates, fear and disorder measures are taken from the 2000 British Crime Survey (henceforth BCS, Hales et al., 2000) across 889 sample points,[4] the sample points being quarter postcode sectors.

Property crime rate is an aggregate count of burglaries (including attempts), thefts from property and thefts of or from vehicle. This crime type was selected for a number of reasons. Apart from vehicle crime, the area of its occurrence is known, and subsequently property crimes can be linked to area's profile (see below). They are also better explained by area characteristics (Kershaw and Tseloni, 2005), while they are just as distressing to the victims as personal crimes are (Norris et al., 1997). The incidence rate of an area's property crime is examined. "Incidence rates" are defined as the average number of crime incidents per household per calendar year. As the focus was on predicted average local area rates, respondents who moved during 1999 have been excluded from the analysis. Their experience of crime may well not reflect typical risk for the area they have moved to. Vehicle crime rates were calculated over vehicle owning households only. Again as the intention was to predict average *local* area risks, any incidents which happened outside 15-minute walks from a respondent's home have been excluded.

Measures of fear of crime and disorder problems have been constructed from scoring BCS respondents' answers on questions on "worry about crime" and "problems in your area," respectively. In particular, the fear measure was based on six questions that ask respondents how worried they are about "having your home broken into and something stolen," "being mugged or robbed," "being raped," "being physically attacked by strangers," "being insulted or pestered by anyone, while in the street or any other public place," and "being subject to a physical attack because of your skin colour, ethnic origin or religion." A score is built up from responses to each question, with any "very worried" response adding 2 to the score, any "fairly worried" adding 1 to the score and other responses adding zero (these being "not very worried," "not at all worried" or "not applicable").

The disorder measure is based on answers to four questions that ask respondents how much of a problem are "teenagers hanging around in the street," "vandalism, graffiti or other deliberate damage to property," "people being attacked or harassed because of their race or colour" and "people using or dealing drugs." A score is built up with any "very big problem" response adding 3 to the score, a "fairly big problem" adds 2, a "not very big problem" adds 1 and "not a problem at all" adds zero following the standard Home Office (UK) coding (Budd and Sims, 2001). Apart from the first one, these disorders point to identifiable crime types. In theory they consist of "indirect victimisation," namely fear-inspiring impact of local crime which is spread via communication of victimless crimes or those suffered by others (Taylor and Hale, 1986).[5] In practice they relate to the crime-bordering types of anti-social behaviour as they are defined by the Home Office (2004). The last three lines of Table 2 in the results section below give some descriptive statistics of the empirical distributions of the dependent variables of this study.

While the following discussion appears to take property crime rates and measures of fear of crime at face value, the measurement issues of these constructs from survey data should not be overlooked (see for instance Farrall et al., 1997). Non-Response and response bias (including telescoping) may distort the level estimates of crime rates (Schneider, 1981). It is also well known that surveys do not measure the true value of fear of crime (for instance, Jackson, 2004) while perceived disorders are just that, i.e., subjective. Intuitively one might argue that area-level aggregates such as the ones employed here would tend to cancel out over- and under-reporting across individuals within an area.

2.2. Area Characteristics and Region

The area characteristics are derived from the 1991 census.[6] The census variables have been rescaled by the BCS fieldwork contractor[7] with normalisation[8] and addition of a random term with 5% of the variance of the census variable, this being done to ensure respondent confidentiality.[9]

A large number of variables may be used to describe community context, and, not surprisingly, they often exhibit high levels of inter-correlation (Osborn et al., 1992). In particular, preliminary work (Tseloni, 2001) with the 1991 census indicated high correlations between variables, which could be thought of as measures of low socio-economic status. Bearing this in mind, an overall area "poverty factor"[10] has been constructed by aggregating the following variables: the percentage of lone parent households, the percentage of households without car, the mean number of persons per room, the percentage of households renting from local authority, the percentages of households with non-manual "head of house-hold," and owner-occupied households. The individual components have been aggregated with the loadings which factor analysis via varimax rotation had indicated. The last two variables carry negative loadings.

The percentage of households in housing association accommodation, which is an additional indicator of low economic status, exhibits low corre-lation with the poverty factor, probably reflecting a wider spread of housing association properties, as compared to those owned by local authority, across both poor and affluent areas. Preliminary analysis also showed low correlation between the poverty factor and other area characteristics con-sidered, these being: percentage Black households,[11] percentage Asian households,[12] percentage of the population aged 16-24 years, percentage single adult non-pensioner households, percentage of persons moved last year and population density. The simple bivariate correlations between these area characteristics are given in Table 1. The highest correlation is observed between the percentage of single-adult non-pensioner households and the percentage of persons who had moved last year (0.64) but, as will be seen in the next sub-section, this correlation is inconsequential to the final estimated models.

Apart from low socio-economic status, the area characteristics of this analysis act as proxies for the (social disorganisation) theoretical concepts of ethnic heterogeneity, residential mobility and urbanisation, while family disruption effects are entangled within those of low socio-economic status due to, as mentioned, the high correlation of the respective census variables. In particular, the percentage of Black and Asian households are constructs of ethnic heterogeneity. Residential mobility is indicated by the percentage of single adult non-pensioner households and persons who had moved in last year, while population density evidently measures urbanisation. The

Table 1: Bivariate Correlations Between Area Characteristics

	Age 16-24	Blacks	Indian-Bangladesh-Pakistani	Movers	Population density	Housing association	Single adult non-pensioners	Poverty[a]
Age 16-24	1							
Blacks	0.285	1						
Indian-Bangladesh-Pakistani	0.351	0.468	1					
Movers	0.528	0.236	0.157	1				
Population density	0.311	0.576	0.402	0.316	1			
Housing association	0.299	0.291	0.278	0.314	0.378	1		
Single adult non-pensioners	0.474	0.437	0.295	0.642	0.566	0.460	1	
Poverty[a]	0.379	0.374	0.282	0.109	0.469	0.382	0.323	1

Note: All correlations are significant at p-value=0.01 (two-tailed).
[a] Aggregate factor calculated as (0.859 percent lone parent households +0.887 percent households without car -0.758 nonmanual -0.877 percent owner occupied households +0.720 mean number of persons per room +0.889 percent households renting from LA).

percentage of population aged 16-24 years old gives the teenage peer groups who may be unsupervised and subsequently may offend and/or induce fear and clues of disorder to other citizens.

The seven individual area attributes discussed here, the poverty factor and nine regional dummy variables, i.e., taking value one for the respective region and zero otherwise, were included in the original regression models for each dependent variable. The regional dummy variables relate to Wales and the eight standard (English) Government Office Regions outside of Greater London. Greater London was chosen as the reference or base region whereupon each dummy's effect is contrasted with it.

3. ESTIMATED MODELS

3.1. Methodology

The statistical specification of the MvMl model is described by Goldstein (1995) and Snijders and Bosker (1999) and is repeated here after making it consistent with the study's empirical model.

Let z_{ij}, with $i=1, 2, 3$ and $j=1, 2, \ldots A$, where A is the total number of postcode sectors in the sample, denote (three) dummy variables, each indicating a response or dependent variable Y_{ij}, i.e., Y_{1j} indicates property crime rate, Y_{2j} fear of crime score, and Y_{3j} perceived disorder score; x_{kj}, with $k=1, 2, \ldots K$, represents K area-level covariates (in this case both area characteristics and regional dummy variables); u_{ij} is the between areas random part of the intercept; and β_{ki}, with $k=0, 1, \ldots K$ a set of coefficients including the intercept for the i-th response variable. The MvMl model, here with 2 levels, i.e., one for the response variable (i) and a second for the postcode sector (j), is formally written as follows:

$$Y_{ij} = \sum_{s=1}^{s=3} \beta_{0s} z_{sij} + \sum_{k=1}^{k=K} \sum_{s=1}^{s=3} \beta_{ks} z_{sij} x_{kj} + \sum_{s=1}^{s=3} u_{sj} z_{sij} \tag{1}$$

$$z_{sij} \begin{cases} 1, s=i \\ 0, s \neq i \end{cases}, \operatorname{var}(u_{ij}) = \sigma_{ui}^2, \text{ and } \operatorname{cov}(u_{sj} u_{ij}) = \sigma_{usi} \text{ for } s \neq i$$

The dummy variable z_{ij} takes the value 1 when the data (on both response and covariates) refer to the dependent variable Y_{ij} and 0 when they do not. Effectively, z_{ij} values are such that only relevant terms are retained in any of the models. σ_{ui}^2 is the unexplained variance of the *i-th* response variable while σ_{usi} is the unexplained covariance between the *s-th* and *i-th* responses after accounting for the covariates' effects (here postcode-level characteristics and regional dummy variables).[13]

Table 2 presents the estimated area and regional effects on property crime rates, fear of crime and perceived disorders as well as the between-areas (unexplained) (co-) variation of the variables in question. The results have been obtained after application of the 2000 BCS weights.[14,15] In particular, Table 2 is divided in three parts: the first presents the estimated coefficients and (multi-parameter) Wald tests for respective groups of predictors as well as the estimated between-areas (unexplained) (co-) variation of the final MvMl models of property crime, fear of crime and perceived disorders; the second part gives a baseline multivariate model (see next sub-section) or the multivariate *empty* model (Snijders and Bosker, 1999, p. 203); and the third, as mentioned in the section on the dependent variables, describes the observed distributions of the three variables of interest without the application of the BCS weights.

Each estimated fixed effect, namely coefficient, or between-areas variance or covariance, in Table 2 has an indication of its statistical significance. This is based on Wald tests, which are χ^2 distributed with one degree of freedom. Any predictor with a Wald test p-value higher than 0.10 in each estimated model was excluded from them. Thus the percentage of single adult non-pensioner households has been dropped from the final models of (the first part of) Table 2.

Multi-parameter Wald tests, which are χ^2 distributed (Greene, 1997; Snijders and Bosker, 1999) with the appropriate degrees of freedom, test for the joint statistical significance of respective groups of predictors. Each set of covariates, i.e., area characteristics and regional dummy variables, is highly statistically significant in comparison with χ^2 distributions with 7 and 9 degrees of freedom, respectively, implying that both meso- (area) and macro- (region) characteristics are important for the prediction of areas' property crime, fear and perceived disorders. The relative importance of these sets of covariates for predicting each dependent variable as well as the relative importance of each covariate for the simultaneous prediction of areas' property crime, fear and disorders will be discussed in the sub-section on area and region effects below.

Table 2: Area Effects on Property Crime Rate, Fear and Disorder from the 2000 British Crime Survey (multivariate multilevel modelling)

Area Characteristics	Property Crime Incidence	Fear of Crime[a]	Perceived Disorders[b]	*Wald test (3 d.f.)*
Estimated Fixed Effects				
Age 16-24	0.12*	0.56**	1.24***	16.74***
Blacks	-0.05**	0.24***	0.01	24.02***
Indian-Bangladesh-Pakistani	0.02	0.44***	0.20**	60.38***
Movers	0.03	-1.24***	-0.89**	29.62***
Population density	0.10***	0.13*	0.27***	36.20***
Housing association	-0.004	0.002	0.14[#]	3.88
Poverty[c]	0.03***	0.13***	0.17***	97.05***
Wald test of area effects (7 d.f.)	181.51***	345.05***	283.42***	-
Regions				
North	-0.03	-0.82***	-1.00***	16.23***
Yorkshire/Humberside	0.16***	-0.45**	-0.70**	23.90***
North West	0.18***	0.50**	-0.08	20.07***
East Midlands	0.11**	0.05	-0.72**	16.87***
West Midlands	0.07	0.14	-0.61**	13.04***
East Anglia	0.09	-0.60**	-0.90**	15.25***
South East	0.13***	-0.15	-0.37[##]	15.13***
South West	0.10**	-0.38*	-0.61**	13.49***
Wales	0.02	-0.88***	-0.84**	17.14***
Wald test of regional effects (9 d.f.)	33.45***	76.18***	26.17***	-
Total Wald test (16 d.f.)	222.83***	589.06***	415.22***	-
Constant	0.27***	3.28***	4.33***	-
Between areas variance-covariance				
Property Crime Incidence	0.098***			
Fear of Crime	0.090***	1.618***		
Perceived Disorders	0.159***	0.932***	2.563***	

(continued)

Table 2 *(continued)*

Area Characteristics	Property Crime Incidence	Fear of Crime[a]	Perceived Disorders[b]	*Wald test* *(3 d.f.)*
BASELINE MODEL				
Constant	0.36***	3.16***	3.84***	
Between areas variance-covariance				
Property Crime Incidence	0.123***			
Fear of Crime	0.201***	2.691***		
Perceived Disorders	0.301***	1.958***	3.760***	
DESCRIPTION[d]				
Mean	0.34	3.00	3.61	
Min/Max	0/18	0/12	0/12	
Standard Deviation	0.92	3.24	2.64	

Note: The 2000 British Crime Survey adult (for fear of crime and disorders) and household (for property crime incidence) weights have been applied to the data before multivariate multilevel regression analysis.
[a] Respondents who reported very and fairly worried enter the calculation of fear with loadings 2 and 1, respectively.
[b] Respondents who reported very, fairly and not a very big problem enter the calculation of disorder with loadings 3, 2 and 1, respectively.
[c] Aggregate factor calculated as (0.859 percent lone parent households+0.887 percent households without car-0.758 nonmanual-0.877 percent owner occupied households+ 0.720 mean number of persons per room+0.889 percent households renting from LA).
[d] The descriptive statistics refer to data without weights.
* $0.05 < \text{p-value} <= 0.10$.
** $0.005 < \text{p-value} <= 0.05$.
*** $\text{p-value} <= 0.005$.
[#] It just misses the 0.10 critical value with $X^2 = 2.67$ rather than 2.71.
[##] It just misses the 0.10 critical value with $X^2 = 2.38$ rather than 2.71.

3.2. Property Crime, Fear and Disorders: Communicated Effects

How much property crime, fear of crime and perceived disorders relate to one another when other effects are ignored is given in a *baseline model*, whereby each dependent variable is regressed to a constant term with all predictors suppressed to zero. In the case of the MvMl specification this is also called *multivariate empty model* (Snijders and Bosker, 1999, p. 203) and is presented in the middle part of Table 2. The constant term of the baseline model gives the mean predicted values of property crime incidence, fear and disorders (0.36, 3.16 and 3.84, respectively) for an area with nationally average characteristics. These are essentially equal to the 2000 BCS national average values (0.34, 3.00 and 3.61, respectively) for crime, fear and disorders with the small difference of 0.2 being possibly due to the application of the 2000 BCS weights (see also note d below Table 2). The multivariate empty model includes also estimates of the between areas variance matrix of each dependent variable. Property crime shows the highest between-areas variation, while fear of crime and disorders vary considerably less. The employment of area predictors and region reduces the between-areas unexplained variation of property crime and crime perceptions (see the estimated variances in the first part of Table 2).[16] Thus, areas of England and Wales experience very different property crime rates, while their perceptions of fear of crime and disorder are rather similar.

Does accounting for area characteristics and region reduce the (unexplained) covariance of crime rates and perceptions? This is answered in the affirmative. Comparing the final model with the empty (baseline) model there is considerable difference between the associated variance-covariance matrices, with the final model apparently accounting for roughly half the between-areas (unexplained) covariation of property crime, fear and disorders. The covariances of property crime with fear or disorders drop from 0.20 to 0.09 and 0.30 to 0.16, respectively, while that between fear and disorders declines from 1.96 to 0.93 (see Table 2). The remaining unexplained (co-) variation may be partly due to individual characteristics which by design are omitted from this analysis (see also introduction and concluding discussion).

The estimated bivariate correlations of the areas' property crime, fear and perceived disorders when no area characteristics or region are accounted for are 0.35 and 0.44 between crime and fear or disorders, respectively, and 0.62 between levels of fear and disorders[17] while the respective correlations from the final MvMl model are 0.23, 0.32 and 0.46. Thus roughly one-fourth of the between-areas correlation of levels of fear of crime and perceived disorders as well as property crime and disorders is due to the demographic and socio-economic characteristics of the areas and regional idiosyncrasy. Areas' profile and region is also responsible for about one third of the between-areas correlation of property crime and fear of crime.[18]

3.3 Area Effects

The constant term of the final MvMl models gives an estimate of what the property crime rate, fear of crime and level of disorders would be in an area located in Greater London (i.e., the region for which no dummy variable was created) that had also the national average area characteristics. The estimated mean value of property crime incidence (0.27) for such a hypothetical location is marginally lower than the 2000 BCS observed national property crime rates (0.34). By contrast, the estimates for fear and disorders (3.28 and 4.33, respectively) are higher than the respective observed national average levels from the 2000 BCS. These deviations are due to a Greater London effect.

Regional dummies are by far most relevant for predicting fear of crime, rather than property crime and disorders, with the respective Wald test values being 76.18, 33.45 and 26.17 with 9 degrees of freedom. Apart from the North West all regions have significantly lower levels of disorders, while most regions (i.e., North, Yorkshire/Humberside, East Anglia, South West and Wales) also show lower fear of crime than Greater London. By contrast, areas in the North West register significantly higher fear of crime while most regions have significantly higher property crime incidence rates than London.

Area characteristics are more important for the prediction of areas' levels of fear of crime and disorders than property crime (respective Wald values of 345.05, 283.42 and 181.51 with 7 d.f.). The most important predictor of property crime, fear and disorders *jointly* is Poverty (Wald test equal to 97.05 with 3 degrees of freedom). The estimated effect of a unit increase of Poverty on the dependent variables is 0.03, 0.13 and 0.17, respectively. The second most (jointly) significant area predictor is the percentage of Asian households (Wald test equal to 60.38 with 3 degrees of freedom) of which an additional standard deviation[19] increases fear of crime and disorders by 0.44 and 0.20, respectively, while it is inconsequential for property crime. The remaining area characteristics effects are given immediately below in descending order of their (joint) statistical significance.

A standard deviation increase of population density is estimated to boost property crime, fear and disorders by 0.10, 0.13 and 0.27, respectively. Similar increase of the percentage of persons moved last year is related to actually lower fear and disorders by 1.24 and 0.89, respectively, while it does not affect property crime. A standard deviation rise of the percentage of Black households reduces property crime by 0.05 but increases fear by 0.24, while it is essentially irrelevant for perceived disorders. An additional standard deviation of the percentage of population aged 16-24 years old raises property crime, fear and disorders by 0.12, 0.56 and 1.24,[20] respectively. The percentage of young population, despite being highly statistically significant, is the least important for the prediction of all the dependent variables (Wald statistic equal to 16.74 with three degrees of freedom).

4. DISCUSSION

In the preamble to this chapter the author intended to identify the interdependence of local (property) crime rates, fear of crime and perceived disorders, which is due to common area characteristics and region, via the multivariate multilevel statistical specification. In doing so more efficient estimates of area and region effects on crime rates and perceptions have been produced than via single-equation modelling of each dependent variable (Snijders and Bosker, 1999).

To summarise, this study evidences that area characteristics predict fear of crime and disorders better than property crime rates, which is in agreement with previous work (Kershaw and Tseloni, 2005). "The better prediction for fear and disorder may reflect less variable attitudes between individual respondents within similar areas' compared to 'their' own 'experience' of crime (e.g., residents in an area may well tend to agree on the problems that afflict their area, but will not tend to have the same experience of crime)" (Kershaw and Tseloni, 2005, p. 17). Previous research on property crime incidence alone shows that its between-households variability is 9.5 times greater than its between-areas variability (Tseloni, 2006). This being said, few area characteristics are important predictors of property crime.

Low socio-economic status and urbanisation (indicated in the models here via poverty and population density) significantly increase local property crime rates. Both effects are in broad agreement with theory (Shaw and McKay, 1942) and previous empirical research (Kennedy and Forde, 1990; Osborn et al., 1992; Osborn and Tseloni, 1998; Tseloni, 2006). This study's negative effect of an area's ethnic minority (via the percentage of Black households) on property crime contradicts the social disorganisation theory (Shaw and McKay, 1942) and also seems counter-intuitive. Nevertheless cumulative previous empirical research indicates this negative relationship between area's ethnic minority population and local or household property crime *rates* without, to the best of my knowledge, counter-evidence (with one exception).[21] In particular, Osborn et al. (1992) evidence that a standard deviation increase of ethnic minority households reduces area's property crime incidence by 0.18 when other area characteristics remain the same. A similar rise of the percentage of Asian households in an area reduces the mean number of resident households' property crimes by 0.12% (Osborn and Tseloni, 1998), while the mean number of burglaries and thefts drops by 0.10% due to an additional standard deviation of the percentage of Black households (Tseloni, 2005) under the assumption of identical household and other area characteristics.

Local crime perceptions are positively related to poverty, ethnic heterogeneity, urbanisation and the percentage of 16-24 years old, while areas with higher residential mobility actually register lower levels of fear of crime and perceived disorders in broad agreement with previous empirical work (see for instance Hale et al., 1994). This study's results on fear of crime confirm previous evidence that individuals' worries about victimisation are greatly influenced by perceived (here, economic and social) vulnerability and perceived (lack of) social cohesion or trust, and consequently they are partly expressions of concern for the community (see, for instance, Jackson, 2004; Spelman, 2004; Taylor and Hale, 1986). *The lack of an effect* of the percentage of single adult non-pensioner households on local levels of fear here or its negative effect on individuals' fear (Hale et al., 1994) further supports this conclusion. In light of the absence of previous research,[22] the above theoretical discussion also refers to perceived disorders. All the area characteristics of this study affect both crime perceptions in the same direction except for the percentage of Black households, which is essentially not related to disorders. The result that, apart from the North West, most regions register significantly higher property crime rates but lower crime perceptions than Greater London is arguably an additional indication that community concern is channelled through crime perceptions.

The main contributions of this work are:

- estimating the proportion of respective covariances and bivariate correlations of property crime, fear of crime and perceived disorders which is due to area characteristics and region; and,

- estimating the relative importance of each area characteristic for jointly predicting property crime, fear and disorders.

How can crime prevention initiatives benefit from this or methodologically similar work? Crime initiatives informed by estimated MvMl models may select the most influential area characteristic depending on whether they focus on one or multiple targets. For instance crime initiatives, which address only property crime, would employ their (usually limited) resources most efficiently if they allocate them across areas with high population density. If property crime is targeted *together with* fear of crime, concentrating on poverty would be most effective, according to the results of this study (ironically population density and poverty do not in reality operate as in the fictitious case given in the introductory section). Such a policy would further appease perceptions of disorders owing to diffusion of benefits. Were initiatives designed to tackle high levels of both crime perceptions apart from poverty, they should take into account the percentage of Asian households, the percentage of persons moved last year and the percentage of young population, in that order.

Most area characteristics, which have been used here, are associated with property crime and perceptions in the same direction, thus leading to diffusion of benefits of crime prevention or public reassurance initiatives, which readily address only one issue. According to the estimates of Table 2 above, displacement can only occur between property crime and fear if initiatives employ the percentage of Black households, which affects the two responses with opposite sign. Diffusion/displacement effects of crime prevention or public reassurance policies between more than one target, such as those discussed above, are due to the estimated associations of area characteristics with crime rates and perceptions. The estimated residual covariance between crime rates, fear of crime and perceived disorders invariably consists of an additional source of diffusion of benefits, especially between fear of crime and perceived disorders. Thus, considering both estimated direct effects of area characteristics on each response variable and indirect ones via the between-responses residual covariance, policies which by design are implemented to reduce one problem, i.e., crime rates or fear or disorders, would most likely reduce all three.

The results also show that there are regional differences in crime, fear of crime and disorder. For example, we see that compared to London, Yorkshire has an increased crime incidence rate, but on average the residents have less fear of crime and problems with perceived disorder. This demonstrates the importance of place and context in policy development; there is no "one size fits all" solution. For example, it could be advisable to change the relative balance of policy in Yorkshire to have a greater emphasis on actual crime prevention and less emphasis on fear reduction than in London.

Finally, the results raise an interesting debate about the initial motivations and pre-conceptions of practitioners. In the past, they may have had a hunch that their property crime scheme may also have an impact on fear of crime, or they may have incorrectly assumed a synergy between schemes where there was in fact a conflict, or they may have been in ignorance of any displacement or diffusion effects between crime reduction and problem perception reduction. Results of the type reported above, if disseminated, would give practitioners a chance to consider the possible knock-on effects of a scheme in a particular type of area before implementation. Hence implementation could be planned with these effects in mind.[23]

The estimated unexplained random variances and covariances of the models of this study entail the effects of individual characteristics, which by design have been left out of this analysis (see the introductory section). Employing MvMl modelling on individual victimisation, levels of fear and perceived disorders while accounting for, apart from area, individual characteristics and prior victimization experiences is the obvious extension of this research in order to estimate the proportion of the (so-far unexplained) covariance between crime rates and perceptions, which is due to individual characteristics and experiences. Finally, estimating any spatial autocorrelation via MvMl models of crime rates and perceptions could have completed the picture of displacement/diffusion effects in terms of crime prevention geography. Such an analysis however is not possible with the present data set, which conceals identification of postcode sectors to preserve statistical confidentiality.

Address correspondence to: Andromachi Tseloni, Criminology, Public Health and Policy Studies, Nottingham Trent University, Burton Street, Nottingham NG1 4BU, U.K., e-mail: andromachi.tseloni@ntu.ac.uk

Acknowledgments: This work was initiated while the author was a visiting academic at the Home Office Research, Development and Statistics Directorate. I would like to acknowledge the encouragement and assistance of Dr Chris Kershaw and Home Office staff in undertaking this work, as well as the Home Office for funding the visit. Many thanks are due to the invited editors and reviewers of an earlier version for their insightful comments and helpful editing. All remaining errors are mine.

The views expressed in this paper are those of the author, not necessarily those of the Home Office (nor do they reflect Government Policy).

NOTES

1. To be precise, the respective effects are 86% and 89%. The term odds ratio refers to the ratio of two probabilities: the probability or likelihood of occurrence, in this instance of reporting fear of crime, over the probability of non-occurrence.

2. The term "multilevel," which is equivalent to "hierarchical," modelling is employed here. The models of this study are pseudo- multilevel or pseudo- hierarchical (see also later endnote no. 12) because the units of analysis are not clustered into higher-level ones.

3. Note that here we are discussing displacement or diffusion caused by policies affecting issues other than those directly targeted (for example, a crime prevention policy positively affecting fear of crime in the area) and not displacement as it is more traditionally defined in the criminological literature (e.g., Reppetto, 1976).

4. 16 sample points have been dropped from this analysis as they consisted of combined small postcode sectors for which census-based area characteristics could not be reliably ascribed.

5. The remaining BCS questions on neighbourhood problems, which were excluded from this analysis, include perceiving rubbish/litter, rundown homes, noisy neighbours, abandoned cars and people sleeping rough. They allude to the theoretical concept of social vulnerability (Skogan and Maxfield, 1981), while according to anti-social behaviour classification they refer to "nuisances" rather than "criminal acts" (Home Office, 2004).

6. Results for the 2001 Census were not available at the time the data file was constructed.

7. The 2000 BCS fieldwork contractor was the National Centre for Social Research, with around half the interviews subcontracted to the Office for National Statistics.

8. Values of each census variable were normalised by subtracting their mean and dividing by their standard deviation. A 5% error has also been added to ensure confidentiality.

9. Linking the actual census variables to the data could allow the Home Office and others to infer the exact location of the postcode sec-

tors used in sampling. This would contravene the National Centre for Social Research policy for safeguarding respondent confidentiality.

10. One might question the use of the "poverty" factor, which is derived via principal component analysis of the correlated census variables, instead of direct application of any deprivation index. According to a BCS stratification analysis, which was carried out contemporarily to this study, census variables perform better than deprivation indices (Smith and Loyd, 2001). The use of deprivation indices in this analysis was also hindered because they relate to administrative geography.

11. By Blacks we refer to African-Caribbeans.

12. By Asians we refer to persons of Indian/Bangladesh/Pakistani ethnicity.

13. The model of this analysis is not truly multilevel since apart from the pseudo level 1, which indicates the multivariate structure (i.e., the fact that more than one dependent variable exists) and has no random part (Snijders and Bosker 1999), there is only one unit of analysis, namely the postcode sector. The estimated MvMl models below have been obtained via the software package MLwiN (Goldstein et al., 1998).

14. The 2000 BCS adult and household weights have been applied to crime rates, fear and disorder appropriately.

15. All variables of this study were tested for Gaussian approximation. Indeed, the observed distribution of property crime rate from the 2000 BCS and area characteristics from the 1991 Census are skewed. Power or logarithmic transformations (Marsh, 1988), which best improved its skewness and kurtosis, were applied to the original data. The so transformed data improved the linearity of the estimated model of property crime, which also produced fewer outliers compared to the model based on the original crime variable. By contrast, the overall explanatory power and predicted distribution was not affected. To simplify the interpretation of the results the models discussed here employ the original data after application of the BCS weights. The estimated model of property crimes, which employs transformed data, can be made available to interested readers upon request.

16. The respective coefficients of (unexplained) variation for property crime, fear of crime and disorders before and after area-level effects are 0.97, 0.52 and 0.50 (calculated as $[(\sqrt{0.12})/0.36])$ $[(\sqrt{2.69})/3.16]$

and [($\sqrt{3.76}$)/3.84], respectively) and 1.16, 0.39 and 0.37 (respective calculations: [($\sqrt{0.10}$)/0.27], [($\sqrt{1.62}$)/3.28] and [($\sqrt{2.56}$)/4.33]) respectively. The coefficient of (unexplained) variation from the final MvMl model of property crime is surprisingly higher than that from the model without covariates. This can possibly be justified by that most regions have higher estimated property crime rates than Greater London under the assumption of similar area characteristics (see next section).

17. The bivariate correlations between the response variables, i.e., property crime and fear, property crime and disorders, and fear and disorders are calculated from the baseline model as [$0.20/(\sqrt{0.12}\sqrt{2.69})$], [$0.30/(\sqrt{0.12}\sqrt{3.76})$], and [$1.96/(\sqrt{3.76}\sqrt{2.69})$], respectively. Not surprisingly, the estimated correlations from the multivariate empty model equal the respective simple bivariate correlations from the 2000 BCS.

18. In particular, area characteristics and region reduce the (unexplained) correlation between areas' property crime and levels of fear or perceived disorders by 34% and 28%, respectively, and that between areas' fear of crime and perceived disorders by 26%.

19. A unit of any census variable actually represents one standard deviation since their values are standardised (see above end note #7).

20. The high estimated effect of the percentage of population 16–24 years old on perceived disorders is not surprising since the latter entails "teenagers hanging around in the street."

21. Kershaw and Tseloni (2005), who evidence a positive effect of the percentage of Asian (as well as a *negative* effect of the percentage of Black) households on local property crime rates, is the only exception. Since they employ the same data set as here in a single-equation framework this (partial) inconsistency may be due to different methodology.

22. The only published work on perceived disorders to date is at the individual level by Wood (2004), who employs the 2003/04 BCS. Kershaw and Tseloni (2005), who employ the same data set as here, do not offer independent confirmation to this research evidence.

23. This is at least how I see the policy implications of this work presently. Since Ken Pease, who is a perpetual source of crime prevention ideas has – at the time of writing – yet to see this analysis, this discussion is only tentative.

REFERENCES

Browne, W. J., & Draper, D. (2000). A comparison of Bayesian and likelihood-based methods for fitting multilevel models (https://www.soe.ucsc.edu/~draper/Browne-Draper2.pdf).

Budd, T., & Sims, L. (2001). *Antisocial behaviour and disorder: Findings from the British Crime Survey*. Home Office Research Findings #145. London: Home Office.

Farrall, S., Bannister, J., Ditton, J., & Gilchrist, E. (1997). Measuring crime and the "fear of crime": Findings from a methodological study. *British Journal of Criminology, 37*, 658-679.

Goldstein, H. (1995). *Multilevel statistical models* (2nd ed.). London: Arnold.

Goldstein, H., Rasbash, J., Plewis, I., Draper, D., Browne, W., Yang, M., Woodhouse, G., & Healy, M. (1998). *A user's guide to MLwiN*. London: Institute of Education.

Greene, W. H. (1997). *Econometric analysis*. Upper Saddle River, NJ: Prentice Hall.

Griffiths, P. L., Brown, J. J., & Smith, P. W. F. (2004). A comparison of univariate and multivariate models of repeated measures of use of antenatal care in Uttar Pradesh. *Journal of the Royal Statistical Society, Series A, Statistics and Society, 167*, Part 4, 597-611.

Hale, C., Pack, P., & Salked, J. (1994). The structural determinants of fear of crime. *International Review of Victimology, 3*, 211-234.

Hale, C. (1996). Fear of crime: A review of literature. *International Review of Victimology, 4*, 79-150.

Hales, J., Henderson, L., Collins, D., & Becher, H. (2000). *2000 British Crime Survey (England and Wales): Technical report*. London: National Centre for Social Research.

Home Office. (2004). *Defining and measuring anti-social behaviour*. Crime Reduction. Home Office Development and Practice Report 26. London: Home Office.

Jackson, J. (2004). Experience and expression: Social and cultural significance in the fear of crime. *British Journal of Criminology, 44*, 946-966.

Judge, G. G., Hill, R. C., Griffiths, W. E., Lutkepohl, H., & Lee, T.-C. (1988). *Introduction to the theory and practice of econometrics*. New York: John Wiley & Sons.

Kennedy, L. W., & Forde, D. R. (1990). Routine activities and crime: An analysis of victimisation in Canada. *Criminology, 28*, 137-152.

Kershaw, C., & Tseloni, A. (2005). Predicting crime rates, fear and disorder based on area information: Evidence from the 2000 British Crime Survey. *International Review of Victimology, 12*, 295-313.

Lynn, P., & Elliot, D. (2000). *The British Crime Survey: A review of methodology*. London: National Centre for Social Research.

Marsh, C. (1988). *Exploring data: An introduction to data analysis for social scientists*. Cambridge: Polity Press.

Norris, F. H., Kaniasty, K., & Thompson, M. P. (1997). The psychological consequences of crime: Findings from a longitudinal population-based study. In R. C. Davis, A. J. Lurigio, & W. G. Skogan (Eds.), *Victims of crime* (pp. 146-166). Thousand Oaks, CA: Sage.

Osborn, D. R., Trickett, A., & Elder, R. (1992). Area characteristics and regional variates as determinants of area crime levels. *Journal of Quantitative Criminology*, 8, 265-285.

Osborn, D. R., & Tseloni A. (1998). The distribution of household property crimes. *Journal of Quantitative Criminology*, 14, 307-330.

Pease, K. (1998). *Repeat victimisation: Taking stock*. Crime Detection and Prevention Series Paper No. 90. London: Home Office.

Reppetto, T. (1976). Crime prevention and the displacement phenomenon. *Crime & Delinquency*, 22, 166-177.

Sampson, R., & Groves, C. (1989). Community structure and crime: Testing social disorganisation theory. *American Journal of Sociology*, 94, 774-802.

Schneider, A. L. (1981). Methodological problems in victim surveys and their implications for research in victimology. *Journal of Criminal Law and Criminology*, 72, 818-838.

Shaw, C. R., & McKay, M. D. (1942). *Juvenile delinquency and urban areas*. Chicago: Chicago University Press.

Skogan, W., & Maxfield, M. (1981). *Coping with crime: Individual and neighbourhood reactions*. Beverly Hills, CA: Sage.

Smith, P., & Loyd, R. (2001). *BCS stratification analysis: Preliminary findings*. BCS/Tech/3/1. London: British Market Research Bureau.

Snijders, T. A. B., & Bosker, R. J. (1999). *Multilevel analysis: An introduction to basic and advanced multilevel modeling*. London: Sage.

Spelman, W. (2004). Optimal targeting of incivility-reduction strategies. *Journal of Quantitative Criminology*, 20, 63-88.

Taylor, R. B., & Hale, M. (1986). Testing alternative models of fear of crime. *Journal of Criminal Law and Criminology*, 77, 151-190.

Tricket, A., Osborn, D. R., & Pease, K. (1992). What is different about high crime areas? *British Journal of Criminology*, 32(1), 81-90.

Tseloni, A. (2001). *2000 British Crime Survey: Report on postcode sector predictions to the Home Office, RDS*. Unpublished report.

Tseloni, A. (2002). Fear walking alone in one's neighbourhood: Regression and multilevel analysis. In C. Zarafonitou (Ed.), Ο Φόβος του Εγκλήματος *[Fear of Crime]* (pp. 156-207, 232-235),Μελέτες Ευρωπαϊκής Επιστήμης/European Studies in Law, Αθήνα-Κομοτηνή: Εκδόσεις Αντ. Σάκκουλα. [Athens: Sakkoulas Publishers.]

Tseloni, A. (2006). Multilevel modelling of the number of property crimes: Household and area effects. *Journal of the Royal Statistical Society, Series A, Statistics and Society*, 169, Part 2, 1-29.

Tseloni, A., & Pease, K. (2004). Repeat personal victimisation: Random effects, event dependence and unexplained heterogeneity. *British Journal of Criminology*, 44, 931-945.

Wood, M. (2004). *Perceptions and experience of antisocial behaviour: Findings from the British Crime Survey 2003/4*. Online Report No. 49/04, London: Home Office (http://www.homeoffice.gov.uk/rds/).

Yang, M. Goldstein, H., Browne, W., & Woodhouse, G. (2002). Multilevel multivariate analyses of examination results. *Journal of the Royal Statistical Society, Series A, Statistics and Society*, 165, Part 1, 137-153.

The Cambridge Evaluation of the Effects of CCTV on Crime

David P. Farrington
University of Cambridge

Trevor H. Bennett
University of Glamorgan

and

Brandon C. Welsh
University of Massachusetts-Lowell

Abstract: *An evaluation of the effects of CCTV in Cambridge city center is described, using before and after measures of crime in experimental and control areas. CCTV had no effect on crime according to survey data, and an undesirable effect on crime according to police records. It is suggested that CCTV may have had no effect on crime in reality but may have caused increased reporting to and/ or recording by the police. It is concluded that more high-quality evaluations are needed that seek to disentangle the effects of CCTV from other plausible hypotheses and to investigate moderators and mediators of these effects.*

Ken Pease has made outstandingly thoughtful, innovative, and original contributions to many areas of crime prevention. Among these is his important evaluation in volume 10 of *Crime Prevention Studies* of the impact of closed-circuit television (CCTV) on crime in Burnley (Armitage et al.,

1999). This was particularly significant because it was the first CCTV evaluation study to compare before and after crimes in experimental areas with adjacent and non-adjacent control areas in order to assess displacement and diffusion effects. In the same volume, Ken Pease also presented a landmark, thought-provoking review of the effects of improved street lighting on crime (Pease, 1999).

Our concern in this chapter is with the effects of CCTV on crime. In the last 15 years, there has been a tremendous growth in the use of CCTV cameras in Great Britain. According to the *Sunday Times* (April 18, 2004):

> People in Britain are monitored by more surveillance cameras than anybody else in the world, according to research. There are believed to be more than 4 million closed-circuit television cameras – one for every 14 people in the country.

In the second half of the 1990s, CCTV accounted for more than three-quarters of total spending on crime prevention by the Home Office (Koch, 1998, p. 49). Hence, it is important to assess the effects of CCTV on crime.

Two of us (Welsh and Farrington) have completed systematic reviews of the literature on the effects of CCTV on crime (as well as of the effects of improved street lighting on crime; see Farrington and Welsh, 2002a, 2002b, 2004, 2006; Welsh and Farrington, 2002, 2004a, 2004b, 2006a, 2006b). We only included evaluations with before and after measures of crime in experimental and comparable control areas, because this is the minimum quality of evaluation design that is interpretable (see Cook and Campbell, 1979). Briefly, our conclusion was that existing evaluations showed that CCTV caused a substantial and significant decrease (41%) in crime in car parks (parking lots), a small but significant decrease (7%) in city centers and public housing, but no significant decrease (6%) in public transportation settings such as metro stations.

The most important methodological problem was that nearly all evaluations measured crime using official records. It is possible that one effect of CCTV is to increase the probability that crimes will be detected, reported, and recorded. Hence, it is desirable that crimes before and after the introduction of CCTV should be measured using both official records and victim surveys, to distinguish real changes in crime from changes in reporting and recording. The Cambridge evaluation project described later in this chapter was the first ever to measure both police-recorded and victim-survey crimes before and after the introduction of CCTV in experimental and control areas.[1]

The highly significant effects of CCTV on crime found in previous car park evaluations were largely attributable to the work of one researcher (Tilley, 1993). In all car park evaluations, the introduction of CCTV was confounded with other interventions, such as improved lighting in particular. Hence, it is unclear whether the observed effects on crime were in fact caused by these other interventions rather than by CCTV.

It is important to assess the methodological quality of evaluation projects using widely accepted criteria, focusing on statistical conclusion validity, internal validity, construct validity, and external validity (Cook and Campbell, 1979; Farrington, 2003; Shadish et al., 2002). We will assess the methodological quality of the Cambridge CCTV evaluation project using these criteria.

THE CAMBRIDGE CITY CENTER EVALUATION

The main aim of this project (commissioned and funded by Cambridge City Council) was to assess the effects of CCTV on crime, disorder and fear in Cambridge City Center. The control area was a secondary shopping centre (the Grafton Centre) which had no cameras on the streets. Basically, the whole central area of the city was partitioned into adjacent experimental and control areas. Thirty CCTV cameras became operational in Cambridge city center in August 1997. They were well publicized in the local newspaper. Their effects on crime were evaluated in two ways: *first* by comparing police-recorded crimes in the 11 months before (August 1996 to June 1997) and 11 months after (August 1997 to June 1998); *second*, by surveys of people during a one-week period in the two areas before (in June 1994) and after (in July 1998) the CCTV cameras became operational.

Police-recorded Crimes

Table 1 shows recorded crimes in the police beats covering the experimental and control areas. This table is based on case-level data provided by the police to the researchers. Total crimes decreased by 14% in the experimental area but by 27% in the control area. The odds ratio (OR) of 0.85 was statistically significant (95% confidence interval 0.72 - 0.99; $z = 2.00$, $p = .046$). Hence, recorded crime decreased by 15% in the control area compared with the experimental area, and CCTV appeared to have had undesirable effects on crime.[2] This was also true of all types of crime other than burglary, although the decrease in the control area was not

Table 1: Effects of CCTV on Recorded Crimes

Crime Types	Experimental			Control			
	Pre	Post	% Change	Pre	Post	% Change	Odds Ratio
Violence	151	142	-6	77	51	-34	0.70
Burglary	224	155	-31	108	79	-27	1.06
Vehicle	224	105	-53	250	115	-54	0.98
Other Theft	1738	1447	-17	744	533	-28	0.86
Damage	146	177	+21	76	73	-4	0.79
Other	117	216	+85	69	117	+70	0.92
Total	2,600	2,242	-14	1,324	968	-27	0.85*

Note: Violence = assault, robbery. Vehicle = theft of and from vehicles.
* $p < .05$, two-tailed.

significantly greater than in the experimental area for any specific type of crime. For comparison, police-recorded crime in the remainder of the city decreased by 20% during this time period.

Crime and Disorder According to the Survey

The main aim of the survey was to interview adults (aged 16 or over) in the experimental and control areas before and after the intervention, to investigate whether crime and disorder had changed according to their reports. Since the funding provided by the City Council was very small (£4,000 for the "before" survey and £5,000 for the "after" survey), the only practical way of obtaining reasonably representative samples was by quota sampling. The quotas were based on the demographic characteristics of residents of the city center: 52% male, 40% aged 16-29, and 92% White. Quota sampling is less satisfactory than random sampling (e.g., for tests of significance), but it was the most appropriate method to use in this case. The interviews were carried out in the streets by two cohorts of postgraduate criminology students, lasted 10 minutes on average and were distributed evenly over the days of the week and hours of the day (from 10:00 am to 8:00 pm). The students were told simply that this was a public opinion survey; they were not told that the research was concerned with the effects of CCTV.

Table 2: Effects of CCTV on Survey Victimization

	Experimental		Control	
	Pre	Post	Pre	Post
No. Surveyed	710	989	376	497
Demographics				
% Male	52.1	50.7	52.1	52.0
% Young	40.0	38.3	49.7	40.0
% White	91.9	92.9	91.8	91.9
% Victimized				
Crime	10.2	13.8	4.0	6.4
Disorder	20.7	20.3	8.5	10.2
Total	26.4	28.5	11.4	13.6

Note: Young = aged 16 to 29. Crime = threatened, assaulted, mugged. Disorder = insulted or bothered.
Likelihood Ratio Chi-Squared Interaction Term = 0.27 (crime), 1.15 (disorder), 0.34 (total); none significant.

Table 2 shows that the number of people interviewed in the experimental area was 710 before and 989 after CCTV became operational, while the number of people interviewed in the control area was 376 before and 497 after.[3] As a rule of thumb, about 325-400 people in each of two areas are required to detect a 10% difference between the areas in the probability of victimization (see, e.g., Painter and Farrington, 1997, p. 216). Because the City Council were more interested in the experimental area, they specified that there should be about twice as many interviews in this area as in the control area. Generally, the demographic distributions of participants were close to the quotas, except that 50% of those in the control area before were young (compared with the quota of 40%).

Participants were shown maps and were asked whether they had been insulted or bothered, threatened, assaulted or mugged in the previous year in the area (e.g., August 1997 to July 1998 in the after survey). Table 2 shows that 26.4% of those in the experimental area reported being victimized before, compared with 28.5% after; and 11.4% of those in the control area reported being victimized before, compared with 13.6% after.

In order to test whether the change in the experimental area was significantly different from the change in the control area, a logistic regression analysis was carried out. In this analysis, the demographic variables were first entered into the equation, then the main effects (pre-post and experimental-control) and then the interaction term (pre-post by experimental-control: see Farrington, 1997; Painter and Farrington, 2001). If the LRCS (Likelihood Ratio Chi-Squared) interaction term is significant, this shows that the change in the experimental area was significantly different from the change in the control area after controlling for pre-existing differences in demographic characteristics of the samples. Since none of the interaction terms was significant, it can be concluded that CCTV had no significant effect on victimization.

Opinion Questions

The survey participants were also asked a number of opinion questions. In the post survey, the percentages who said they thought that disorder had increased in the area in the last 12 months were not significantly different in the two areas (27.2% in the experimental area and 24% in the control area); most thought that there had been no change. In response to specific questions about whether aggressive begging and unruly youths were fairly or very common in the area, participants thought that these were somewhat more common in the post survey, but the change in the experimental area was similar to the change in the control area (Table 3). There was no change in the perceived prevalence of drunks in either area.

There was little change over time in the percentage of participants who felt unsafe after dark in the two areas. Virtually no one (about 1%) felt unsafe during the day. The percentage who were worried about crime (being threatened, assaulted or mugged) and disorder (being insulted or bothered) increased somewhat in both areas, but the change in the experimental area was similar to the change in the control area.

The majority of participants in both areas thought that CCTV would help to catch and deter criminals. Again, there was no differential effect of CCTV on this opinion. In the after survey, 81.1% of those in the experimental area and 80.8% of those in the control area thought that CCTV would reduce crime. Fewer thought that CCTV would reduce disorder (51.1% in the experimental area and 54.1% in the control area).

Most participants thought that CCTV was a good idea. Participants in the experimental area became even more convinced that it was a good idea after CCTV was installed (LRCS = 15.54, p<.0001). However, the percentage who thought that CCTV would (or did) make them feel safer

Table 3: Effects of CCTV on Opinion Questions

	Experimental		Control		
Percent	Pre	Post	Pre	Post	LRCS
Aggressive begging is common	33.3	42.4	17.6	28.7	ns
Unruly youths are common	37.7	44.2	31.3	35.1	ns
Drunks are common	55.3	55.6	35.9	34.4	ns
Feel unsafe after dark	31.0	30.1	33.7	35.3	ns
Worried about crime	15.9	26.7	14.2	22.0	ns
Worried about disorder	19.3	22.2	14.9	19.8	ns
CCTV helps catch criminals	75.9	85.5	85.8	89.2	ns
CCTV helps deter criminals	68.9	77.4	76.3	81.3	ns
CCTV is a good idea	65.8	87.9	78.6	86.0	15.54
CCTV makes me feel safer					
- during the day	37.4	31.0	40.1	43.0	4.04
- after dark	64.4	38.7	71.0	66.2	19.81
CCTV makes me visit the area more frequently					
- during the day	7.7	4.2	6.7	10.6	11.41
- after dark	21.3	4.7	27.6	21.2	32.50
First choice for crime prevention:					
- Police patrols	69.1	62.6	68.5	60.9	ns
- Street lighting	25.1	23.5	22.6	22.0	ns
- CCTV	4.1	11.7	7.8	14.8	ns
- Private patrols	1.8	2.2	1.1	2.2	ns

Note: Crime = threatened, assaulted, mugged.
Disorder = insulted or bothered.
LRCS = Likelihood Ratio Chi-Squared Interaction term.
LRCS = 3.84 is significant at p=.05 (two-tailed);
LRCS = 10.83 is significant at p= .001 (two-tailed);
ns = not significant.

during the day or after dark decreased significantly more in the experimental area, perhaps as a result of experience with CCTV. Similarly, the percentage who thought that CCTV would (or did) make them visit the area more frequently during the day or after dark decreased significantly more in the experimental area. Therefore, experience with CCTV made participants realize that they did not feel safer and did not visit the area more frequently.

Participants were asked to rank four possible crime prevention measures in order of priority: more police officers patrolling on foot, more or brighter street lights, more CCTV cameras in public places, and more private security patrols. Table 3 shows that participants in both areas at both times preferred more police patrols, followed by improved street lighting. Very few people chose private security patrols. The popularity of CCTV increased somewhat over time, but there was no differential change in the experimental compared with the control area.

Methodological Quality

Because of limited funding, the Cambridge CCTV evaluation was not comprehensive and had to make methodological compromises. Nevertheless, it will be assessed according to the methodological quality criteria in Table 4. We would argue that its statistical conclusion validity was adequate. Statistical tests showed that CCTV had an undesirable effect on crime according to police records and no effect according to the survey. The sizes of the survey samples were adequate for statistical power.

We would also argue that the internal validity of this evaluation was adequate. Having a control area dealt with many threats to internal validity, such as instrumentation (e.g., changes in police recording procedures). The survey was similar at both times and the quota sampling was carried out in the same way at both times. The logistic regression analyses controlled for selection effects (pre-existing differences between experimental and control areas), at least in major demographic variables. Since the researchers monitored changes in the areas during the project period, history (the effects of other interventions) could be excluded. For example, there were street lighting improvements in the city center before the first survey and after the second survey, but not coincidentally with CCTV. The main motivation behind the installation of CCTV cameras in the city center was not a crime wave but the prospects of obtaining Home Office funding for this intervention at this time. National trends in crime (according to police records and the British Crime Survey) were declining during this time period (1994-1998), but this would have affected both the experimental and the control areas.

It was not possible to throw much light on the mediators between CCTV and crime. Given the discrepancy between the police statistics and

Table 4: Methodological Quality Criteria

Type	Explanation	Threats
Statistical conclusion validity	Were the intervention and outcome related? Effect size and statistical significance should be measured	Insufficient statistical power (small N), inappropriate statistics
Internal validity	Did the intervention cause a change in the outcome? What are mediators?	Selection (pre-existing differences between experimental and control), history, maturation (continuation of pre-existing trends), instrumentation, testing, regression, causal order
Construct validity	Adequacy of operational definition and measurement of constructs underlying intervention and outcome	Treatment fidelity, implementation failure, validity and reliability of outcome measures, bias caused by knowledge of intervention, displacement and diffusion of benefits
External validity	Generalizability of causal relationships across persons, places, times, interventions and outcome measures. What are moderators?	Interaction of causal effect with types of persons, places, times, interventions and outcomes, bias because researchers have a stake in the results

Source: Based on Cook and Campbell (1979), Shadish et al. (2002), and Farrington (2003).

the victimization survey results, it is plausible to suggest that crime did not change but that reporting to the police and/or recording by the police increased (relatively) in the experimental area. Unfortunately, participants were not asked whether they did or would report crime or disorder to the police. However, since the vast majority were very optimistic about the ability of CCTV to catch criminals, it is plausible that this may have increased. The survey results suggested that CCTV did not increase pedestrian usage of the experimental area.

We would argue that the construct validity of this evaluation is adequate. Thirty CCTV cameras were installed and monitored, so there was no implementation failure. In the post survey in the experimental area, 74% of respondents said that they had seen CCTV cameras in the area.

Crime was measured not only by police records but also by a victim survey. The students who carried out the interviews were not told anything about what kinds of results might be expected. The limited resources made it impossible to investigate crime displacement or diffusion of benefits, but the absence of any desirable impact of CCTV means that these effects could not occur.

The external validity of CCTV evaluations is probably best established by systematic reviews. The Cambridge evaluation suggests that victimization did not change but police-recorded crimes were greater (in relative terms) after CCTV. A systematic review of nine evaluations showed that CCTV caused a small (13%) non-significant decrease in crime in city centers (Welsh and Farrington, 2004b). Thus, the Cambridge evaluation is consistent with prior research in showing no significant desirable effect of CCTV on crime in city centers. It should perhaps be pointed out that the City Council raised many critical questions about the findings, and did not wish to publicize them. Thus, it cannot be argued that the results were positively influenced by the biases of the sponsor.

DISCUSSION

More high-quality evaluations are needed to inform criminal justice policy about CCTV and many other interventions (see Farrington and Painter, 2003). In evaluating the effects of CCTV on crime, ideally several experimental areas should be compared with several comparable control areas. Crime should be measured in several different ways, including police records, a victimization survey, self-reports, and (if possible) by systematic observation. A statistical power analysis should be carried out before any evaluation is mounted, to establish the numbers of crimes and numbers of persons that are needed to detect the likely effects of CCTV. It is important to disentangle the influence of CCTV from the influence of other interventions and factors that influence crime, partly by design (having comparable control areas) and partly by statistical control. The comparability of control areas should be established by survey and archival data. Ideally, the effects of CCTV on crime should be investigated after controlling (e.g., in a regression equation) not only for prior crime but also for individual and community factors that influence crime.

It is important to study territorial displacement of crime and diffusion of crime prevention benefits. In order to investigate these topics, the minimum design requires one experimental area, one adjacent area, and one non-adjacent control area. As mentioned, Ken Pease pioneered this design in the evaluation of CCTV. If crime decreased in the experimental area, increased in the adjacent area, and stayed constant in the control area, this might be evidence of displacement. If crime decreased in the experimental and adjacent areas and stayed constant or increased in the control area, this might be evidence of diffusion of benefits.

Ideally, prospective longitudinal research is needed. Long time-series before and after CCTV interventions would help to establish whether the intervention followed an unusually high crime rate, and hence would help to exclude regression to the mean as a plausible alternative explanation of observed effects. A long-term follow-up would help to establish whether immediate effects were similar to or different from delayed effects, and hence whether the effects of CCTV wore off over time. It is important to monitor experimental and control areas over time to investigate historical events and other interventions (e.g., police initiatives) that might influence crime.

Research is needed to help identify the active ingredients of successful CCTV schemes and the causal mechanisms (mediators) linking CCTV to reductions in crime. To the extent that active ingredients are known, their effects could be investigated in a Latin Square design (e.g., CCTV alone, improved lighting alone, CCTV plus improved lighting, neither). This would make it possible to investigate whether these ingredients had interactive or merely additive effects. Surveys of potential offenders are needed to test hypotheses about changes in their behavior (e.g., about the deterrent effects of CCTV), and similarly surveys of potential victims are needed to test hypotheses about changes in their behavior (e.g., about increasing security precautions or reporting to the police). Surveys are also useful in testing hypotheses about other topics such as community pride, and systematic observation would be useful in testing hypotheses about pedestrian use of areas. Research is also needed on many other issues, including the monetary costs and benefits of CCTV in preventing crime and associated social problems, preferably in comparison to other possible interventions (Welsh and Farrington, 1999).

Very recently, the results of a large-scale, multi-site national evaluation of CCTV in the U.K., funded by the Home Office, have been published (Gill and Spriggs, 2005). This is the most extensive and methodologically sophisticated evaluation of CCTV that has ever been conducted. Seventeen CCTV schemes were evaluated, covering residential areas, town and city centers, car parks, and a hospital. In agreement with our previous meta-analyses, the researchers found that CCTV caused a decrease in crime in (station) car parks but nowhere else. However, once again, the introduction of CCTV in car parks was accompanied by improved street lighting and other interventions such as increased security and fencing, so that it was difficult to isolate the specific impact of CCTV on crime.

In conclusion, more high-quality, rigorous evaluation research is needed that seeks (a) to establish the effects of CCTV on crime by excluding plausible alternative hypotheses and threats to validity; (b) to investigate moderators (factors that influence the effects) and mediators (mechanisms by which CCTV has effects); and (c) specifically to assess the effects of CCTV in conjunction with or separately from other interventions such as improved lighting. Ideally, experiments should be carried out in which a large number of areas are randomly allocated to have CCTV cameras or not, or to have alternative periods with or without CCTV coverage (e.g., using mobile cameras). Future research should include interviews with actual or potential offenders and should seek to determine how CCTV can be implemented most effectively in order to justify the massive amounts of public and private money expended on it.

Address correspondence to: Professor David P. Farrington, Institute of Criminology, University of Cambridge Sidgwick Site, Cambridge CB3 9DT, UK; e-mail: dpf1@cam.ac.uk

Acknowledgments: We are very grateful to Dr. Loraine Gelsthorpe, who managed the Cambridge survey, organized the students to collect the data, and provided helpful comments on a first draft of this chapter. As mentioned, the survey was commissioned and funded by Cambridge City Council.

NOTES

1. Skinns (1998) measured police-recorded crimes in experimental and control areas and victim-reported crimes in experimental areas.
2. The odds ratio (OR) was used as the measure of effect size. The OR has a very simple and meaningful interpretation. It indicates the

proportional change in crime in the control area compared with the experimental area. The OR is calculated from the following table:

	Before	After
Experimental	a	b
Control	c	d

where a, b, c, d are numbers of crimes.

OR = ad/bc

For total crimes, the odds of a crime after CCTV compared with before in the control area were 968/1324 or 0.73. The corresponding odds in the experimental area were 2242/2600 or 0.86. The odds ratio was therefore 0.73/0.86 or 0.85. The variance of the OR is usually calculated from the variance of LOR (the natural logarithm of OR): V(LOR) = 1/a + 1/b + 1/c + 1/d. This is based on the assumption that total numbers of crimes have a Poisson distribution. Thirty years of mathematical models of criminal careers (see e.g., Blumstein et al., 1986; Piquero et al., 2003) have been dominated by the assumption that the commission of crimes can be accurately modeled by a Poisson process; for a more detailed discussion of this topic, see Farrington and Welsh (2004). If the number of crimes has a Poisson distribution, its variance should be the same as its mean. However, the large number of extraneous factors may cause overdispersion; that is, where the variance of the number of crimes VAR exceeds the number of crimes N:

D = VAR/N

specifies the overdispersion factor. Where there is overdispersion, V(LOR) should be multiplied by D. Farrington et al. (2005) estimated VAR from monthly numbers of crimes and found the following equation:

D = .0008N + 1.2

D increased linearly with N and correlated .77 with N.

For total crimes, the average number of crimes in an area was about 1,800, corresponding to an overdispersion factor of 2.6. This is an overestimate, because the monthly variance is inflated by seasonal variations, which do not apply to N and VAR. However, even using this overdispersion factor, the OR of 0.85 was statistically significant (z = 2.00, p = .046).

3. Some results obtained in the before survey in the experimental area were published by Bennett and Gelsthorpe (1996).

REFERENCES

Armitage, R., Smyth, G., & Pease, K. (1999). Burnley CCTV evaluation. In K. A. Painter and N. Tilley (Eds.), *Surveillance of public space: CCTV, street lighting and crime prevention*. Crime Prevention Studies, vol. 10. Monsey, NY: Criminal Justice Press.

Bennett, T. H., & Gelsthorpe, L. R. (1996). Public attitudes towards cctv in public places. *Studies on Crime and Crime Prevention*, 5, 72-90.

Blumstein, A., Cohen, J., Roth, J. A., & Visher, C. A. (Eds.), (1986). *Criminal careers and "career criminals,"* vol. 1. Washington, DC: National Academy Press.

Cook, T. D., & Campbell, D. T. (1979). *Quasi-experimentation: Design and analysis issues for field settings*. Chicago: Rand McNally.

Farrington, D. P. (1997). Evaluating a community crime prevention program. *Evaluation*, 3, 157-173.

Farrington, D. P. (2003). Methodological quality standards for evaluation research. *Annals of the American Academy of Political and Social Science*, 587, 49-68.

Farrington, D. P., Gill, M., Waples, S. J., & Argomaniz, J. (2005). *The effects of CCTV on crime: Meta-analysis of an English national quasi-experimental multi-site evaluation*. Unpublished paper.

Farrington, D. P., & Painter, K. A. (2003). How to evaluate the impact of CCTV on crime. *Crime Prevention and Community Safety*, 5(3), 7-16.

Farrington, D. P., & Welsh, B. C. (2002a). *Effects of improved street lighting on crime: A systematic review*. Research Study No. 251. London: Home Office.

Farrington, D. P., & Welsh, B. C. (2002b). Improved street lighting and crime prevention. *Justice Quarterly*, 19, 313-342.

Farrington, D. P., & Welsh, B. C. (2004). Measuring the effects of improved street lighting on crime: A reply to Dr. Marchant. *British Journal of Criminology*, 44, 448-467.

Farrington, D P., & Welsh, B. C. (2006). Improved street lighting. In B. C. Welsh and D. P. Farrington (Eds.), *Preventing crime: What works for children, offenders, victims and places*. Dordrecht, Netherlands: Springer.

Gill, M., & Spriggs, A. (2005). *Assessing the impact of CCTV*. Research Study No. 292. London: Home Office.

Koch, B. C. M. (1998). *The politics of crime prevention*. Aldershot, UK: Ashgate.

Painter, K. A., & Farrington, D. P. (1997). The crime reducing effect of improved street lighting: The Dudley Project. In R. V. Clarke (Ed.), *Situational crime prevention: Successful case studies* (2nd ed.). Monsey, NY: Criminal Justice Press.

Painter, K. A., & Farrington, D. P. (2001). Evaluating situational crime prevention using a young people's survey. *British Journal of Criminology*, 41, 266-284.

Pease, K. (1999). A review of street lighting evaluations: Crime reduction effects. In K. Painter and N. Tilley (Eds.), *Surveillance of public space: CCTV, street lighting, and crime prevention.* Crime Prevention Studies, vol. 10. Monsey, NY: Criminal Justice Press.

Piquero, A. R., Farrington, D. P., & Blumstein, A. (2003). The criminal career paradigm. In M. Tonry (Ed.), *Crime and justice,* vol. 30. Chicago: University of Chicago Press.

Shadish, W. R., Cook, T. D., & Campbell, D. T. (2002). *Experimental and quasi-experimental designs for generalized causal inference.* Boston: Houghton-Mifflin.

Skinns, D. (1998). *Doncaster CCTV surveillance system: Second annual report of the independent evaluation.* Doncaster, UK: Faculty of Business and Professional Studies, Doncaster College.

Tilley, N. (1993). *Understanding car parks, crime and cctv: Evaluation lessons from safer cities.* Crime Prevention Unit Series Paper No. 42. London: Home Office.

Welsh, B. C., & Farrington, D. P. (1999). Value for money? A review of the costs and benefits of situational crime prevention. *British Journal of Criminology, 39,* 345-368.

Welsh, B. C., & Farrington, D. P. (2002). *Crime prevention effects of closed circuit television: A systematic review.* Research Study No. 252. London: Home Office

Welsh, B. C., & Farrington, D. P. (2004a). Evidence-based crime prevention: The effectiveness of CCTV. *Crime Prevention and Community Safety,* 6(2), 21-33.

Welsh, B. C., & Farrington, D. P. (2004b). Surveillance for crime prevention in public space: Results and policy choices in Britain and America. *Criminology and Public Policy,* 3, 497-525.

Welsh, B. C., & Farrington, D. P. (2006a). CCTV and street lighting: Comparative effects on crime. In A. E. Perry, C. McDougall & D. P. Farrington (Eds.), *Reducing crime: The effectiveness of criminal justice interventions.* Chichester, UK: Wiley.

Welsh, B. C., & Farrington, D. P. (2006b). Closed-circuit television surveillance. In B. C. Welsh & D. P. Farrington (Eds.), *Preventing crime: What works for children, offenders, victims and places.* Dordrecht, Netherlands: Springer.

Burglary Prediction:
The Roles of Theory,
Flow and Friction

by

Shane D. Johnson

and

Kate J. Bowers
Jill Dando Institute of Crime Science,
University College London

Abstract: *One requisite of efficient crime prevention is an understanding of where crime will most likely happen next. Accordingly, understanding the spatial and temporal distribution of crime is one of the primary aims of environmental criminology. There have been many advances, both theoretical and empirical. However, whilst many of the theories generated and the respective findings are often complimentary, a greater understanding of how to predict the future locations of crime could potentially be reached if it were possible to unify the central ideas. In this chapter our aim is to conceptualise one way in which this may be achieved for the crime of burglary, focusing on the generation of short-term predictions – what happens in the next few days – rather than on yearly or monthly forecasts. To do this, some of the main theories and approaches to studying crime will be discussed and a simple way of bringing them together suggested.*

Two distinct approaches to studying spatial and temporal patterns of crime are currently adopted. First are top-down approaches with which most readers will be entirely familiar. Here, the goal is to understand how crime patterns emerge, and how offenders make target choices by studying the actual patterns, such as burglary hotspots themselves. Thus, the analysis begins with knowledge of the outcome, or what happened, and hypotheses regarding offender decision making are inferred. Second are "bottom-up" modelling[1] approaches which work in the opposite direction. For example, more recently adopted in the social sciences, computer simulation techniques are used to simulate complex social systems, such as offender behaviour, to test theoretical models. In what follows, we will begin by reviewing some of the research concerned with crime pattern theory and spatial concentrations of crime, and then discuss how a bottom-up approach might enhance our understanding of, and ability to predict, future patterns of crime.

Theories of Crime Concentration

Two related theories have been particularly influential in our understanding of spatial and temporal patterns of crime and, in particular, why crime might be concentrated in some areas and not others. In the original formulation of *routine activities theory*, Cohen and Felson (1979) discuss how criminal activities are strongly related to the rhythms of legitimate activities in space and time, and that crime occurs when there is a convergence in these two dimensions of a motivated offender, potential targets for crime and the absence of capable guardians against it. Moreover, this convergence of what Felson refers to as the "chemistry for crime" is a product of social structures. For example, crimes will occur at locations where many people gather for legitimate purposes as this will naturally provide an abundance of both potential victims and offenders. Brantingham and Brantingham (1995) refer to such locations as crime generators. These are distinct from crime attractors, which are areas to which offenders travel to for the sole purposes of committing crime. Crime pattern theory projects routine activity theory in a spatial dimension, encapsulated by maps of individuals' awareness spaces. These cognitive maps encode the areas with which offenders are most familiar, and places where these align with good opportunities for crime is where they will be most likely to offend.

Interestingly, although both theories were motivated by offender decision making, they have traditionally tended to inspire top-down research. An example is the study of crime hotspots. The operational relevance of this work hinges on the assumption that current and past trends are good predictors of future ones. This approach is, of course, used in a variety of other disciplines, such as economics and medicine. Evolving from early work concerned with the outbreak of cholera (see, e.g., Tufte 2001), research into hotspots of crime has sought not only to identify areas with high concentrations of crime but, by contrasting the socio-demographic composition of these and other areas, to examine the factors that may contribute to making an area criminogenic.

Sophisticated methods of analysing and displaying hotspots have been developed (e.g., see Ratcliffe and McCullagh, 1998). Importantly, Geographical Information Systems (GIS), the computer software typically used to generate or display hotspots, are now fairly commonplace in police forces (Weisburd et al., 2003). However, although this approach can be useful for identifying general areas likely to experience high rates of crime over long periods of time, such as one year, for predicting more precisely when and where crimes will occur (e.g., on which streets they will they occur tomorrow), problems with this type of analysis have been acknowledged. For instance, it has been noted that hotspots are intrinsically retrospective (Groff and La Vigne, 2002; Johnson and Bowers, 2004) and that analyses based on data from even the recent past may be of limited value (Townsley and Pease, 2002).

A further area of research which continues to gain momentum is concerned with *repeat victimisation* (RV) prevention, the story of which begins with and continues to be written by Ken Pease. The central conclusions of this research are that: for every type of crime studied, only a small proportion of the population is victimised and these victims experience a disproportionate amount of crime (for a review, see Pease, 1998); the risk of victimisation increases significantly following an initial event (e.g., Polvi et al., 1991; Farrell and Pease, 1993); and where RV occurs, it does so quickly, offering a narrow window of opportunity for intervention (e.g., Polvi et al., 1991; Johnson et al., 1997). Research also demonstrates that RV is most prevalent in deprived areas (Johnson et al., 1997), and within hotspots of crime (e.g., Johnson et al., 1997; Townsley et al., 2000), suggesting that RV may generate geographical hotspots of crime.

Perhaps most importantly, research has shown that compared to other available variables (e.g., household and area demographics) the crime event is itself the greatest predictor of future risk (Budd, 1999). This finding is further supported by evaluations of crime prevention schemes, which demonstrate that the targeting of previous victims represents an effective crime reduction strategy (e.g., Anderson et al., 1995). Thus, it is apparent that RV is of considerable interest both for academic theory and practical policy making.

Nevertheless, while the predictive value of prior victimisation is undisputed, self-evidently RV provides no predictions for those as yet unvictimised (Johnson and Bowers, 2004), and hence it focuses on (current) victims but not (current) non-victims. An advance in this area, inspired by Ken's notion of "virtual" repeats (Pease, 1998), addresses this criticism. Drawing upon an epidemiological model, researchers in the U.K. (Johnson and Bowers, 2004) and Australia (Townsley et al., 2003) have examined whether or not the risk of burglary is communicable – which may be demonstrated by showing that properties proximate to a burgled home are temporarily victimised at a rate disproportionate to what would be expected on the basis of chance (hereafter, "near repeats"). The possibility that burglary may exhibit this feature was prompted by offender reports that having burgled one property they prefer to re-victimise this location, or select the next most similar one, such as premises that share architectural features or security precautions (Ashton et al., 1998).

The results of studies (e.g., Johnson and Bowers, 2004; Townsley et al., 2003) have confirmed that burglary does exhibit this feature of communicability. To illustrate, Figure 1 shows how burglary risks were communicated at the street level in the county of Merseyside (UK) over the time period 1995-2000. Adapted from Bowers and Johnson (2005a),[2] the data show that following an initial incident, the burgled home is at an elevated risk, and so too are neighbouring households. However, this elevation in risk appears to be temporary and it diminishes as the distance from the burgled property increases: a pattern of temporal-spatial distance-decay. More detailed analyses showed that this increase in risk was communicated to houses up to 400 meters away and for a period of one-month after a reference event.

An interesting question raised by these findings is whether burglaries that occur close together in both space and time are committed by the same offender, or by their associates. This relates directly to the long-debated "flag" or "boost" question in RV research. According to the former, vulnerable properties signal (flag) their vulnerability and hence are repeatedly victimised by a number of different offenders. The alternative is that only when a property is victimised is its potential as a particularly good target revealed (Pease, 1998) and the likelihood of further victimisation (by the same offender) boosted. The most direct way of testing this would be to obtain full and accurate data regarding offender activity, which homes

Figure 1: The Communicability of Burglary Risk

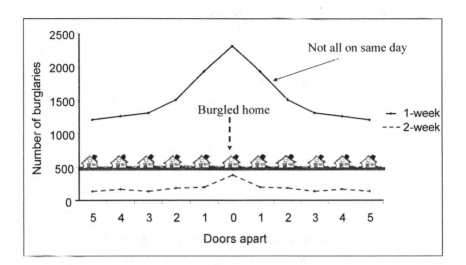

they burgled and when. However, data concerned with offending activity is typically incomplete. For this reason in a recent paper (Bowers and Johnson, 2004) we adopted an alternative approach, comparing the consistency of the modus operandi of near repeats with all other pairings of burglaries. The results demonstrated a space-time interaction for the consistency with which entry was gained (point and mode of entry), with events that occurred closest to each other in space and time most frequently converging. This provides tentative evidence that at least some near repeat events are committed by the same offender.

These findings have clear implications for crime prevention theory and practice, and have subsequently been used by the current authors and Ken (Bowers et al., 2004; Johnson et al., 2005) to derive a method for producing *prospective* crime maps. The approach taken essentially integrates the theory and findings from the near repeat studies with the basic approach undertaken in the generation of retrospective hotspot crime maps. The latter involves the production of a *risk surface* using an approach known as the moving window technique (Bailey and Gatrell, 1995). To do this, a two-dimensional grid (with n x n equal sized cells) is generated and overlaid on the study area. An estimation of the likelihood of crime occurring within each cell, an index of *risk intensity*, is generated using a recursive algorithm. For each cell, every crime event that occurred within a certain radius, or bandwidth, of the centre of the cell is identified. In traditional hotspot research the bandwidth used is typically arbitrary, being around 200 meters. A weighting is then given to each crime event, derived on the basis of the distance of the point to the centre of the cell, with those closest being assigned the greatest weighting. The weightings of each crime event are then summed to produce a risk-intensity measure. These values will, of course, be affected by how much historic data is used in the generation of the risk surface. This varies, with some people using as little as two weeks worth of data, others more.

In contrast, to generate prospective hotspots, Bowers et al. (2004) developed an algorithm for which the selection of the bandwidth was based upon a theoretical model. Our earlier findings suggested that a series of crimes may be seen as a constellation of events from which meaningful predictions can be made. Thus, we used the parameters that defined the communicability of risk for the area studied to calibrate the algorithm. First, to take account of the distinct time signature of near repeats (and RV), cell weightings were derived using not only the distance of the crime event from the centre of the cell, but also *when* the crimes occurred (a temporal bandwidth). An inverse multiplicative function was used such that burglaries that occurred a long time ago and a long distance away were given less prominence than those that occurred recently and nearby. Moreover, the spatial bandwidth used was 400 meters, which reflected the distance over which victimisation has an impact for the area studied. An evaluation of the predictive efficacy of this technique demonstrated that it substantially outperformed retrospective hotspot techniques, correctly identifying the spatial location of 62% of burglaries that occurred two days after the map was created. To evaluate the external validity of the method, in collaboration with Ken we are currently in the process of testing this model in a different region of the U.K.

Collectively, the above findings suggest that patterns of risk operate across at least two levels. First, different areas appear to generate or attract crime (Brantingham and Brantingham, 1995) to different extents, and second, at least a proportion of the risk of victimisation appears to propagate through areas in relatively predictable ways. Together, these findings help us to understand where hotspots may form, and why they might do so.

However, current methods of generating both retrospective hotspots and prospective maps assume a uniform opportunity surface for the geographical area studied. This will rarely accord with reality. For instance, some areas will have a higher target density than others (i.e., more homes); they may have less attractive targets; and they may have more heterogeneous housing (with implications for offender awareness and target attractiveness); while others still will be less easy to access. Thus, consideration should be given to factors that facilitate the communication or flow of crime risk and to those factors that generate a form of friction. The focus of this chapter will now turn to these factors. Before doing so it is worth noting that to date, our work with Ken has drawn upon principles and techniques from the disciplines of geography and epidemiology. In order to implement what is proposed here, the methods used will additionally draw upon approaches developed in the field of mathematics, particularly graph theory.

Friction and Opportunity Surfaces

The classic example of crime related friction is, of course, distance, with research consistently demonstrating that the frequency of offences committed by an offender is inversely related to the distance travelled (e.g., Rengert et al., 1999). The algorithms which are used to produce both prospective and retrospective hotspot maps do take this type of friction into account, but ignore other factors that might influence the direction in which crime risk is likely to flow. To illustrate the problem with this, a limited number of factors and their likely influence on crime flow will be discussed.

Natural Physical Environment

When considering the likely location of crime, one important factor of the physical environment, as discussed by Felson (2001), is topology. In much the same way that castles (with moats, etc. and other medieval structures) were designed, Felson discusses the way that environmental features that surround a property may either protect it or increase its vulnerability. This concept also has been discussed by Brantingham and Brantingham (2000), who consider how natural features such as rivers and forests, as well as man-made features including roads and bridges, may impact on an offender's choices of which properties to target. The theory is that where features that would be difficult to circumvent intersect an offender's journey to a particular property or area, he will be less likely to choose that area than more accessible ones. So, for instance, if an area was encapsulated by a river, offenders living on one side of the river would be less likely to target properties on the other.

Crime Prevention Activity

Whilst crime prevention schemes do not make properties immune to crime, they can significantly increase the effort involved in victimising them. Consequently, it is likely that where the risk of victimisation is communicated into such locations it will be impeded.

It is important to raise the issue of crime displacement here, as it has obvious implications for our discussion of crime flow and friction. One way of conceptualising displacement is to view it as the deflection of crime flow, caused by crime prevention. However, along with others we dispute that this kind of deflection will normally be absolute, as this implies a reverse wave as powerful as its forward movement. Where displacement does occur, perhaps it would be better conceptualised as a form of refraction, similar to the way light waves slow down as they enter denser mediums, such as water. Thus, whilst some activity may be displaced, inertia to seek out new opportunities in less familiar or optimal areas may limit this.

A related idea is the concept of familiarity decay (Eck, 1993). Originally conceived to predict the places that offenders might target if geographically displaced by crime prevention activity, Eck suggests that under such conditions offenders will select the next most similar or familiar targets available. Where such alternative targets do not exist locally, offending may be deterred. For burglars, such targets might simply be those near by, or those nearest to protected households that share the most similar features. In addition to being an explanatory parameter in relation to the spatial displacement of crime, this could also help explain offender target selection choices, or crime placement (Barr and Pease, 1990) more generally.

Support for this idea comes from interviews with offenders, who sometimes express a preference for targeting properties that share features or are replicas of those successfully burgled in the past, a pattern that Ken refers to as virtual repeat victimisation (Pease, 1998). This finding also correlates with the Brantinghams' (1981) idea that offenders generate templates or schemas which, like a menu, describe the optimal ingredients for the commission of a crime. For some offenders, one salient factor in this type of decision process could well be the type of houses available for burglary (e.g., detached, flats, terraced/row homes).

Housing Characteristics

One hypothesis that follows from this discussion is that if near repeats are committed by the same offenders who have preferences for the types of houses targeted, risk should be communicated not only to those proximate in space and time but also in terms of architecture. The relevance of an affirmative finding would be that data concerned with housing type and location could be used as one layer of an opportunity surface to enhance prediction. In the absence of existing empirical data, we explore this here.

Ideally, to examine this hypothesis data concerned with the types of homes burgled, the proximity of the events in space and time, and the type of properties not burgled would be analysed. This would allow the expected and observed frequencies of near repeats for different types of housing to be compared. However, data concerned with the spatial distribution of different types of housing were unavailable, and so a variant of this approach was adopted. Using a sample of recorded burglary data for the county of Merseyside (N=6,000), each burglary was compared with every other, and the spatial and temporal distance between each pairing calculated. Additionally, for each pairing the types of homes burgled (detached home, semi-detached home, terraced/row home, or, flat/apartment), as defined in a structured Modus Operandi field for each burglary event, was compared. The results are shown as Figure 2. The y-axis shows the percentage of comparisons for which the houses burgled were of the same type (e.g., two detached houses). Thus, a value of 0.50 indicates that for 50% of comparisons within a particular distance-time category the types of homes burgled were concordant.

In line with the first law of geography,[3] there was an association between the similarity of the houses targeted and the distance between them. More importantly, there was a space-time interaction such that for those burglaries that occurred closest together in *both* space and time, relative to those committed close to each other in space but not time, the types of houses targeted tended to align with higher probability. Add to this earlier findings (Bowers and Johnson, 2005a) that houses on the same side of the street are at a greater risk of victimisation than those opposite, and that near repeats are particularly a feature of areas with homogeneous housing (Townsley et al., 2003), and it would appear that the risk of burglary communicates in a way that is consistent with Eck's theory of familiarity decay and Ken's concept of virtual repeats, placing those nearest and most similar to the burgled home at the greatest risk of victimisation.

Figure 2: Similarity of Types of Houses (e.g., semi-detached or flat) Burgled

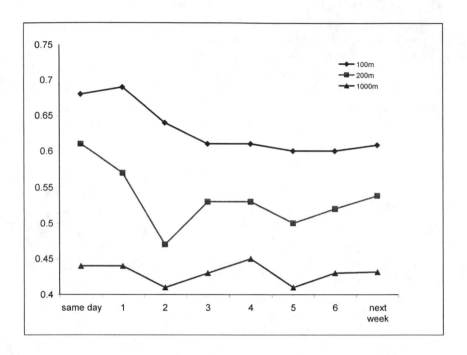

The Street Network

A further factor that may influence how burglary risk is communicated is the permeability of an area or street. This can be conceptualised in different ways, but essentially it is concerned with how easy places are to access. In relation to crime pattern theory, this is important as it impacts upon people's routine movements and their cognitive maps of different areas. In their study, Beavon et al. (1994) examined how the risk of victimisation varied at different street segments in Vancouver and whether this was related to the ease with which people could access each segment via the street network. One measure of permeability was derived by calculating how many turnings there were onto each segment from other roads. The operational definition used is illustrated in Figure 3, using examples at the extremes of the index (each segment could have between 1 to 6 ways of

Figure 3: Examples of the Accessibility Measure Used by Beavon et al. (1994)

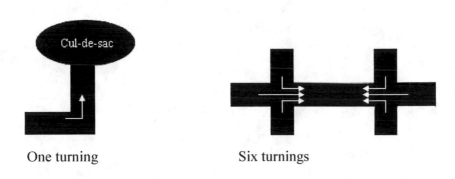

One turning   Six turnings

accessing it). The results revealed a positive correlation between this measure of permeability and crime risk for a series of property crimes, including burglary, suggesting that the accessibility of an area affects the risk of victimisation. This issue is extended and further validated in the chapter by Rachel Armitage in this volume using data for West Yorkshire in the U.K., demonstrating the external validity of the pattern.

In the development of a model of burglary flow and friction this is of clear importance. Permeability as so defined could affect victimisation risk in two ways. First, it is possible that burglary risks will communicate more easily to those street segments or areas that are more permeable – a general effect. However, this takes no account of the direction from where risk may be communicated. Thus, in addition, it is plausible that for any particular location there will exist optimal vectors through which the risk of crime is communicated. For instance, the risk of burglary may be communicated with greater potency from a home located on one street segment to a property located on another segment if the two roads are more easily linked than others, or if they have a greater number of direct routes between them.

This section has provided a short introduction to some of the factors, other than crime itself, that are likely to accelerate or dampen the evolution of burglary problems in an area. As far as the authors are aware, none of these factors have so far been considered in any models that attempt to predict future patterns of crime on a day-to-day basis. Later in this chapter, we explain how opportunity surfaces for these factors may be derived and used to enhance crime forecasting methods. Before doing so, currently evolving research which adopts a bottom-up approach to studying crime will briefly be discussed. For a more detailed discussion, the interested reader is referred to Brantingham and Brantingham (2004). There is also a discussion of complex systems in the chapter in this volume by John Eck et al.

Simulation Modelling in Three Paragraphs

In a nutshell, computer simulation, which has only recently been applied to the study of crime, allows the testing and refining of theories. Different methodologies exist, but perhaps the most useful is agent-based simulation. A fascinating method to see in action, agents (which represent offenders, potential victims and guardians) are brought to life using an interface between a GIS and software that simulates the environment and the agents' interactions with it. The agents wander around the simulated area making discrete (partly stochastic) choices and commit crimes when the conditions are right, which is defined by a set of parameters that articulate the theory tested. The agents' activity is simulated over a number of iterations, and the cumulative patterns of offending in space and time are known as the emergent properties of the simulation. The ecological validity of the model, that is to say how closely this resembles reality, can then be assessed by comparing the emergent properties with patterns of crime typically observed in the real world.

A number of studies are underway (e.g., Birks et al., forthcoming) and, despite being in their infancy, are producing exciting and plausible findings. However, for a variety of reasons, it is beyond the scope (or purpose) of these models to forecast the exact spatial and temporal distribution of crime on a day-to-day basis in a way that could be used in an operational context. One reason for this is that to replicate real crime patterns precisely (in terms of the exact locations and timings of offences) would require accurate and detailed data on active populations (offenders, guardians, and targets) within an area. Such data are difficult to obtain and validate, and subject to change. So, even if patterns of crime for a simulated environment with many of the features of a real area such as the land use, road structure and number of offenders were generated, it would be unlikely that any current agent-based model would be able to generate the exact distribution of crime events as observed in the real world.

Currently then, the principle aim of research that uses agent-based simulation is to test the validity of theoretical models. Representing complex systems as they do, the results of agent-based simulations can generate surprising results not previously anticipated even for fairly simple interactions. Thus, further questions that could usefully be addressed using this approach in the near future would be the likely (general) impacts on crime of changes in the physical environment, the implementation of crime prevention or changes in the number of capable guardians against crime (see Brantingham and Brantingham, 2004). However, what is so far beyond the scope of these models is the accurate prediction of where crimes will occur next in the non-simulated world.

A Different Approach?

Thus top-down and bottom-up approaches typically focus on static crime patterns and area characteristics, and simulated patterns of offender choices, respectively. What we propose here lies somewhere between the two. One way of thinking about the approach is to consider crime events as disease agents that, like pathogens without a host, do not live for very long. While a disease agent is active, risk is communicated across and *interacts* with the opportunity surface. Consequently, some cells within the surface will be affected more than others. Instead of using a stochastic model, as would be applied in agent-based simulation, for now a deterministic model is proposed, although the model could later be adapted to include a random element. In some cases, generating a prediction for one point in time a large number of times might identify that a few areas could be at risk, under different conditions.

Returning to the general approach, one way of visualising the way crime events affect the risk surface is to think of them as an erupting volcano. When the event occurs, lava flows rapidly from the mouth of the volcano: as it flows the combination of friction and cooling limit the distance over which it travels (like the distance decay associated with criminal activity). In addition, features of the landscape facilitate or repel the lava – interacting with and – influencing the direction of flow. Thus, obstacles or barriers divert or terminate the flow of the lava, whereas open channels allow the molten rock to flow freely and open channels with a gradient will facilitate the flow over greater ranges.

Assuming a finite volume of lava (produced by a single event or eruption), compared to a uniformly even surface, where obstacles block certain vectors, others will experience a greater volume of lava. Similar effects may be apparent with the communicability of risk, as it is reasonable to assume that risk will communicate to those areas where the opportunities attract the (crime) disease agent and be repelled by those that do not. In the next section we will discuss how opportunity surfaces may be produced to help model crime risk, and then move on to discuss how to incorporate the concept of communication vectors and friction.

Generating Opportunity Surfaces

The first step will be the generation of opportunity surfaces that encapsulate the relevant "layers" most likely to impact upon the communication of risk. Some of these have been discussed above (e.g., permeability), others are discussed in accompanying chapters of this volume and elsewhere. However, one technical challenge is how to operationalise this information in a predictive model. In a recent study, Groff and La Vigne (2001) developed a method for generating opportunity surfaces and illustrated the technique for the crime of burglary. This involved generating a grid like those discussed above and using a GIS to produce a series of layers, one for each opportunity factor chosen. Ten factors considered included land use (residential versus other types), housing tenure (renter versus owner occupied), and proximity to likely offenders (nearby or not). For each layer, cells were attributed a value which indicated the presence or absence of the relevant factor (e.g., residential land) in that cell or those immediately adjacent (to reflect the fact that surrounding cells might also affect crime risk at a location).

Next, the resulting layers were added together to produce a single surface for which cells with the smallest (largest) values represented those where the risk of crime should be lowest (greatest). The accuracy of the model was subsequently tested using 12 months of burglary data. The results were particularly promising in relation to the prediction of cold cells, with only 6% of burglaries occurring in locations with opportunity scores 1-2 standard deviations below the mean score. For the hot cells (those with opportunity scores one or more standard deviations above the mean), 20% of the burglaries and 50% of the repeats occurred in these cells. However, the majority of crimes (72%) occurred within cells that were within (+/-) 1 standard deviation of the mean score. Thus, the model appeared to be better at predicting where crimes would not occur than where they would.

Groff and La Vigne's study represents the first attempt that the current authors are aware of to generate an opportunity surface of this kind, and hence their work represents an important first step. One likely reason why the model was less accurate at predicting locations of crime was that it did not to take account of the flux of crime and the communication of risk. For this reason, our discussion will now turn to how this may be done.

One simple way of calibrating a prospective model that incorporated an opportunity surface would be to generate the risk intensity value for a cell by comparing the opportunity parameters for that cell with those in which each contributing crime event (disease agent) within the specified bandwidth is located. This would represent a similarity decay function, calculated using multiple parameters. All other things being equal, cells with more similar profiles to cells in which crimes occur would have a greater risk intensity value than those for which greater differences exist.

To illustrate this approach consider the simple example shown in Figure 4. To calculate a risk intensity value for cell *a*, it is necessary to consider the influence of all events (disease agents) within the bandwidth of the cell. For simplicity, assume that both of the crime events shown are. However, the crime event above and to the right of cell *a* has a more similar profile in terms of the housing in the area in which it occurred than the other. Thus, for this surface, this event would contribute more

Figure 4: Example of a Single Friction Surface

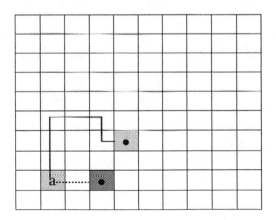

- Paths between cells
• Crime events
Terraced housing
Detached housing

than the burglary that occurred in the area with a different housing profile. In Figure 4 we have illustrated only one factor, but it is easy to see how this would be extended using a variety of different layers, such as those used by Groff and La Vigne (2001).[4] The key advance with what is proposed is that the interaction between the disease agents and the opportunity surface would be explicitly modelled.

Using graph theory, a more complicated variant of the procedure would consider how connected the cells of the surface are. To do this, each cell would represent a node of a network, and the paths (roads/footpaths) between every node would be identified and weighted according to how permeable the connection is. Permeability could be modelled in a variety of ways. For example, a number of reasonable routes from one cell to another could be computed using what are known as greedy algorithms such as Dijkstra's or the nearest neighbour algorithms. Each of the paths would be assigned a friction cost associated with travelling along it. Cost would most likely be the distance of travel, but could include other factors such as the estimated time of travel,[5] the risk of identification, and the level of crime prevention activity in an area. For instance, paths which have a simple linear geometry (see the dotted line in Figure 4) would be less costly than those that are more convoluted with many turns and a longer path (the solid line in Figure 4). Such a cost is easily computed using the greedy algorithm. Thus, the degree to which two cells are connected, and how much the communication of risk can flow, would be a function of the number of routes between them and how sinuous each path is. All other things being equal, those pairings with the greatest number of short routes would be identified as the most easily connected, and consequently would have the highest likelihood of crime risk flowing between them.

Using graph theory in this way would mean that the simple Euclidian (as the crow flies) distance-decay function currently used in the prospective model could be dispensed with as the process that it currently crudely models would be accounted for in a more precise way.

Of course, the results this type of analysis would represent only one of a number of layers used to construct the opportunity surface, and the challenge in generating the risk-intensity surface will lie in estimating how the disease (crime) agents interact with each of them. The simple example shown in Figure 4 illustrates the importance of this. Here, in terms of the influence on cell *a*, the cell in the top right of the surface would have the highest risk value for the housing parameter, but the lowest for the network parameter (because of the greater friction). Thus, for this surface, the two cells may contribute the same or a similar intensity to the overall value for the cell a. Other cells, particularly those with more similar housing characteristics to, and more directly connected with, the cells with crime events in them would have higher risk intensity values to cell a.

Final Thoughts

To recapitulate, where research has considered opportunity surfaces in the past, the surface used remained static over time and the temporo-spatial distribution of recent crimes was excluded from the analysis. Consequently, this approach took no account of the flux of crime and the communicability of risk. In contrast, approaches that do consider recent crime patterns take no account of opportunity surfaces, and hence research that considers the interaction between the two should be of clear benefit. Determining the extent to which different layers enhance predictive efficiency is an empirical question that can only be answered by testing variations of the model in a stepwise fashion, adding one new layer to the model at a time and testing the main effect of so doing. By testing the model in this way, it will be possible to eliminate layers which we might have expected to increase predictive accuracy but that do not, and to incorporate only those that appear to enhance the model (with a preference for parsimony). This helps to not only improve the model but also to refine theories of crime patterns. Moreover, if fully realised, as well as helping to predict where crime is most likely to next occur, the potential short term side-effects (e.g., diffusion of benefit) of new crime reduction interventions or policing strategies might be anticipated by manipulating the relevant opportunity layers.

A further potential application of this kind of approach would be in the future development of geographic profiling methodology. The task for the latter is to predict the home location of an offender based upon the spatial constellation of their crimes. The current methods used (e.g., Canter et al., 2000; Rossmo, 2000) essentially identify a probability surface using a similar approach to kernel density estimation, but using only those crimes believed to be committed by one offender. Some of the thinking discussed here could inform this endeavour. For instance, it may be possible to link unsolved crimes with more reliability by considering their temporal as well as spatial distribution. Moreover, the application of graph theory and the consideration of opportunity surfaces (see also Bernasco, 2006), perhaps using different environmental features selected on the basis of the crimes considered and relevant theory, may help reduce the search area currently identified by the methods as currently conceived.

It would be incomplete to conclude this chapter without a short discussion on the importance of model testability. It is important to stimulate debate on how the predictive efficiency of hotspot maps can be most accurately tested, something that as far as we are aware has received little attention within the research literature. In the context of the current research agenda we know exactly what we are looking for. As the methodology develops and additional layers are added, we would expect to observe an associated increase in predictive efficiency for some but perhaps not all factors. But how is accuracy best measured?

Equally important is consideration of the context (for a discussion, see Pawson and Tilley, 1997) of the model, as it may be that one formula works almost perfectly for one area and time, but loses a great deal of predictive power in other situations. It will therefore be important to test the external validity of the models generated, using data for different times and places.

In this chapter, we have discussed a way of drawing upon a number of theories of offending and victimisation to predict future crime patterns and a way of operationalising this in a mathematical model. With Ken, we hope to report in the near future our first empirical findings from this stream of research.

Address correspondence to: shane.johnson@ucl.ac.uk

NOTES

1. Bottom-up modeling approaches are known by several names including agent based modeling (see, Axelrod, 1997).
2. The data are presented as a mirror image here to emphasize the pattern in an easy to understand format.
3. This states that things which are closest to each other in space tend also to be more similar to each other than things separated by some distance.

4. Note that different layers would be handled differently. For example, in a simple model the location of crime prevention activity may be represented by a weighted surface, with an analysis of cell to cell similarity being an unnecessary step – the communication of risk to cells in which there was crime prevention simply being lower irrespective of the location from which risk was communicated.
5. The authors would like to thank Richard Block for pointing this out during a presentation of this work at the American Society of Criminology annual conference, 2004.

REFERENCES

Anderson, D., Chenery, S., & Pease, K. (1995). *Biting back: Tackling repeat burglary and car crime*. Crime Detection and Prevention Series Paper No 58. London: Home Office.

Ashton, J., Brown, I., Senior, B., & Pease, K. (1998). Repeat victimisation: Offender accounts. *International Journal of Risk, Security and Crime Prevention*, 3(4), 269-279.

Axelrod, R. (1997). *The complexity of cooperation*. Princeton: Princeton University Press.

Bailey, T. C., & Gatrell, A. C. (1995). *Interactive spatial data analysis*. Longman, Harlow.

Barr, R., & Pease, K. (1990). Crime placement, displacement and deflection. *Crime and Justice: A Review of the Research*, 12, 277-318.

Beavon, D. J. K., Brantingham, P. L., & Brantingham, P. J. (1994). The influence of street networks on the patterning of property offenses. In R. V. G. Clarke (Ed.), *Crime prevention studies*, vol. 2. Monsey, NY: Criminal Justice Press.

Bernasco, W. (2006). The usefulness of measuring spatial opportunity structures for tracking down offenders: A theoretical analysis of geographic offender profiling using simulation studies. *Psychology, Crime and Law*, in press.

Birks, D. J., Donkin, S., & Wellsmith, M. (forthcoming). Synthesis over analysis: Towards an ontology for volume crime simulation. In L. Liu and J. Eck (Eds.), *Crime analysis systems: Using computer simulations and geographic information systems*. Hershey, PA: Idea Group PLC.

Bowers, K. J., & Johnson, S. D. (2004). Who commits repeats? A test of the boost explanation of near repeats. *Western Criminology Review*, 5(3), 12-24.

Bowers, K. J., & Johnson, S. D. (2005a). Domestic burglary repeats and space-time clusters: The dimensions of risk. *European Journal of Criminology*, 2(1), 67-92.

Bowers, K. J., Johnson, S. D., & Pease, K. (2004). Prospective hot-spotting: The future of crime mapping? *The British Journal of Criminology*, 44(5), 641-658.

Brantingham, P. J., & Brantingham, P. L. (Eds.), (1991). *Environmental criminology* (rev. ed.). Prospect Heights, IL: Waveland.

Brantingham, P. J., & Brantingham, P. L. (1995). Criminality of place: Crime generators and crime attractors. *European Journal on Criminal Policy and Research*, *3*(3), 1-26.

Brantingham, P. L., & Brantingham, P. J. (2000). *A conceptual model for anticipating crime displacement*. Paper presented at the American Society of Criminology Annual meeting, San Francisco.

Brantingham, P. L., & Brantingham, P. J. (2004). Computer simulation as a tool for environmental criminologists. *Security Journal*, *17*(1), 21-30.

Budd, T. (1999) *Burglary of domestic dwellings: Findings from the British Crime Survey*. Home Office Statistical Bulletin 4/99. London: Home Office.

Canter, D. V., Coffey, T., Huntley, M., & Misson, C. (2000). Predicting serial killers' home base using a decision support system. *Journal of Quantitative Criminology*, *16*(4), 457-478.

Cohen, L. E., & Felson, F. (1979). Social change and crime rate trends: A routine activity approach. *American Sociological Review*, *44*, 588-608.

Eck, J. (1993). The threat of crime displacement. *Criminal Justice Abstracts*, *25*, 527-546.

Farrell, G., & Pease K. (1993). *Once bitten, twice bitten: Repeat victimisation and its implications for crime prevention*. Crime Prevention Unit Paper 46. London: Home Office.

Felson (2001). The topography of crime. *Crime Prevention and Community Safety*, *4*(1), 47-52.

Groff, E. R., & La Vigne, N. G. (2001). Mapping an opportunity surface of residential burglary. *Journal of Research in Crime and Delinquency*, *38*(3), 257-278.

Groff, E. R., & La Vigne, N. G. (2002). Forecasting the future of predictive crime mapping. In N. Tilley (Ed.), *Analysis for crime prevention*. Crime Prevention Studies, vol. 13. Monsey NY: Criminal Justice Press.

Johnson, S. D., & Bowers, K. J. (2004). The burglary as clue to the future: The beginnings of prospective hot-spotting. *European Journal of Criminology*, *1*(2), 237-255.

Johnson, S. D., Bowers, K., & Pease, K. (2005). Predicting the future or summarising the past? Crime mapping as anticipation. In M. Smith and N. Tilley (Eds.), *Launching crime science*. London: Willan.

Johnson, S. D., Bowers, K., & Hirschfield, A. (1997). New insights into the spatial and temporal distribution of repeat victimisation. *British Journal of Criminology*, *37*(2), 224-244.

Liu, L., Xuguang, W., Eck, J., & Liang, J. (2005). Simulating crime events and crime patterns in a RA/CA model. In F. Wang (Ed.), *Geographic information systems and crime analysis*. Reading, PA: Idea Publishing.

Pawson, R., & Tilley, N. (1997). *Realistic evaluation*. London: Sage.

Pease, K. (1998). *Repeat victimisation: Taking stock*. Crime Detection and Prevention Series, Paper 90. Home Office: London.

Polvi, N., Looman, T., Humphries, C., & Pease, K. (1991). The time course of repeat burglary victimisation. *British Journal of Criminology*, *31*(4), 411-414.

Ratcliffe, J. H., & McCullagh, M. J. (1998). Aoristic crime analysis. *International Journal of Geographical Information Science*, *12*(7), 751-764.

Rengert, G. F., Piquero, A. R., & Jones, P. R. (1999). Distance decay reexamined. *Criminology, 37*(2), 427-446.

Rossmo, D. K. (2000). *Geographic profiling.* Boca Raton, FL: CRC Press.

Townsley, M., Homel, R., & Chaseling, J. (2000) Repeat burglary victimisation: Spatial and temporal patterns. *Australian and New Zealand Journal of Criminology, 33*(1), 37-63.

Townsley, M., Homel, R., & Chaseling, J. (2003). Infectious burglaries: A test of the near repeat hypothesis. *British Journal of Criminology, 43,* 615-633.

Townsley, M., & Pease, K. (2002). Hot spots and cold comfort: The importance of having a working thermometer. In N. Tilley (Ed.), *Analysis for crime prevention.* Crime Prevention Studies, vol. 13. Monsey NY: Criminal Justice Press.

Tufte, E. (2001). *The visual display of quantitative data.* Cheshire, CT: Graphics Press LLC.

Weisburd, D., Mastrofski, S. D., McNally, A. M., Greenspan, R., & Willis, J. J. (2003). Reforming to preserve: Compstat and strategic problem solving. *Criminology & Public Policy, 2*(3), 421-456.

Risky Facilities:
Crime Concentration in
Homogeneous Sets of
Establishments and Facilities

by

John E. Eck
University of Cincinnati

Ronald V. Clarke
Rutgers University

and

Rob T. Guerette
Florida International University

Abstract: *The concentration of much crime in a few members of any group of homogeneous facilities is quite common and follows a well-known pattern found throughout the physical, biological and social sciences. Like repeat victimization (a closely related phenomenon), risky facilities provide opportunities for prevention. We explore a variety of explanations for risky facilities; examine measurement problems associated with studying them; list policy options; and conclude by exploring the hypothesis that crime concentration among groups of homogeneous facilities may be the outgrowth of complex dynamic interactions among individuals – offenders, targets, and place managers.*

Crime Prevention Studies, volume 21 (2007), pp. 225–264.

INTRODUCTION

The fact that crime is heavily concentrated on particular people, places and things has important implications for prevention. It suggests that focusing resources where crime is concentrated will yield the greatest preventive benefits. Researchers have therefore begun to develop concepts intended to guide prevention that capture different aspects of this concentration. These include "repeat offenders" – who commit a disproportionate amount of total recorded crime (Spelman, 1994); "hot spots" – places with high rates of crime (Sherman et al., 1989; Weisburd et al., 1992); "crime generators" – places that are high in crime because they are exceptionally busy (Brantingham and Brantingham, 1995); crime attractors" – places that contain many suitable crime targets without adequate protection (Brantingham and Brantingham, 1995); "repeat victims" – who suffer a series of crimes in a relatively short period of time (Farrell and Pease, 1993); and "hot products" – which are stolen at much higher rates than other products (Clarke, 1999).

In this paper, we add another related form of crime concentration: *for any group of similar facilities (for example, taverns, parking lots, or bus shelters), a small proportion of the group accounts for the majority of crime experienced by the entire group.* As we will demonstrate, this is a highly general phenomenon that deserves more attention from researchers than it has so far received. Naming a phenomenon helps to attract attention and we suggest it should be called "risky facilities."

Risky facilities might show up as hot spots in a city's crime map. Indeed, hospitals, schools and train stations are well known examples. But treating these facilities simply as hot spots (or even as crime attractors or crime generators) is to miss an important opportunity for analysis: a comparison of the risky facilities with the other members of their set could reveal many important differences between them, which account for the differences in risk and which might provide important pointers to preventive action.

Risky facilities can be treated as an extension of the concept of repeat victimization. This extension differentiates between the people being victimized and the location at which this occurs (Eck, 2001). Thus, a tavern that repeatedly calls for police assistance to deal with fights among its patrons is not itself repeatedly victimized (unless it routinely suffers damage in the course of these fights or the staff are regularly assaulted). Even those directly involved in the fights might not be "repeat" victims, as different patrons might be involved each time. Indeed, no one need be victimized at all, as would be the case if the calls were about drug transactions, prostitution solicitations, or the sales of stolen property. Calling attention to the tavern directs attention to the role of management in facilitating the behaviors leading to illicit acts. Thus, when a tavern with many fights is compared with others nearby, it might be found that its layout and management practices contribute substantially to the problem, and that if these were altered the fights might greatly decrease.

In this paper, we will review the evidence showing that the concept of risky facilities is of wide application and that many different kinds of facilities show this form of crime concentration. We then offer some explanations of why risky facilities exist and consider empirical issues that must be addressed in the study of risky facilities. Next, we turn to the preventive implications of the concept. In our conclusions we propose that distributions of facility risk may be emergent properties of complex dynamic systems.

RISKY FACILITIES IN THE LITERATURE

The term "facilities" suggests large buildings and areas of land (often closed to the public), such as docks, water treatment plants and trash burning incinerators. When modified by "public" it suggests libraries, hospitals, schools, parking lots, railway stations, shopping centers and so forth. We use the term for both these kinds of large facilities. We also intend it to cover a wide range of much smaller private and public establishments such as taverns, convenience stores, banks, betting shops, Social Security offices, etc.

Our literature search for risky facilities was not intended to be exhaustive. We were not trying to identify every kind of facility where the concept holds, but we simply wanted to show that it is of wide application. We looked for studies describing crime (including disorder and misconduct) in specific kinds of facilities, and then looked to see whether the study contained evidence that a small proportion of the facilities studied accounted for a large proportion of crime experienced by the whole group. This was rarely the focus of the original studies, but many of them contained data that allowed us to judge whether it was the case. We did not define precisely what we meant by a "small" proportion of facilities or a "large" proportion of the crime. This has not been done for the other forms of crime concentrations discussed above, though it is not unusual to see figures like "Five percent of offenders account for fifty percent of crime" or "Four percent of victims suffer forty percent of personal crimes" – and we were looking for similar proportions in the literature we examined.

Unfortunately, data were sometimes not presented in this form, but instead the studies reported differences between facilities in crime numbers or rates – for example, "Four percent of banks had robbery rates 4 to 6 times that of other banks." While consistent with "risky facilities," these figures do not satisfy a key component of the definition of the concept – they do not demonstrate that a small number of high-risk banks account for a large part of the robbery problem. Put another way, such studies show that some facilities have more crime than other like facilities, not that most crime is located at these few extreme facilities.

The concentration of crime we are looking for can be represented as a J-curve (Allport, 1934; Clarke, 1996; Clarke and Weisburd, 1990; Hertwig et al., 1999; Simon, 1955; Walberg et al., 1984). As we will see, this curve is closely related to distributions described by power laws (Schroeder, 1991), a well-known variant of which is Zipf's Law[1] (Gell-Mann, 1994; Zipf, 1949). To reveal a J-curve, the number of crimes in a given time period at each facility needs to be known, and then the facilities ranked from those with the most crimes to those with the fewest. If a bar chart of the crime frequency is drawn, a few facilities at the left end of this distribution will have many crimes, but as one moves to the right there will be a steep drop-off in crimes that flattens out at a very few or no crimes for the majority of the facilities. The resulting graph resembles a reclining J. A number of such distributions will be shown below.

The concentration represented by the J-curve is not peculiar to crime and disorder, but is practically a universal law (Bak, 1999). A small portion of the earth's surface holds the majority of life on earth. Only a small proportion of earthquakes cause most of the earthquake damage. A small portion of the population holds most of the wealth. A small proportion of police officers produce most of the arrests resulting in prosecution (Forst et al., 1982; Forst et al., 1977). In more popular terms, this kind of distribution is commonly referred to as the 80-20 rule: 20% of some things are responsible for 80% of the outcomes (Kock, 1999). In practice, it is seldom exactly 80-20, but it is always a small percentage of something or some group involved in a large percentage of some result. As we will see in the final section of this paper, the J-curve is symptomatic of a class of processes that can help explain how crime concentrations form.

Our literature search identified 37 studies of specific kinds of facilities that included data about variations in the risks of crime, disorder or misconduct (see the Appendix). The studies cover a wide range of different facilities (for example, banks, bars, schools, sports facilities and parking structures) and many different kinds of crime and deviance (for example, robbery, theft, assaults and disorder). While all studies reported considerable variations in risks, not all provided clear evidence that risks were highly skewed so that a small proportion of the facilities accounted for a large proportion of the crime disorder or misconduct. Those that do (in some cases data were recalculated to show this) are identified in the Appendix with an asterisk in order to distinguish from those that merely establish that some facilities were of higher risk than others. This does not mean that risks for the second group were not highly skewed – only that the data did not allow the distribution of risk to be examined.

From this review, it appears that crime in any population of similar facilities in a geographic area and time period will be highly concentrated in a few facilities, while most of the facilities will have relatively few or even no crimes. When crimes are infrequent and short time periods are examined, this concentration will not be readily apparent (e.g., a year's worth of data may be sufficient to detect J-curves for disorders and many types of thefts, but for homicides and stranger rapes, many years of data may be required for a J-curve to become evident).

VARIETIES OF CONCENTRATION AT FACILITIES

Let us look at some examples of facility analysis drawn from data supplied by crime analysts in several cities across the United States. These examples illustrate, again, the ubiquity of the J-curve, but we must offer this caveat. This is not a test of a hypothesis because we requested these data to show how common this phenomenon is. Consequently, these examples are further demonstrations of the plausibility of a hypothesis.

Figure 1 shows the distribution of calls to the police for all 15 bars located in Shawnee, Kansas for over two years. These bars are ranked from highest to lowest. We have substituted letters for the names of each bar. Two things to note about the chart: (1) most bars have few calls, and (2) a very few have many calls. In this example, the worst three bars (F, M, and J) comprise 20% of the bars but account for 62% of reports.

The same pattern can be seen in Figure 2. This figure shows shoplifting reports made by 78 stores in Danvers, Connecticut. Seventeen out of 78 stores had three or more shoplifting incidents. In addition to these stores, there were 7 stores with 2 cases, 28 stores with 1 incident, and 26

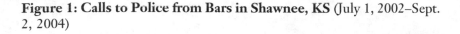

Figure 1: Calls to Police from Bars in Shawnee, KS (July 1, 2002–Sept. 2, 2004)

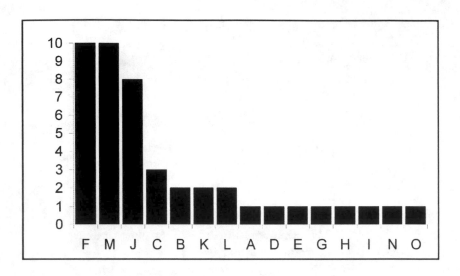

stores with no reported shoplifting. Over all, 20.3% of the stores contribute 84.9% of the shoplifting cases.

These examples have not differentiated among crime types. Yet as can be seen in Figure 3, when crimes are differentiated (in this case property and violent crimes), the J-curve persists. In this example, from Jacksonville, Florida, we are looking at 269 apartment complexes, each with over 50 units. We are examining only complexes with one or more calls, unlike the previous examples where we looked at all facilities in the jurisdiction. In each panel of Figure 3, 20% of the apartment complexes contribute about 47% of the crime (clearly, the concentration would be more extreme if apartment complexes with no calls to the police were included). Though we expect the J-curve to persist when we become more crime-specific, we do not expect that each type of crime will be equally concentrated. That is, we always expect a J-curve, but some of the curves may be more pronounced than the others.

What occurs when we become more facility-specific and subdivide the places? The Chula Vista (CA) Police Department conducted a study of motel crime. The data, graphed in Figure 4, suggests an answer. Panel

Figure 2: Shoplifting Reports from Stores in Danvers, CT (Oct. 1, 2003–Sept. 30, 2004)

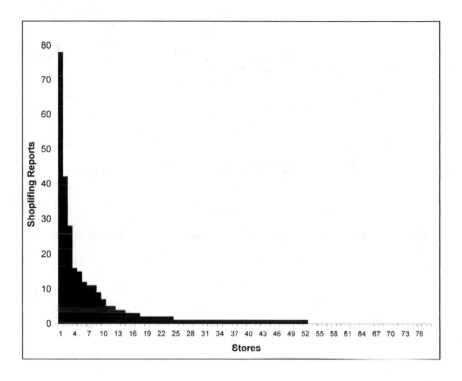

A shows the J-curve for all 26 motels in the city. The top 5 (19%) of the motels contribute 51.1% of the motel calls. Some of the 26 motels are locally owned and some are parts of national chains. The two groups of motels contributed about equal numbers of calls in 2003 (1,106 from the 16 locals and 983 from the 10 national chains). When we examine both types of motels separately, we see the same shape distribution. The top 20% of the local motels contributed about 50% of the calls from these types of motels. The top 20% of the national chain motels contributed 53.6% of the calls from national chain motels.

Though there is overall similarity between the chain and non-chain distributions, an examination of the source of the concentration reveals an important difference. The concentration of the national chain motels

Figure 3: Crime Incidents from Apartment Complexes with Over 50 Units, Jacksonville, FL (Sept. 1, 2003–August 31, 2004)

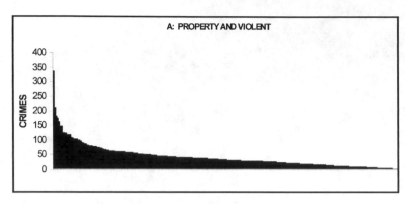

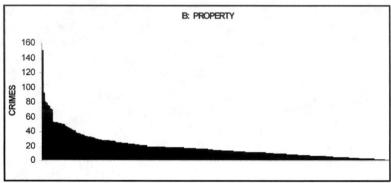

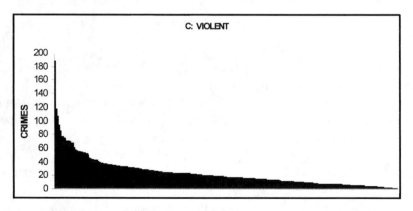

Figure 4: Calls from Motels, Chula Vista, CA – 2003

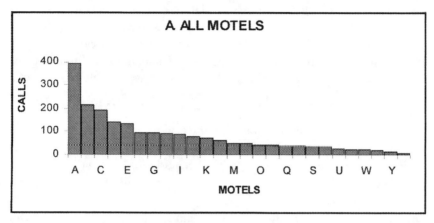

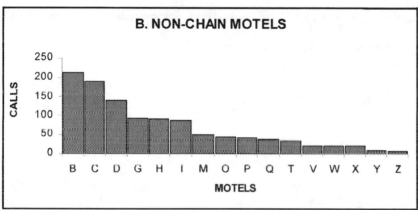

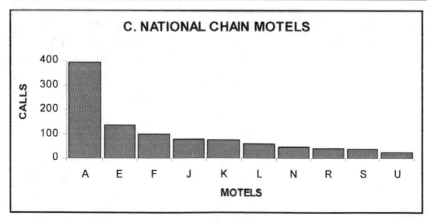

is largely due to one motel (A), whereas the concentration in the local motels is shared among several motels.

Though we will discuss the practical implications of this sort of analysis later, it is worth pointing out a specific implication. By separating the type of motel, crime prevention professionals can locate the locus of control, and this has implications for attaining improvements in facility practices. Getting a local business owner to change practices is likely to involve a different sort of persuasion than getting a national chain to change practices.

These four examples demonstrate the prevalence of the concentration of crime in facilities. We should expect to find the J-curve; the exceptions will be when it is not found. Further, we hypothesize that the J-curve will be found in every form of specificity: crime type, facility type, time period, geographic area, and other subdivisions. In most cases the J-curve will only disappear when the numbers of facilities or crimes become few in number (e.g., a street corner with three gas stations will not reveal a J-curve of gas station robberies because there will be too few robberies and gas stations, but given an area with a large number of gas stations, and sufficient time for a large number of robberies to occur, the J-curve will appear). There may be exceptions to this rule, but we believe that such exceptions will be relatively uncommon.

WHAT CAUSES RISKY FACILITIES?

Are there differences in the characteristics of the facilities at the left and right ends of these J-curves that cause the differences in crime? Answering this question should give us some insight into what can be done to reduce crime. In this section we will look at five possible answers: random variation, crime reporting, targets, offenders, and place management. We do not expect one of these answers to be true (and the others false) in all circumstances, rather we expect that in any given circumstance some of these answers will be more relevant than in other circumstances. As we will explain, it is virtually impossible to have only one answer.

Random Variation

This explanation simply claims that the distribution of crimes across facilities is a fluke: If one looked at a group of facilities at different time periods, the facilities with the most (and least) crime would radically change. In short, there is nothing systematically different about the high crime and low crime facilities. In some circumstances this is likely to be the case. And in such circumstances the appropriate crime reduction approach is to ignore the high crime facilities: They will get better on their own and other facilities will get worse, and we will not be able to predict which will get better or worse, and how much.

The evidence from studies of geographic hot spots suggests that this explanation cannot be discounted; some hot spots improve on their own and new ones appear. But these studies also show that some crime concentrations are stable over long periods (Spelman, 1995a, 1995b; Weisburd et al., 2004).

There are two ways of testing for random instability. The first is to apply a significance test to determine if the observed distribution is sufficiently different from a randomly generated distribution; if it is not, we cannot reject the possibility that random fluctuation is the cause of the observed distribution. However, when examining very large numbers of facilities and crimes, significance tests will reject randomness as a plausible answer. So significance tests are most useful when the numbers of facilities and crimes are few and crime is only slightly concentrated.

A second approach is to examine the distribution at different time periods. If facilities do not radically change position – those on top tend to stay on top and those at the bottom tend to stay at the bottom – then we can reject the hypothesis that random instabilities are an important cause. One example is provided by Clarke and Martin (1975), who examined absconding rates in three groups of training schools for juvenile offenders in the United Kingdom: 17 "senior" schools for boys aged 15-17 on admission; 22 "intermediate" schools for boys aged 13-15; and 20 "junior" schools for boys aged up to 13 on admission. There was wide variation in the absconding rates for each group: for example, the rates of absconding in the senior schools ranged between 10% and 75% of those resident in each school during 1964. This variation was highly stable between 1964 and 1966: for senior schools it was 0.65, for intermediate schools 0.56 and for junior schools 0.43. Very few of the same boys would have been in each school during the two years compared, which suggested that regime variables, rather than random variations or "offender" variables, were the main determinants of the stability in absconding rates.

Reporting Processes

The variation in shoplifting reports from Danvers (CT) stores could be due to store policies regarding the detection of shoplifting and bringing shoplifters to police attention. It might not have much to do with the actual distribution of thefts from these stores (e.g., a store at the extreme right end of the distribution might have as many or more shoplifting incidents as one at the extreme left end, but the store fails to detect the thefts, or if they do detect them, they do not report them to the police). This is an example of the reporting process causing the distribution. Any time the managers of facilities control the reporting process, this hypothesis is a plausible contender.

Careful examination of how facility managers discover crime and the circumstances under which they report it is the best method for diagnosing this particular cause. Some reporting variation among facilities is to be expected, particularly as police presence is often perceived as having an adverse economic consequence. But the ability of facility managers to suppress crime reporting probably varies across facilities. The managers of the Chula Vista mobile home parks, for example, probably cannot control crime reports to the extent that Danvers store managers can control shoplifting reports. And managers may have more control over some crimes than others. The Danvers store managers probably can control shoplifting reports more than they can control reports of vehicle thefts from their parking lots.

Targets

The quantity and quality of targets can also be a cause of extreme variation in crime within a set of facilities. Some facilities are larger than others. Everything else being equal, we would expect big facilities to have more crime than smaller facilities, and if there are many small facilities of a given type, and few large ones, this might account for the J-curve we observe. Paul and Patricia Brantingham refer to places with high numbers of crime due to many targets as *crime generators* (Brantingham and Brantingham, 1995). It is easy to dismiss the concept of risky facilities based on target numbers, but size is often not the full explanation.

The simplest test for whether size is an important contributor is to divide the crimes by the size of each facility to get a measure of risk. If risk is constant, then size is the most important explanation. But if targets in some facilities have higher risks than in other facilities, then size is not the entire explanation. Figure 5 shows two risk distributions, one for Chula Vista motels and one for Jacksonville apartment complexes. Both graphs show that some facilities have much higher risks than others, indicating that in these examples, the number of targets is at best an incomplete explanation.

The "quality" of targets may also make a difference. If some vehicles are particularly desirable to thieves, and these cars tend to cluster in some parking lots, then such parking facilities might have a very high level of vehicle theft, even if the overall number of vehicles in these lots is relatively small. Stores that stock "hot products" (Clarke, 1999) may have many more thefts than similar stores that do not.

Similarly, high crime facilities may differ from otherwise similar low crime facilities by having more repeat victims. The total number of possible victims may be about equal, but for some reason there are a few victims who are repeatedly attacked at the high crime facilities. And repeat victims are infrequent at the low crime facilities.

The test for the target quality explanation is to examine the distribution of crime across facilities for specific target types. One would want to examine both the number of crimes and the rate of crime, relative to the specific targets being examined. If particular targets are the cause, then facilities with such targets will have both a higher number of crimes and a higher rate of crime for these particular targets relative to other targets at the same locations.

Offenders

All crimes need offenders; just as they need targets. So offenders must be part of any explanation, but this will never be the complete explanation. There are two types of offender explanations. First, some facilities may attract many offenders. The Brantinghams call such places *crime attractors* (Brantingham and Brantingham, 1995). However, we do not need many offenders to produce many crimes at a facility; just a few highly active offenders will be sufficient.

As important as these explanations are, they raise more questions than they answer. In particular, why are many offenders attracted to a few facilities and not to many other similar facilities? Why are a few offenders so highly active in a few places but not in many other similar facilities? In short, what makes the few high crime facilities so attractive to offenders?

Traditionally, criminologists have answered such questions by suggesting that the few high crime places are located near areas with many

Figure 5: Two Examples of the Effect of Size on Risky Facilities

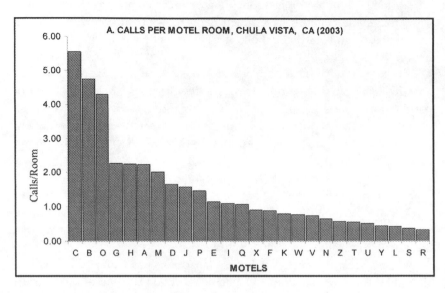

A. CALLS PER MOTEL ROOM, CHULA VISTA, CA (2003)

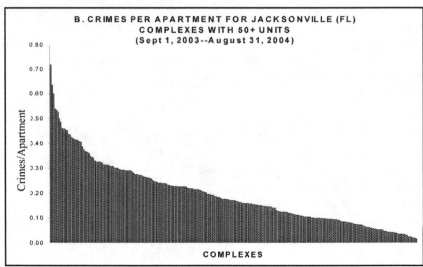

B. CRIMES PER APARTMENT FOR JACKSONVILLE (FL) COMPLEXES WITH 50+ UNITS (Sept 1, 2003--August 31, 2004)

offenders, but most of the similar low crime places are located somewhere else. This explanation is probably true in some circumstances, but like each explanation we have discussed, it is unlikely to be anything close to a universal rule. When the Chula Vista Police Department looked at the locations of motels they found that all of them – high and low crime – were located in high crime areas (Chief's Community Advisory Committee, 2004).

This explanation can be tested in two ways. First, one can look at facilities in close proximity to each other. If all close-by similar facilities have similar levels of crime, but their crime levels are different from similar facilities in other neighborhoods, then proximity to offenders is a potentially useful explanation. However, if crime levels vary a great deal with the neighborhood, or crime levels are similar across neighborhoods then this is a less useful explanation.

Second, if the people caught committing crimes in the high crime facilities live near these facilities, but the people committing crimes in the low crime places traveled further, then proximity to offender populations may be part of the explanation. But if offenders travel about the same distances to both types of facilities, then proximity is an unlikely explanation.

Another offender explanation is that they are differentially attracted by facilities. That is, some facilities have features that help offenders, but most do not. One feature that might attract offenders is many targets, or particularly desirable targets. These are both target-related explanations, which we have examined earlier. Another feature that offenders might find attractive is the lack of place management: the owners and operators of the few high crime facilities are not as scrupulous about regulating conduct at their facilities compared to most similar facilities. Or the physical layout of the high crime facilities makes offending easier than is the case with the low crime facilities. These are both place explanations, which we will come to next.

Place Management

Just as targets and offenders have a role in explaining high crime facilities, so do place characteristics. Place characteristics are under the control of the people who own and manage the facility (Eck, 2003). In stores, this includes the products stocked, the way they are displayed, the opening and closing hours, and a host of other characteristics. In bars, management controls: how drinks are dispensed; the prices charged; what entertainment is provided; how bartenders handle intoxicated patrons; the types of customers being catered to; the employment, training, and rules for bouncers, bar tenders, and other staff; and many other conditions (Homel and Clark, 1994). At motel and hotels, management controls: how reservations are taken; whether ID is examined at check-in; the establishment and enforcement of rules; hours of staffing; and many other things. In all facilities, management controls many aspects of the physical layout of the location. And management has a strong influence over the security of the site against a wide variety of crimes. So place management directly influences many things related to targets and offenders, as well as how they can interact at the location. We have termed places where management practices allow crime to occur, *crime enablers* (Clarke and Eck, 2003).

Comparing the way similar facilities with different crime levels are managed can test crime enabling. If compared to low crime facilities, the high crime locations have fewer rules, lax enforcement, easy access, poor security, and other features that help offenders detect targets, commit crimes, and get away, then place management is an important explanation. If the high crime facilities have many targets or more highly desirable targets (either hot products or repeat victims) compared to low crime facilities, but managers do little to enhance target protection, this also suggests place management is at the heart of the problem.

There is no single universal explanation for why a few facilities have far more crime than most other facilities. For any particular set of facilities the full explanation will involve a combination of the five explanations we have discussed, though the relative contribution of each explanation will vary. Crimes cannot occur without the interaction of offenders, targets and places. There will always be some level of instability. And when using official police records, the crime reporting process will have some influence. So the concentration of crime at a few facilities can seldom be dismissed as a random fluke or "just a lot of targets" or active offenders. On the other hand, the combinations of factors that contribute to such concentrations suggest multiple approaches to reducing crime at the high crime facilities.

MEASURING CONCENTRATION ACROSS FACILITIES

Throughout this discussion we have taken measurement as an assumption. Here we want to briefly describe seven issues that need to be considered in empirical examinations of risky facilities. These issues are common to the family of crime concentration concepts.

Frequency of Events

If the events being examined are common, then it will be relatively easy to describe the distribution of crimes per facility. It will be harder to empirically describe the J-curve for rare events. We would hypothesize that stranger sexual assaults in public parks follow a J-curve. But testing this hypothesis will be difficult because sexual assaults are not common. Many years of data will be required before the curve becomes apparent (see Time Window).

Time Windows

The longer the time period over which a homogeneous set of facilities is studied the more accurate the depiction of the J-curve. This is particularly true when the events under consideration are scarce. Short period estimates with rare events are unlikely to show a crime distribution distinguishable from random variation. Over a sufficiently long time, almost all facilities will have some crime event, but even if it is difficult to distinguish between the zero-event and one-event facilities, there still will be a big difference between the left and right extremes on the J-curve. However, very long time periods can produce results confounded by changes in facilities – some may go out of business, others may come into being, and others may be altered, both physically and managerially.

Address Matching

Any study of crime concentration depends on accurate attribution of crime events to the people, places, or things of interest. This is no less true of risky facilities. Two types of errors are possible. The first is underreporting. This will result in an underestimate of crime concentration. Over reporting is also possible. Corner locations may be assigned more crimes in police reports, for example, if police find it easier to record the address to intersections. This will overestimate crime concentration (Farrell and Pease, 2003).

Frequency of Facility Types

Some facilities are more common than others in any area. If the number of facilities in an area is very small, then the J-curve may not be readily apparent. In a moderate sized city, there will be very few hospitals, for example. Given at least two facilities, it is likely that one has more crime events (of any particular type) than the other. This may have some very practical consequences, but for examining the overall distribution the population is too small. Using a much larger region might be productive.

Zero-event Facilities

Our thesis is that given any sufficiently large population of homogeneous facilities the modal number of crime events will be zero. But zero-event facilities may be invisible if police data is the sole source of information. This is because police data only shows locations with one or more events. If a regulatory authority licenses the facilities under study (for example, locations that serve alcohol), then data from the regulatory agency can be compared to the police data to estimate the number of zero-event facilities. It may be difficult to get accurate counts of facilities that are not required to register with some authority.

Facility Size

If we are trying to estimate the risk of the average target at each facility, then we will need some indicator of how many targets are found at each facility. Target counts are usually unavailable. One reason is that the number of targets may be variable – the number of vehicles in a parking facility will vary by time of day, day of week, and season of the year, for example. One option is to hand count targets at multiple time periods. Another is to estimate average target numbers from business records (for examples, motel room occupancy rates adjusted for average number of occupants per room). A third is to use an indirect measure of targets, such as counting parking spaces in downtown parking facilities as a proxy for vehicles at risk of theft or break-in (Clarke and Goldstein, 2001).

Crime Event Data Sources

There is no single best source of crime event data for examining risky facilities. Police reports are useful because the data is readily available for a wide variety of crime events. However, reporting problems (see address matching) and lack of information about facilities without crime (see zero-event facilities) may seriously distort J-curve estimates. Business surveys based on samples of facilities can avoid many of the reporting and zero-event problems. And surveys can be used to collect information on size and targets at risk. However, sample surveys may not have sufficient numbers of the types of facilities needed, or might not collect sufficient information to classify accurately facilities by type. And unless the sample size is very large, it is likely to exclude the rare many-event facilities. Rather than make a strong (and only weakly defensible) claim for a particular data source, we take a more pragmatic approach. Any study must be able to defend the data source relative to the particular questions being asked, the feasible alternatives available, and likely errors in estimates.

FACILITIES AND PREVENTION

The first, and most important, implication from this discussion is that it is productive to divide places by facility type and focus prevention on homogeneous sets of facilities. This is a logical extension of the first principle of Situational Crime Prevention: be crime-specific. Analysis of crime across a heterogeneous set of places is far less likely to reveal effective interventions than analysis that controls for facility type. This may seem contrary to our argument that the J-curve can be found when analyzing crime in any homogeneous set of facilities, and our argument that all five explanations we have examined contribute to producing J-curves. Indeed, there may very well be a common process that leads to J-curves, regardless of type of facility or crime. Nevertheless, details are all-important when it comes to selecting preventive measures.

The second implication is that focusing on the most troublesome facilities will have greater payoff than spreading prevention across all facilities, most of which have little or no crime. This is an extension of the principle that one should focus on the most active offenders, most victimized victims, and the hottest places.

The third implication is that any prevention measure will have to involve the people who own and run the facilities. Whether the concentration of crime is largely due to reporting, targets, offenders, or place management, the people with the obligation and authority to make changes that can prevent crime, are the people who control the space (Laycock, 2004; Scott, 2005).

The very fact that only a few facilities, in a set of similar facilities, have a great deal of crime raises several questions. What are place managers at most facilities doing that is not being done at the high crime locations?

Why aren't these things being done at the high crime facilities? And how can one get the high crime facilities to adopt necessary crime prevention? There are five general answers.

Circumstances

The high crime facilities may face different circumstances than the low crime facilities. Even though they follow the same practices, the practices are ineffective at the high crime places. Special crime prevention efforts for the few high crime facilities need to be created in these circumstances.

Ignorance

Place managers at the high crime facilities may be unaware of what they should be doing. This might occur when communications among facility managers and owners is limited. Training programs to transfer information from the knowledgeable low crime facilities to high crime facilities could help here.

Cost

The high crime facilities might face higher costs for prevention than the low crime facilities. This could occur if the high crime facilities are in older structures that are more costly to adapt to modern crime prevention standards. Old structures, for example, sometimes contain lead pipes, asbestos, and other materials that are costly to handle. Newly built structures do not contain these materials, making renovation easier and cheaper. Similarly, high crime facilities might have less revenue to spend on prevention than newer facilities. The lack of prevention may be a cost cutting method. This is most likely when the cost of crime falls more on place users than facility owners. Intimidation is the threat of a cost. Place managers might be reluctant to change if they expect to bear a high cost imposed by offenders. Lowering the costs of prevention to the facilities' owners might help in these circumstances. Examples of this include subsidized toxic waste removal to facilitate renovation, low interest loans, extra police protection, and other similar efforts.

Profit

Owners might profit from the criminal activity. At the extreme, they may be involved directly in its production. Owners might not be involved, but their employees are. However, owners might simply feed off of deviant activity, without them or their employees having any direct involvement. For example, drug dealers and buyers might make up a disproportionate share of the customers to a convenience store and account for most of the sales. Though the store's owner might wish they were involved in a legitimate activity, he might ignore their illegal pursuits because the offenders are his best customers.

Accountability

All of the above remedies (with the partial exception of the last) assume that place managers will do the right thing if they are provided with the ability. This assumption is not always valid. It is usually cheaper to shift responsibility for a crime problem to someone else, such as the police. Consequently, it is often useful to make facility owners responsible and accountable for crime on their property. There are several methods for this, all of which increase the cost of non-compliance.

1. *Publicity.* The much greater risk of using a particular facility than of using other similar facilities, could be made known to the public. If the public acts on this information, then the facility could loose business.

2. *Sanctions.* Local governments use civil procedures to shut down facilities that are persistent trouble spots and whose owners do not attempt to address the problem. There is considerable evidence that the threat of civil sanctions can be quite effective (Eck, 2002). Sanctions can vary from fines, loss of operating licenses, to closure of the facility.

3. *Certification programs.* The police or local authority might certify premises and facilities for their security. These certification programs could be voluntary or compulsory. Police in the U.K. operate a voluntary safe car parks scheme of this kind.

4. *Voluntary codes of practice.* The managers or owners of a class of facilities in a particular region or locality might agree to follow certain practices designed to reduce crime. Examples would be the "accords" made between the managers of pubs and clubs in entertainment districts in Melbourne, Surfers Paradise (Homel et al., 1997), Geelong (Felson et al., 1997), and elsewhere in Australia to reduce drink-related violence.

5. *Performance Standards.* Recently, the Chula Vista Police Department has been experimenting with the use of performance standards (Chief's

Community Advisory Committee, 2004). Based on the analysis of crime frequency and negations, a maximum number of crimes is established for facilities of a particular type. This standard may be expressed as a rate, to account for size. Facilities that exceed the performance standards are sanctioned.[2] Along the same lines, the Oakland Police Department (2003) in California entered into an agreement with a motel chain that the chain would significantly reduce crime and disorder at one of its problem motels in the city. This agreement was guaranteed by a "performance bond," which required the chain to pay $250,000 to the city if the goal were not reached within two years. It was left to the motel chain to decide which security measures to introduce, and it decided to upgrade lighting and fencing, replace the managers and security guards, conduct pre-employment background checks on all new employees, establish strict check-in procedures with a list of banned individuals, and prohibit room rentals for more than 30 days. Crime was greatly reduced by this initiative, which earned the project the Herman Goldstein Award for Excellence in Problem-Oriented Policing for 2003.

In practice, a combination of approaches might be the best strategy. One reason for this is that facility owners can be politically powerful, and it is far easier to reduce crime if they are cooperative than if one has to engage in a political battle. So providing both carrots and sticks might be the best strategy.

TO A THEORY OF RISKY FACILITIES

In this paper we have argued that the distribution of crime across a population of similar facilities follows a J-curve: a few of the facilities account for most of the crime in these facilities. We suggest that this distribution is the norm and that regardless of how one subdivides the crime or the facilities one is interested in, the distribution will have the same basic J-shape. The implications of this are straightforward: focus on the high crime members of the facility set and, if one is successful at driving down crime at these locations, the overall crime level for all facilities in the set will decline. The flip side of this argument is just as obvious: focusing on all the facilities, and particularly the low crime facilities, will have little impact and will have greater costs per crime prevented than the recommended approach. How one addresses the high crime facilities depends on why these facilities have more crime than their cousins. We have provided five interrelated explanations – as well as diagnostic tests – for why some facilities have far more crime than most similar facilities. We have argued that to address any of these underlying causes (with the exception of instability) will require the involvement of the owners and managers of these places. And in the previous section we have described a number of strategies for dealing with owners.

Throughout our discussion we have compared the facilities at the two ends of the distribution – what characteristics do the high crime facilities possess that are not possessed by the low crime facilities? Such characteristics suggest explanations for the crime discrepancies. These types of comparisons can be readily carried out using case-control studies. Case-control studies, unlike most other study designs, stratify and select cases based on the dependent variable. They are particularly useful when the outcome of interest is relatively rare (Loftin and McDowall, 1988). This is certainly true with risky facilities. The high crime facilities are rare relative to the norm so a probability sample will have to be large if a sufficient number of the risky facilities are to be found in the sample. In a case-control study, one selects a sample of high and of low crime facilities, thus assuring that there are sufficient cases in both categories to make useful distinctions. One then collects data on the relevant independent variables (e.g., size, management practices, physical characteristics, neighborhood, etc.). Such studies have been used to examine drug dealing locations (Eck, 1994) and convenience store robberies (Hendricks et al., 1999).

Cross-sectional studies of facility populations at one time period can tell us how high and low crime facilities differ and suggest what forms of interventions make the most sense. But such studies cannot provide a full explanation. They do not explain how the distribution of facilities came to be J-shaped. Given the prevalence of this distribution, an explanation is necessary.

We have assumed that facilities in a given population are independent of each other; for example, that the bars in Shawnee (Figure 1) can be treated as separate entities. This assumption may hide a deeper understanding. As we mentioned at the outset, concentrations like those we have been examining among facilities are common throughout nature. As noted at the beginning of this paper, the J-shaped distributions like those we have been examining often can be described by a power function. Recent theories of physics and biology suggest that power functions and their distributions are the result of the interaction of multiple agents in complex adaptive systems (Cowan et al., 1999).

Consider a crime pattern that has received extremely little attention but is familiar (in part) to every university-based academic: student party disturbances in rental apartments. The basic components of this problem are a street network around a university; a population of apartment complexes containing variable numbers of apartments; landlords who rent these properties to students; students who rent them; students who host parties; students who attend parties; and other users of the area around the campus. Though we have no data to demonstrate this point, we predict that if one collected the relevant data, one would observe a variety of J-curves: for both apartment units and complexes; the frequency of parties; the size of parties; noise level generated by parties; calls to the police about such parties; and a host of other related phenomena.[3] These distributions would be the result of the complex interactions of the agents as: students sort themselves among rental units, parties, and other students; landlords make decisions on how they will regulate tenant behavior and where they will purchase rental housing; and other agents (e.g., non-student residents of the area, local businesses, and police) make individual decisions. The individual, and largely uncoordinated, decisions among all these agents, in the same area, will create a situation in which most rental properties have few, small, quiet parties, but a few will have many, large, noisy parties. At the far extreme will be alcohol-related student disturbances.

In short, *the J-curves of crime are an emergent macro property of the interaction of individual decisions.* Offenders, targets, and place managers make choices, which other offenders, targets and place managers respond to. The choices of owners of bars, apartment complexes, motels, gas stations, or other facilities have impacts on the choices of offenders and targets. For example, a bar owner who selects country music is not likely to attract many patrons who prefer hip-hop. If offenders congregate at a convenient storefront, scaring off other customers, then the storeowner may decide to cater to their needs. If some drivers avoid high theft parking lots, the drivers who continue to park in these lots will either have to choose to invest in better vehicle security, or become repeat victims. The security-conscious drivers who refuse to park in these lots will park in other locations, reinforcing the security choices of these lot owners.

The developing field of complexity describes the processes we have been describing: " . . . (C)omplex systems contain many relatively independent parts which are highly interconnected and interactive and that a large number of such parts are required to reproduce the functions of truly complex, self-organizing, replicating, learning, and adaptive systems" (Cowan, 1999). If we are correct, then researchers need to examine populations of facilities as parts of larger systems, and policy makers (including crime analysts and other police officials) should similarly focus on sets of facilities rather than attempting to understand each high crime facility as a separate problem.

Address correspondence to: john.eck@uc.edu

Acknowledgments: We would like to thank Tracey Belledin, Christopher Bruce, Nanci Plouffe, Karin Schmerler, Susan Wernicke, and Matt White for their considerable assistance as well as two anonymous reviewers for their insightful comments.

NOTES

1. Power Law, Zipf's Law and Pareto's Law functions are three closely related concepts (Adamic, no date; also see, Simon, 1955). Following Adamic we will illustrate this relationship using risky facility terminology. When we want to know the number of crimes at the rth ranked facility, we need to apply Zipf's Law. This is stated as, $C \sim r^{-b}$, where C is the number of events at a facility ranked r by the number of events at that place and b is a shape parameter (the symbol ~ indicates "is proportional to"). Note that we began by ordering all facilities from biggest to smallest by the number of crimes of interest. The rank of each in this ordered list is r, so the facility with the most crimes is the first facility (with r=1). Thus, as the rank increases, the number of crimes in each subsequent facility declines non-linearly. If instead, we are interested in the number of crimes at all facilities that have more than a given number of crimes, then we need to apply Pareto's Law. This law is summarized as, $P(C>c) \sim c^{-k}$, where $P(C>c)$ is the number of crimes, C, at all facilities with more than c crimes. Finally, if we want to know the exact number of crimes at facilities with C crimes, we use a power function, $P(C=c) \sim c^{-a}$, where $P(C=c)$ is the number of crimes at all facilities that have exactly c crimes and a = k+1. The Pareto Law function is a cumulative probability function of a power law and the power function, a probability distribution function. The Zipf Law function is an inverted Pareto Law function – the c and r simply switch axes (Adamic, no date).

2. A variation on this is to adopt a recent innovation in pollution control; creating a market for pollution permits (Stavins, 2002; Tietenberg, 1980). Facilities could be issued permits for a prescribed crime level that they can sell to other facilities. This gives an incentive to reduce crime to below the permit level. Facilities that cannot do so, buy the permits of low crime facilities. If the number of permits is adequately set, then crime would be driven down, low crime facilities would be rewarded, and high crime facilities would pay a penalty (through the market price) for continuing to enable crime.

3. Though far beyond the scope of this enquiry, following recent studies in economics (Axtell, 2001; Luttmer, 2004) we would also predict that the distribution of landlords would by J-shaped: a few landlords owning a large percentage of the student rental properties (whether measured by numbers of buildings, apartments, or square footage), and many landlords owning a few rental properties each.

REFERENCES

Adamic, L. A. (no date). *Zipf, power-laws, and Pareto: A ranking tutorial*. Retrieved March 31, 2005 from: www.hpl.hp.com/research/idl/papers/ranking/ranking. html

Allport, F. H. (1934). The J-curve hypothesis of conforming behavior. *Journal of Social Psychology, 5*, 141-183.

Austin, C. (1988). *The prevention of robbery at building society branches* (vol. 14). London: Home Office.

Axtell, R. L. (2001). Zipf distribution of U.S. firm sizes. *Science, 293*, 1818-1820.

Bak, P. (1999). Self-organized criticality: A holistic view of nature. In G. Cowan, D. Pines and D. Meltzer (Eds.), *Complexity: Metaphors, models, and reality*. Cambridge, MA: Perseus Books.

Bowers, K., Hirschfield, A., & Johnson, S. (1998). Victimization revisited: A case study of non-residential repeat burglary in Merseyside. *British Journal of Criminology, 38*, 429-452.

Brantingham, P. L., & Brantingham, P. J. (1995). Criminality of place: Crime generators and crime attractors. *European Journal on Criminal Policy and Research, 3*, 1-26.

Burquest, R., Farrell, G., & Pease, K. (1992). Lessons From schools. *Policing, 8*, 148-155.

Burrows, J., Anderson, S., Bamfield, J., Hopkins, M., & Ingram, D. (1999). *Counting the cost: Crime against business in Scotland*. Edinburgh, SCOT: Scottish Executive Justice Department.

Chakraborti, N., Gill, M., Willis, A., Hart, J., & Smith, P. (2002). The victimisation of petrol service stations: Crime patterns and implications. *Crime Prevention and Community Safety: An International Journal, 4*, 37-48.

Chief's Community Advisory Committee (2004). *The Chula Vista Motel Project*. Chula Vista, CA: Chula Vista Police Department.

Clarke, R. V. (1996). The distribution of deviance and exceeding the speed limit. *The British Journal of Criminology, 36*, 169-181.

Clarke, R. V. (1999). *Hot products: Understanding, anticipating and reducing demand for stolen goods*. London: Home Office, Research Development and Statistics Directorate.

Clarke, R. V., & Bichler-Robertson, G. (1998). Place managers, slumlords and crime in low rent apartment buildings. *Security Journal, 11*, 11-19.

Clarke, R. V., & Eck, J. E. (2003). *Become a problem-solving crime analyst: In 55 small steps*. London: Jill Dando Institute of Crime Science.

Clarke, R. V., & Goldstein, H. (2001). Thefts from cars in center-city parking facilities: A case study in implementing problem-oriented policing. In J. Knutsson (Ed.), *Problem-oriented policing: From innovation to mainstream*. Crime Prevention Studies, vol. 15. Monsey, NY: Criminal Justice Press. (Accessible online at: www.cops.usdoj.gov.)

Clarke, R. V., & Goldstein, H. (2002). Reducing theft at construction sites: Lessons from a problem-oriented project. In N. Tilley (Ed.), *Analysis for crime prevention*. Crime Prevention Studies, vol. 13 (pp. 89-130). Monsey, NY: Criminal Justice Press.

Clarke, R. V., & Martin, D. N. (1975). A study of absconding and its implications for the residential treatment of delinquents. In J. Tizard, I. Sinclair & R. V. Clarke (Eds.), *Varieties of residential experience*. London: Routledge and Kegan Paul.

Clarke, R. V., & Weisburd, D. (1990). On the distribution of deviance. In D. M. Gottfredson & R. V. Clarke (Eds.), *Policy and theory in criminal justice* (pp. 10-27). Hants, England: Aldershot.

Cowan, G. (1999). Conference opening remarks. In G. Cowan, D. Pines and D. Meltzer (Eds.), *Complexity: Metaphors, models, and reality* (pp. 1-4). Cambridge, MA: Perseus Books.

Cowan, G., Pines, D., & Meltzer, D. (Eds.), (1999). *Complexity: Metaphors, models, and reality*. Cambridge, MA: Perseus Books.

Eck, J. E. (1994). *Drug markets and drug places: A case-control study of the spatial structure of illicit drug dealing*. Unpublished doctoral dissertation, University of Maryland, College Park, MD.

Eck, J. E. (2001). Policing and crime event concentration. In R. Meier, L. Kennedy and V. Sacco (Eds.), *The process and structure of crime: Criminal events and crime analysis* (pp. 249-276). New Brunswick, NJ: Transactions.

Eck, J. E. (2002). Preventing crime at places. In L. W. Sherman, D. Farrington, B. Welsh & D. L. MacKenzie (Eds.), *Evidence-based crime prevention* (pp. 241-294). New York: Routledge.

Eck, J. E. (2003). Police problems: The complexity of problem theory, research and evaluation. In J. Knutsson (Ed.), *Problem-oriented policing: From innovation to mainstream*. Crime Prevention Studies, vol. 15 (pp. 67-102). Monsey, NY: Criminal Justice Press.

Farrell, G., & Pease, K. (1993). *Once bitten, twice bitten: Repeat victimization and its implications for crime prevention*. London: Home Office.

Farrell, G., & Pease, K. (2003). Measuring and interpreting repeat victimization using police data: An analysis of burglary data and policy for Charlotte, North Carolina. In M. J. Smith and D. B. Cornish (Eds.), *Theory for practice in situational crime prevention*. Crime Prevention Studies, vol. 16 (pp. 265-289). Monsey, NY: Criminal Justice Press.

Felson, M., Berends, R., Richardson, B., & Veno, A. (1997). Reducing pub hopping and related crime. In R. Homel (Ed.), *Policing for prevention: Reducing crime, public intoxication and injury*. Crime Prevention Studies, vol. 7 (pp. 115-132). Monsey, NY: Criminal Justice Press.

Fisher, B., & Looye, J. (2000). Crime and small businesses in the Midwest: An examination of overlooked issues in the United States. *Security Journal, 13*, 45-72.

Forst, B., Leahy, F., Shirhall, J., Tyson, H., Wish, E., & Bartolomeo, J. (1982). *Arrest convictability as a measure of police performance*. Washington, DC: U.S. Department of Justice.

Forst, B., Lucianovic, J., & Cox, S. (1977). *What happens after arrest?* Washington, DC: Institute for Law and Social Research.

Gell-Mann, M. (1994). *The Quark and the Jaguar: Adventures in the simple and the complex*. New York: W. H. Freeman.

Gill, M. (1998). The victimisation of business: Indicators of risk and the direction of future research. *International Review of Victimology, 6*, 17-28.

Hendricks, S. A., Landsittel, D. P., Amandus, H. E., Malcan, J., & Bell, J. (1999). A matched case-control study of convenience store robbery risk factors. *Journal of Occupational and Environmental Medicine, 41*, 995-1104.

Hertwig, R., Hoffrage, U., & Martignon, L. (1999). Quick estimation: Letting the environment do some of the work. In G. Girgerenzer, P. M. Todd & A. B. C. R. Group (Eds.), *Simple heuristics that make us smart* (pp. 209-234). New York: Oxford University Press.

Hirschfield, A., & Bowers, K. (1998). Monitoring, measuring and mapping community safety. In A. Marlow & J. Pitts (Eds.), *Planning safer communities* (pp. 189-212). Lyme Regis, UK: Russell House Publishing.

Homel, R., & Clark, J. (1994). The prediction and prevention of violence in pubs and clubs. In R. V. Clarke (Ed.), *Crime prevention studies*. Crime Prevention Studies, vol. 3 (pp. 1-46). Monsey, NY: Criminal Justice Press.

Homel, R., Hauritz, M., McIlwain, G., Wortley, R., & Carvolth, R. (1997). Preventing drunkenness and violence around nightclubs in a tourist resort. In R. V. Clarke (Ed.), *Situational crime prevention: Successful case studies* (2nd ed., pp. 263-282). Monsey, NY: Criminal Justice Press.

Hope, T. (1982). *Burglary in schools: The prospects for prevention*. London: Home Office.

Hopkins, M., & Ingram, D. (2001). Crimes against business: The first Scottish business crime survey. *Security Journal, 14*, 43-59.

Johnston, V., Leitner, M., Shapland, J., & Wiles, P. (1994). *Crime prevention on industrial estates*. London: Home Office.

Kock, R. (1999). *80-20 principle: The secret to success by achieving more with less*. New York: Doubleday.

La Vigne, N. G. (1994). Gasoline drive-offs: Designing a less convenient environment (pp. 91-114). In R. V. Clarke (Ed.), *Crime Prevention Studies*, vol. 2. Monsey, NY: Criminal Justice Press.

Laycock, G. (1977). *Absconding from borstals*. London: Home Office.

Laycock, G. (2004, October 30). *Clarifying responsibility for crime and safety problems: Who is responsible for what?* Paper presented at the 15th Annual Problem-Oriented Policing Conference, Charlotte, NC.

Laycock, G., & Austin, C. (1992). Crime prevention in parking facilities. *Security Journal, 3*, 154-160.

Lindstrom, P. (1997). Patterns of school crime: A replication and empirical extension. *British Journal of Criminology, 37*, 121-130.

Loftin, C., & McDowall, D. (1988). The analysis of case-control studies in criminology. *Journal of Quantitative Criminology, 4*, 85-98.

Luttmer, E. G. J. (2004). *The size distribution of firms in an economy with fixed and entry costs* (Working Paper 633). Minneapolis, MN: Federal Reserve Bank of Minneapolis, Research Department.

Matthews, R., Pease, C., & Pease, K. (2001). Repeat bank robbery: Theme and variations. In G. Farrell & K. Pease (Eds.), *Repeat victimization*. Crime Prevention Studies, vol. 12 (pp. 153-164). Monsey, NY: Criminal Justice Press.

Mirrlees-Black, C., & Ross, A. (1995). *Crime against retail and manufacturing premises: Findings from the 1994 Commercial Victimisation Survey*. London: Home Office.

National Association of Convenience Stores. (1991). *Convenience store security report and recommendations*. Alexandria, VA: National Association of Convenience Stores.

Newton, A. (2004). *Crime and disorder on busses: Toward an evidence base for effective crime prevention*. Unpublished doctoral dissertation, University of Liverpool, Liverpool.

Oakland Police Department (2003). *Oakland Police Department Beat Health Unit*. Oakland, CA: Author.

Perrone, S. (2000). *Crimes against small business in Australia: A preliminary analysis*. Canberra: Australian Institute for Criminology.

Ramsey, M. (1986). Preventing disorder. In K. Heal & G. Laycock (Eds.), *Situational crime prevention: From theory into practice* (pp. 81-89). London: Her Majesty's Stationery Office.

Schroeder, M. (1991). *Fractals, chaos, power laws: Minutes from an infinite universe*. New York: W. H. Freeman.

Scott, M. S. (2005). Policing for prevention: Shifting and sharing the responsibility to address public safety problems. In N. Tilley (Ed.), *Crime prevention handbook*. Cullompton, Devon, UK: Willan.

Sherman, L. S., Gartin, P. R., & Buerger, M. E. (1989). Hot spots of predatory crime: Routine activities and the criminology of place. *Criminology, 27*, 27-55.

Sherman, L. S., Schmidt, J. D., & Velke, R. J. (1992). *High crime taverns: A RECAP Project in Problem-Oriented Policing*. Washington, DC: Crime Control Institute.

Simon, H. A. (1955). On a class of skew distribution functions. *Biometrika, 42*, 425-440.

Smith, D. J., Gregson, M., & Morgan, J. (2003). *Between the lines: An evaluation of the Secured Park Award Scheme*. London: Home Office Research, Development and Statistics Directorate.

Snyder, H., & Sickmund, M. (1999). *Juvenile offenders and victims: 1999 national report*. Washington, DC: U.S. Office of Juvenile Justice and Delinquency Prevention.

Spelman, W. (1994). *Criminal incapacitation*. New York: Plenum.

Spelman, W. (1995a). Criminal careers of public places. In J. E. Eck & D. Weisburd (Eds.), *Crime and place*. Crime Prevention Studies, vol. 4 (pp. 115-144). Monsey, NY: Criminal Justice Press.

Spelman, W. (1995b). Once bitten, then what? Cross-sectional and time-course explanations of repeat victimization. *British Journal of Criminology, 35*, 366-383.

Stavins, R. N. (2002). Lessons from the American experiment with market-based environmental policies. In J. D. Donahue & J. S. N. Jr. (Eds.), *Market-based governance: Supply side, demand side, upside, and downside* (pp. 173-201). Washington, DC: Brookings Institution Press.

Taylor, N. (2002). *Robbery against service stations and pharmacies: Recent trends*. Canberra: Australian Institute for Criminology.

Taylor, N., & Mayhew, P. (2002). *Patterns of victimisation among small retail businesses* (Vol. 221). Canberra: Australian Institute for Criminology.

Tietenberg, T. H. (1980). Transferable discharge permits and the control of stationary source air pollution: A survey and synthesis. *Land Economics, 56*, 391-416.

Townsley, M., Homel, R., & Chaseling, J. (2000). Repeat burglary victimisation: Spatial and temporal patterns. *Australian and New Zealand Journal of Criminology, 33*, 37-63.

Walberg, H. J., Strykowski, B. F., Rovai, E., & Hung, S. S. (1984). Exceptional performance. *Review of Educational Research, 54*, 87-112.

Walker, J. (1996). Crime prevention by businesses in Australia. *International Journal of Risk, Security and Crime Prevention, 1*, 279-291.

Webb, B., Brown, B., & Bennett, K. (1992). *Preventing car crime in car parks*. London: Home Office.

Weisburd, D., Bushway, S., Lum, C., & Yang, S.-M. (2004). Trajectories of crime at places: A longitudinal study of street segments in the city of Seattle. *Criminology, 42*, 283-322.

Weisburd, D., Maher, L., Sherman, L., Buerger, M., Cohn, E., & Petrosino, A. (1992). Contrasting crime general and crime specific theory: The case of hot spots of crime (pp. 45-70). In *Advances in Criminological Theory*. vol. 4. New Brunswick, NJ: Transaction.

Zipf, G. K. (1949). *Human behavior and the principle of least effort: An introduction to human ecology*. Cambridge, MA: Addison-Wesley Press.

Appendix – Research Identifying Crime Concentrations Within Facilities by Type
(*Denotes studies that document a specific level of crime concentration – see text)

AUTHOR/YEAR	SAMPLE	LOCATION	CRIME TYPE	KEY FINDINGS
Apartment complexes				
Clarke & Bichler-Robertson, 1998	Police calls for service at selected properties, 1989-1995.	Santa Barbara, CA, US	All crimes/calls for police service	2 apartment properties owned by one landlord had yearly average calls for service that were 2 to 3 times that of the other apartment properties owned by that landlord.[†]
Banks				
*Austin, 1988	Bank association records comprising 76% of total UK branches (N = 5,236).	UK	Burglaries and robberies	All successful and attempted burglaries and robberies occurred in 5% of building society branches.
Matthews et al., 2001	Police records of attempted and completed robberies from 1992-94.	UK	Robbery	21 (4%) of branches had rates of robbery 4 to 6 times that of other bank branches.[†]

(continued)

Appendix (*continued*)

(*Denotes studies that document a specific level of crime concentration – see text)

AUTHOR/YEAR	SAMPLE	LOCATION	CRIME TYPE	KEY FINDINGS
Bars, pubs, and clubs				
*Homel & Clark, 1994	Purposive observations at 45 sites within 36 facilities conducted in winter 1991. N = 102 incidents of aggression.	Sydney, AUS	Aggressive behavior, violence	11 or 30.5% of the establishments accounted for 83% of physical incidents of aggression.
*Ramsey, 1986	Police records recording crime in public places in 1980, N = 557 incidents.	Central Southampton, UK	All crimes	15% of pubs and clubs accounted for 42% of incidents.
*Sherman et al., 1992	Homicide data, 1980 to 1989; city violation reports, 1960 to 1989; offense reports, 1986 to 1990; police dispatch records, July 1990 to January 1991.	Milwaukee, WI, US	Violent crime	15% of taverns produced over 50% of all tavern crime. 13% of taverns produced 55% of all violent tavern crime. 13% of taverns produced 52% of police dispatch calls.
Bus stop shelters				
*Newton, 2004	Recorded incidents of vandalism (N=15,628) to bus stop shelters (N=3,072) in Liverpool during 2000 to 2002.	Liverpool, UK	Vandalism	25% of bus shelters accounted for 70% of the vandalism.

Appendix (*continued*)

(*Denotes studies that document a specific level of crime concentration – see text)

AUTHOR/YEAR	SAMPLE	LOCATION	CRIME TYPE	KEY FINDINGS
Businesses (various)				
*Burrows et al., 1999	Survey of 2,500 business premises within Scotland.	Scotland	Violent and property crimes	10% of premises experienced 66% of all crimes. 5% of premises experienced 54% of all crimes.
*Fisher & Looye, 2000	Randomly selected survey of small businesses in six states, N=400. Conducted April of 1996.	US	All crimes	12.5% of the businesses experienced all crime incidents.
*Gill, 1998	Survey of 2,618 businesses (sample). Also reports on Small Business and Crime Initiative (SBCI) survey and Commercial Victimisation Survey (CVS).	UK	All crimes	2% of retailers suffered 25% of burglaries and 58% of thefts from vehicles (CVS). 17% of businesses suffered 83% of frauds (SBCI). 3% of businesses suffered 81% of violent attacks (SBCI). 12% of businesses accounted for 76% of burglaries and 92% of the thefts (sample). 5% of businesses experienced 68% of vehicle theft (sample).

(*continued*)

Appendix *(continued)*

(*Denotes studies that document a specific level of crime concentration – see text)

AUTHOR/YEAR	SAMPLE	LOCATION	CRIME TYPE	KEY FINDINGS
*Hopkins & Ingram, 2001	Scottish Business Crime (SBC) survey of 2,500 premises throughout Scotland regarding crime occurring in 1998.	Scotland	All crimes	10% of businesses accounted for 40% of break ins. 10% accounted for 53% incidents of vandalism. 10% accounted for 73% of thefts by non-employees.
Johnston et al., 1994	Survey of 585 tenants on 41 industrial estates performed between April and July of 1990.	UK	Violent and property crimes	A small proportion of industrial estates experienced an annual crime per unit rate reaching 4.9 – the mean crime rate was 0.8.
*Mirrlees-Black & Ross, 1995	National victimization survey of 3,000 commercial premises.	UK	Violent and property crimes	3% of retailers experienced 59% of all retail crime. 2% of manufacturers experienced 25% of all burglaries. 8% of manufacturers experienced almost 75% of all crimes.
*Perrone, 2000	Small Business Crime Survey (SBCS): National survey of small businesses for 1998-99 crimes, N= 4,315.	AUS	All crimes	1% of businesses accounted for 66% of all crime incidents.

Appendix (continued)

(*Denotes studies that document a specific level of crime concentration – see text)

AUTHOR/YEAR	SAMPLE	LOCATION	CRIME TYPE	KEY FINDINGS
*Taylor & Mayhew, 2002	Small Business Crime Survey (SBCS): National survey of small businesses for crimes occurring during the 1998-99 financial year. N= 4,000 businesses.	AUS	All crimes	1.7% of businesses accounted for 24% of burglaries. 1.6% of businesses accounted for 70% of all shoplifting incidents. 6.7% of businesses accounted for 70% of all vandalism.
*Townsley et al., 2000	Police records of 1,750 incidents over 18 months from June 1995 to November 1996.	AUS	Burglary	3% of businesses recorded 20% of burglaries.
*Walker, 1996	National survey of businesses, N=966.	AUS	All crimes	25% of businesses experienced all burglaries.
Construction sites				
*Clarke & Goldstein, 2002	Police records of reported thefts occurring in 1998 in one police district, N = 104. County records of building permits, N = 3,130.	US	Theft	3.3% of houses under construction experienced all of the reported thefts.

(continued)

Appendix (*continued*)

(*Denotes studies that document a specific level of crime concentration – see text)

AUTHOR/YEAR	SAMPLE	LOCATION	CRIME TYPE	KEY FINDINGS
Convenience stores				
*National Association of Convenience Stores, 1991	National survey of convenience stores.	US	Violent crime	6.5% of stores experienced 65% of the robberies.
Fast-food facilities				
*Spelman, 1995b	Police records of calls for service for 34 facilities. between 1990 and 1992. N = 1,801 calls.	San Antonio, TX, US	All crimes	10% of fast food facilities accounted for 32.7% of all crime incidents.
Gas stations				
*Chakraborti et al., 2002	Incident reports of crimes experienced by 4,360 stations. N = 91,969 incidents.	UK	All crimes	28.5% of the *companies* reporting experienced 57% of the incidents.[†]
*La Vigne, 1994	Police records of calls for service from 1988-90.	Austin, TX, US	All crimes	10% of gas stations experienced over 50% of calls for drive offs and drug crimes. 10% accounted for 26% of property crime calls. 10% of stations accounted for 36% of robberies.

Appendix *(continued)*

(*Denotes studies that document a specific level of crime concentration – see text)

AUTHOR/YEAR	SAMPLE	LOCATION	CRIME TYPE	KEY FINDINGS
*Taylor, 2002	National survey of small businesses (SBCS) for 1998-99 crimes; National Crime Statistics; and Recorded Crime Australia.	AUS	Robbery	5% of all gas stations and pharmacies experienced 72% of all reported robberies.
Healthcare facilities				
Bowers et al., 1998	Police records of reported crimes occurring between July 1994 and June 1995. Purposive sample drawn of those experiencing repeat victimizations, N=2,560.	Merseyside, UK	Burglary	17.4% of healthcare facilities experienced revictimization rates that were twice that of 69.6% of all healthcare properties that experienced revictimization.
Hotels				
Oakland Police Department, 2003	Police incident reports and calls for service for 6 area hotels, 1998-2000.	Oakland, CA, US	All crimes/calls for service	1 hotel had incident and arrest rates that were 9 times that of other area hotels.

(continued)

Appendix (continued)

(*Denotes studies that document a specific level of crime concentration – see text)

AUTHOR/YEAR	SAMPLE	LOCATION	CRIME TYPE	KEY FINDINGS
Parking lots				
*Laycock & Austin, 1992	Police records of car crimes in 1983, N = 1427 offences.	Basingstoke, UK	Theft from, of, and damage	5 parking lots accounted for 50% of the crime. Of the 5 parking lots, three accounted for 80% of that 50%.
*Smith et al., 2003	Police records of reported car crimes in 2001 for Nottingham city centre, N=415.	UK	Theft from, of, and damage	21% of parking lots accounted for 44% of crime. 10% of parking lots accounted for 35% of crime.
Webb et al., 1992	Police records of car crimes for three parking lots in three areas of London.	London, UK	Theft from, of, and damage	A few parking lots maintained crime rates that were up to 2.5 times greater than the average rate experienced across parking lots studied.[†]
Schools				
Bowers et al., 1998	Police records of reported crimes occurring from July 1994 to June 1995. Purposive sample drawn of those experiencing repeat victimizations, N=2,560.	Merseyside, UK	Burglary	15.6% of schools experienced revictimization rates that were 3 to 4 times that of over half of all educational properties that experienced revictimization.

Appendix *(continued)*

(*Denotes studies that document a specific level of crime concentration – see text)

AUTHOR/YEAR	SAMPLE	LOCATION	CRIME TYPE	KEY FINDINGS
*Burquest et al., 1992	Police records of 33 schools for 1990	Merseyside, UK	Burglary and criminal damage	18% of the schools (6) reported almost 50% of the crimes.[†]
*Hope, 1982	Official records of incidents. Random sample of 59 comprehensive schools.	London, UK	Burglary	Roughly 33% of the schools experienced 75% of the burglaries.
*Lindstrom, 1997	Police records of 62 randomly drawn and 43 total secondary schools (total N=96) for 1993/94 school year. 1,630 crimes reported.	Stockholm, Sweden	All crimes	10% of schools accounted for 37% of all property crimes. 17% of schools experienced 50% of all school crimes. 8% of schools suffered 50% of violent school crimes.
*Snyder & Sickmund, 1999	National survey of public elementary, middle and high school administrators.	US	Violent crimes	Only 13% of high schools and 12% of middle schools reported incidents of attacks or aggravated assaults. 8% and 5%, respectively, reported robbery and rape or sexual battery. Over all, 21% of high schools and 19% of middle schools reported an incident of serious violent crime to police.

(continued)

Appendix (*continued*)

(*Denotes studies that document a specific level of crime concentration – see text)

AUTHOR/YEAR	SAMPLE	LOCATION	CRIME TYPE	KEY FINDINGS
Sports facilities				
Bowers et al., 1998	Police records of reported crime occurring between July 1994 and June 1995. Purposive sample drawn of those experiencing repeat victimizations, N=2,560.	Merseyside, UK	Burglary	24.6% of sporting facilities experienced rates of revictimization that were 2 or more times that of 47% of all sporting facilities.
Telephone booths (kiosks)				
*Hirschfield & Bowers, 1998	Telephone calls made to police from 1992 to July 1997.	Merseyside, UK	Hoax calls	20% of the hoax calls came from 3% of the phone booths. 51% of the hoax calls came from 14% of the phone booths.
Young offender institutions				
Clarke & Martin, 1975	59 junior, intermediate, and senior training schools	UK	Absconding	A few training schools maintained absconding rates that were 5 to 6 times that of the other schools.
Laycock, 1977	Records from 22 Borstals from 1969 and 1974	UK	Absconding	Some borstals experienced 2 to 4 times the average absconding rate found across all borstals.

† Calculated by present authors.

Repeat Victimization
of Prison Inmates

by

Michael Townsley
**Jill Dando Institute of Crime Science,
University College London**

and

Graham Farrell
**Midlands Centre for Criminology and Criminal Justice,
Loughborough University**

Abstract: *Inspired and led by the work of Ken Pease, research into the prevention of repeat victimization has progressed significantly over the last two decades. Here, a victimization survey of prison inmates is examined. It shows that most victimizations of inmates by other inmates are repeats, that most victimizations of inmates by prison staff are repeats, and that inmates who report victimization of one type are more prone to other types of victimization. Likewise, inmates who report discrimination in their access to facilities and services are more likely to report multiple types of discrimination. Further, inmates who are victimized by other inmates are also more likely to be victimized by prison staff and to be discriminated against. While prison facilities might be expected to be a challenging environment in which to develop the prevention of repeat victimization, this should not preclude some effort.*

Crime Prevention Studies, volume 21 (2007), pp. 265–277.

INTRODUCTION

The study of repeat victimization has progressed significantly in the two decades since Ken Pease directed the Kirkholt burglary prevention project (Forrester et al., 1988; Pease 1991). Types of repeat victimization identified to date are listed in Table 1. The types of repeat often overlap. A repeat bank robbery involves the same target but may also involve the same offender using the same method – even if that method is brandishing a banana in a paper bag to make it look like a gun. Repeat victimization is known to cluster in time, one crime following another in quick succession. Hot spots of spatial repeats are often focused on the same target (Pease and Laycock, 1996), but when different crimes occur in close proximity (such as assaults, robbery, and drug dealing at a bar, or theft and robbery from a store), then it is the spatial repetition of the location that is the common factor of such risky facilities (see Eck et al., this volume).

Much recent progress has built on Pease's (1998) notion of virtual repeats, which ingeniously combined elements of tactical, crime-type, spatial and offender repeats to describe victimization of similar targets in comparable circumstances. The successive mugging of identical twins was his hypothetical limiting case for illustration, but break-ins to identical

Table 1: Types of Repeat Victimization

- *Target repeats* – the repeated victimization of the same target, whether a person, place, vehicle or other target however defined.
- *Tactical repeats* – includes frequent theft of hot products, is an element of burglary of similar-design households, and other repetitive crimes linked by target characteristics and/or *modus operandi*.
- *Spatial repeats* – crime repeated within a certain spatial proximity, captured on maps as hot dots or hot spots, risky facilities, and sometimes involving different types of crime.
- *Crime-type repeats* – offenders repeat the same types of crime because they have the resources, ability and/or skills and experience. Same-crime repeats against the same target or virtual target are more likely.
- *Temporal repeats* – crimes committed quickly to maximize perceived benefits, or perhaps as a spree, often linked to spatial and tactical repetition. Repeats against the same target as well as virtual repeats cluster in time.
- *Offender repeats* – the role and prominence of repeat offending has been well established. Repeats are more likely to be committed by the same offenders.

cars and same-layout houses, or racially-motivated attacks against persons of similar skin color, are the more likely reality (see Townsley et al., 2003 on near-repeat burglaries). High rates of theft of certain hot products (Clarke, 1999), such as mobile phones, computer laptops or SatNav systems, are linked by the repetition of target characteristics as well as, often, the *modus operandi* and the same offenders. While prediction has always been central to preventing repeat victimization, Johnson, Bowers and Pease (2005) took it to a new level by predicting burglary of alike nearby properties (tactical and spatial repeats) which were *not previously victimized* – work which Johnson and Bowers continue in this volume. Prospective prediction should have much research mileage, and many lessons for crime prevention practice, when transferred to other forms of virtual repeat.

The overarching theme of the body of work related to repeat victimization is that crime is remarkably concentrated. Crime's aggregate tendency to cluster appears almost without regard for the context in which, or the dimension along which, it is studied. Unpacking the various types of repeat victimization should facilitate the development of appropriate crime prevention practice, and Table 1 seeks to continue this effort.

A two-dimensional version of Table 1 is conceivable, where the other dimension is the routine activity variables of target/victim, location, and offender (requiring some modification of this initial list), but this is a next step outside the scope of the present study. However, what is clear is that as research relating to repeat victimization has progressed, so too has understanding of the relevant concepts. There are now numerous studies of various types of repeated personal and property crimes covering many countries, diverse sources of data and research methods. A recent addition to the list which is not necessarily intuitively obvious, is the study of repeated kidnapping (Reynald, 2005). Cyberspace is no exception, as Moitra and Konda (2004) demonstrate in relation to repeated computer network attacks. Their study of network root break-ins, account break-ins, denials of service, corruption of information, access attempts, and disclosure of information, found that a quarter of networks had experienced three or more attacks, averaging 12 each, while the top 10 most victimized averaged 369 attacks each. We anticipate crime relating to e-services will result in similar patterns, so that preventing repeat victimization should be used to inform crime prevention in this arena. In the context of progress in the understanding and definition of repeat victimization in recent years, the present study has a modest aim. It seeks to add to the study of repeat victimization of prison inmates.

Prison victimization rates are notoriously high compared to other locations. Cooley (1993) suggests inmate-on-inmate assault rates are three times that of the general community and twice that of a similar demographic group (see Wortley, 2002). Prisons present different victimization possibilities from other locations, although these will vary from prison to prison. Yet the close personal proximities and frequent interaction with the same persons that prison life fosters seem likely to precipitate relationships that can become violent and remain so (see O'Donnell and Edgar, 1996; Edgar and O'Donnell, 1998; Hochstetler et al., 2004). The research presented here is an exploratory analysis of a prison victimization survey. The results of the survey suggest that, reflecting different opportunities, the types of incident which repeat in prison are not necessarily those which repeat elsewhere. While prisons may prove a difficult environment in which to prevent repeat victimization, this should not preclude some effort, and the likelihood of developing situational crime prevention in prisons is promising (Wortley, 2002; Hulley and Smith, 2005).

Method

The analysis is based on a survey of eight UK prisons, the main details and findings of which were published elsewhere (Burnett and Farrell, 1994). The main report of the study did not fully exploit the survey's potential to shed light on the repeated nature of incidents. The survey asked inmates about their experiences in the preceding three months. While a three-month reference period minimizes memory problems that can affect respondent recall, it is a short time-window in which to measure repeated incidents that occur over time. Consequently, it would be expected that the repeat victimization rates reported here are conservative estimates.

Five hundred and one prison inmates from eight penal establishments were interviewed face-to-face. Ethnic minority inmates were over-sampled to facilitate analysis by ethnic group. To account for this, a weighting was applied for the present analysis. The weighting (available upon request from the authors) sought to make the sample representative of the ethnic groups in the national prison population at the time. Weighting a relatively small sample is not unproblematic, but the findings below are presented in the expectation that key patterns will prove sufficiently robust to justify this exploratory analysis.

FINDINGS

By means of introduction, an overview of the frequency of victimization of inmates by other inmates and by staff is shown in Table 2. About 15% of inmates experienced close to 90% of incidents from each source (those in the row of 5+ incidents). It is not necessarily the same individuals who were victimized by inmates and by staff, but this point is returned to later.

Repeats by Other Inmates

Table 3 shows victimization of inmates by inmates over the three-month reference period, ranked by the concentration rate (the exception to the ranking is Any Type of Incident, which is shown last). The concentration rate is the average number of incidents per victim. Nearly half of inmates (45.5%) had experienced some form of victimization in the previous three months. Generally speaking, victimization concentration did not necessarily increase along with the prevalence of an incident type. Harassment, verbal abuse and exclusion were the types of incident most repeated. Of these three, only verbal abuse was unusually prevalent. Experienced by a quarter of inmates, verbal abuse was repeated an average of 12 times per recipient (that is, approximately once per week over the three month reference period). In contrast, only 3 or 4% of inmates experienced harassment or exclusion by other inmates, but those who did reported an average of around a dozen such incidents. Even though these mean average rates

Table 2: Victimization of Inmates

	By Inmates		By Staff	
Number of Incidents	% of Inmates Victimized	% Incidents	% of Inmates Victimized	% Incidents
0	54.9	0.0	64.6	0.0
1	12.0	2.4	5.2	1.1
2	5.4	2.2	4.9	2.0
3	11.1	6.7	5.4	3.4
4	3.2	2.6	5.0	4.2
5+	13.5	86.1	15.0	89.4
Total	100.0	100.0	100.0	100.0

Table 3: Victimization of Inmates by Inmates

Type of incident	Concentration (incidents per victim)	Prevalence (victims per 100 inmates)	% Repeats (% of total incidents)
Harassment	13.2	3.7	92
Verbal Abuse	12.0	26.1	92
Exclusion	11.5	3.1	91
Bullying	5.5	9.7	82
Taxing	4.5	0.9	78
Robbery	2.6	0.8	62
Sexual Assault	2.5	0.1	60
Assault	1.4	8.5	27
Theft	1.3	17.5	25
Any type of incident	10.9	45.1	91

mask some large outliers (a tiny fraction of inmates reported an incident per day), they give some indication of the unequal distribution of incidents.

One in ten inmates reported having been bullied in the previous three months, but victims experienced an average of more than five incidents each. While taxing (extortion) and robbery were relatively rare, being experienced by one in 100 inmates, victims experienced an average of 4.5 and 2.6 incidents each respectively in the three-month period.

Most incidents were repeats of previous victimizations even during this three-month period (Table 3, final column). Repeat incidents made up over 90% of all incidents, and of harassment, verbal abuse and exclusionary acts. Around 80% of bullying and taxing were repeats, 60 or so percent of robberies and sexual assaults, and around a quarter of thefts and sexual assaults (though the sample size for the latter was tiny so it should be read with caution).

Repeats by Prison Staff

Slightly more than a third of inmates had been victimized by prison staff in the preceding three months (see Table 4). Verbal abuse, bullying and harassment were the most prevalent types of victimization, and the most frequently repeated. Table 4 is ranked by the concentration rate except

Table 4: Victimization of Inmates by Staff

Type of incident	Concentration (incidents per victim)	Prevalence (victims per 100 inmates)	% Repeats (% of total incidents)
Verbal abuse	10.9	22.8	90.9
Bullying	8.6	10.2	88.4
Harassment	7.9	17.6	87.4
Assaults	1.4	2.8	28.0
Theft	1.1	3.6	12.5
Any Type of Incident	13.7	35.4	92.7

for Any Type of Incident, which is shown last. The list of categories of incident type about which information was collected was shorter than for inmate-inmate incidents. Both concentration and prevalence were relatively high for verbal abuse and harassment by staff. The prevalence and frequency of theft and assault were low in comparison to the other types of incident.

Repeated Institutional Discrimination

In what follows, institutional discrimination refers to policies and procedures of a prison rather than the actions of any one individual. When the survey was conducted it sought to assess institutional racial discrimination. For example, if a prison did not provide religious facilities or culturally-appropriate foodstuffs for certain groups of inmates while doing so for others, then this could be due to institutional racial discrimination (see Burnett and Farrell, 1994 for further details). Most inmates (79%) experienced some discrimination with respect to facilities or services. Almost four in ten inmates reported being discriminated against with respect to the types of meals they could obtain, and three in ten in the way their requests and complaints were dealt with (Table 5). Almost a quarter experienced discrimination with respect to how searches (of cells or persons) were conducted or in the availability of canteen products. Note that the weighted averages reported here mask the variation among ethnic groups that produced some of the more prominent findings of the original study.

Information was not requested on the number of times inmates experienced each type of discrimination. However, inmates experienced an aver-

Table 5: Prevalence of Discrimination against Inmates

Type of facility or service	% Inmates
Meals	38.9
Requests and complaints	29.8
Searches (strip or cell)	23.8
Canteen products (food, toiletries, etc.)	23.7
Visits, letters, phone calls	21.8
Job opportunities	20.9
Information or advice	20.9
Cell/dorm/wing allocation	14.0
Clothing and laundry	13.5
Education	11.9
Newspapers or books	10.5
Training opportunities	9.5
Association/recreation	8.5
Gym and sports	8.0
Practising religion	4.8

age of 3.2 types of incidents each. More than a fifth of inmates experienced five or more types of discrimination (Table 6).

Are They the Same Victims?

A natural question arising from the previous sections is whether those inmates experiencing repeated victimization by inmates are the same individuals experiencing repeat victimization by prison staff. The first method we employed to investigate this was a scatterplot of the extent of victimization by inmates versus victimization by staff. Exploratory analysis had revealed an extremely skewed distribution for both dimensions, so the numbers of victimizations were transformed using a base 2 logarithmic function (equivalently log2). The key to interpret a log2 transform is that every unit change in the transformed variable corresponds to a doubling in the original value. It was also noted that many observations shared the same value, which is not surprising given that the data are positive integers. This could cause problems in visualizing the distribution if there was a

Table 6: Number of Types of Discrimination

Number of Types	% Inmates	% Types
0	20.8	0.0
1	21.5	8.5
2	13.7	10.8
3	14.4	17.1
4	8.7	13.7
5+	21.0	49.8
Total	100.0	100.0

tendency for a significant overlap in symbols. To remedy this, a modified scatterplot, known as a *sunflowerplot* (Cleveland and McGill, 1984), was used. Observed points are represented by sunflowers, comprising petals (short, straight line segments) originating from a central point. The number of petals indicates the number of observations sharing those points. Multiple observations, that is, those with petals, are displayed slightly smaller than single observations. Figure 1 displays the bivariate victimization distribution.

A number of features are immediately apparent from the sunflower plot. First, there is a large number of inmates who did not report any victimization by either inmates or staff. This is represented by the intersection of the zero ordinate and zero co-ordinate.[1] The number of observations sharing these values is so large as to render the petals indistinguishable from each other. Second, there appear to be some inmates who suffer victimization only at the hands of other inmates. This feature can be seen by the left-most column of observations (least victimized at the bottom, most at the top). Third, there is a group of inmates who reported no victimization by fellow inmates, only by staff. These are located on the bottom row of the plot (similarly the least victimized are toward the left, chronically victimized to the right). Finally, some inmates experienced victimization by both other inmates and staff (located in the general body of the figure).

Figure 1 helps depict the victimization profile of types of individuals, but it is still far from clear whether victimization by inmates is independent of victimization by staff. If there was a direct link between the two, we could ask if victimization by inmates had a bearing on victimization by staff,

Figure 1: Sunflower Plot of Victimization by Inmates and Staff (in which the number of "petals" refers to the number of observations at each location)

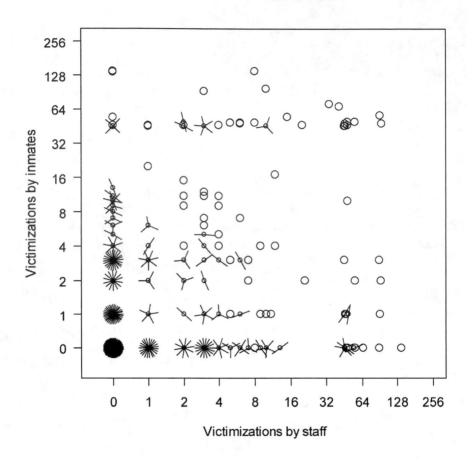

and vice versa. However, the design of the survey precludes establishing temporal precedence. The aim was not to quantify future risk based on exposure, but merely to identify whether one type of victimization status is associated with another type of victimization status. The approach adopted to pursue this further was to cross-classify all respondents by three factors: inmate-on-inmate victimization (yes/no); staff-on-inmate victimization (yes/no); and discrimination (yes/no). Thus, the extent of within-incident type repeat victimization is ignored, and only prevalence remains.

The counts of the observations satisfying all combinations of the three factors was calculated, generating a three-way contingency table ($2 \times 2 \times 2$).

When two categorical variables are cross-classified, the resulting two-way contingency table is usually subjected to a chi-square hypothesis test, in order to determine whether there is a dependent relationship between the two variables (equivalently, the distribution of cell frequencies is not influenced by the values of the two variables). When the dimensionality of a contingency table is greater than two, somewhat different methods are used. A loglinear model (essentially a general linear model of Poisson data – i.e., count data – regressed against a set of categorical variables) was used to examine the independence structure of the contingency table.

The general hypothesis being tested was whether there is dependence between the three independent variables: inmate-on-inmate victimization, staff-on-inmate victimization, and discrimination. This is known as the mutual independence model and it is equivalent in ANOVA terms to testing the main effects while ignoring interaction between variables. It is a conventional two-way hypothesis test extended to a three-way table. The difference between the three-way observed distribution and its corresponding expected distribution under the mutual independence model was statistically large enough to reject the null hypothesis of independence across the three variables (Likelihood Ratio $= 64.03$, df $= 4$, p $\ll .00001$).

A loglinear analysis (not presented here but available from the authors) revealed that there were a greater than expected number of two types of inmates: (a) individuals who did not report any victimization for any source; and (b) inmates who reported victimization of all three types (by other inmates, by staff and, in the form of discrimination). These two groups could be characterised as immune and ubiquitously vulnerable, respectively.

There are two possible interpretations of this finding. Perhaps some inmates present more attractive possibilities for victimization to both other inmates and to staff (some characteristic "flags" their attractiveness as a target). Alternatively, it is possible that, if an inmate was victimized by staff then this could boost the chances of victimization by inmates (see Pease 1998 for the definitive statement on 'flag and boost' explanations of repeat victimisation). Exactly how discrimination fits into the dynamics of victimization is unclear. It could be that those individuals experiencing institutional discrimination are different enough from the inmate population that there is a flag mechanism. On the other hand, staff could perceive those inmates who raise grievances related to institutional discrimination as troublemakers, thereby boosting victimization by staff. The vicious victimization cycle would continue if, in turn, other inmates then believe they can victimize such inmates with impunity.

CONCLUSION

This study scratches the surface of repeat victimization of prison inmates. Repeats accounted for over 90% of victimization experienced against inmates, whether it was committed by other inmates or by prison staff. Victims of inmates were also more likely to be victims of staff and to experience discrimination. There is clearly scope for further examination of these issues.

Preventing repeat victimization by inmates might prove difficult if the victims are unlikely to bring it to the attention of prison staff. The effect would be exaggerated for those inmates also victimized by staff. However, victimization itself can present a tangible anchor for the development of focused crime prevention efforts. Consequently, the particular context of prisons should not preclude some effort to prevent the further victimization of inmates.

Address correspondence to: M.Townsley@ucl.ac.uk

NOTE

1. The transformation of zero by log2 is minus infinity. This issue was avoided by adding a small positive value to all zero observations so they could be included in the plot. The magnitude of this value is immaterial.

REFERENCES

Burnett, R., & Farrell, G. (1994). *Reported and unreported racial incidents in prisons.* University of Oxford Occasional Paper Number 14. Oxford, UK: Centre for Criminological Research, University of Oxford.

Clarke, R. V. (1999). *Hot products: Understanding, anticipating and reducing demand for stolen goods.* Police Research series paper 112. London: Home Office.

Cleveland, W. S., & McGill, R. (1984). The many faces of a scatterplot. *Journal of the American Statistical Association, 79*, 807-822.

Cooley, D. (1993, October). Criminal victimization in male federal prisons. *Canadian Journal of Criminology*, 479-495.

Edgar, K., & O'Donnell, I. (1998). Assault in prison: The victim's contribution. *British Journal of Criminology, 34*(8), 635-650.

Forrester, D., Chatterton, M., & Pease, K. (1988). *The Kirkholt Burglary Prevention Project, Rochdale*. Crime Prevention Unit Paper 13. London: Home Office.

Hochstetler, A., Murphy, D. S., & Simons, R. L. (2004). Damaged goods: Exploring predictors of distress in prison inmates. *Crime & Delinquency, 50*(3), 436-457.

Hulley, S., & Smith, M. (2005). *Reducing prisoner-on-prisoner victimisation in a young offenders institution: A problem-solving approach*. London: Jill Dando Institute of Crime Science, University College London.

Johnson, S. D., Bowers, K. J. Bowers, & Pease, K. (2005). Predicting the future or summarising the past? Crime mapping as anticipation. In M. Smith & N. Tilley (Eds.), *Crime science: New approaches to preventing and detecting crime*. Cullompton, UK: Willan Publishing.

Moitra, S. D., & Konda, S. L. (2004). An empirical investigation of network attacks on computer systems. *Computers and Security, 23*, 43-51.

O'Donnell, I., & Edgar, K. (1996). *Victimisation in prison*. Home Office Research Findings 37. London: Home Office.

Pease, K. (1991). The Kirkholt Project: Preventing burglary on a British public housing estate. *Security Journal, 2*(2), 73-77.

Pease, K. (1998). *Repeat victimisation: Taking stock*. Crime Prevention and Detection series paper 90. London: Home Office.

Pease, K., & Laycock, G. (1996). *Revictimization: Reducing the heat on hot victims*. National Institute of Justice Research in Brief series. Washington, DC: U.S. National Institute of Justice.

Reynald, D. (2005). *A situational profile of kidnapping for ransom in Trinidad & Tobago*. Unpublished MSc thesis. London: Jill Dando Institute of Crime Science, University College London.

Townsley, M., Homel, R., & Chaseling, J. (2003). Infectious burglaries: A test of the near repeat hypothesis. *British Journal of Criminology, 43*, 615-633.

Wortley, R. (2002). *Situational prison control: Crime prevention in correctional institutions*. Cambridge, UK: Cambridge University Press.